SIGNATURE WOUND

Recent Books by G. B. Trudeau

Got War?

Talk to the Hand!

Dude: The Big Book of Zonker

Heckuva Job, Bushie!

Welcome to the Nerd Farm!

Tee Time in Berzerkistan

The Long Road Home: One Step at a Time
Foreword by Senator John McCain

The War Within: One More Step at a Time
Foreword by General Richard B. Myers

Doonesbury.com's The Sandbox:
Dispatches from Troops in Iraq and Afghanistan

Doonesbury.com's The War in Quotes

"My Shorts R Bunching. Thoughts?" The Tweets of Roland Hedley

SIGNATURE WOUND

Rocking TBI

by **G. B. TRUDEAU**

**Andrews McMeel
Publishing, LLC**

Kansas City • Sydney • London

DOONESBURY is distributed internationally by Universal Uclick.

Signature Wound: Rocking TBI copyright © 2010 by G. B. Trudeau. All rights reserved. Printed in the United States of America. No part of this book may be used or reproduced in any manner whatsoever without written permission except in the case of reprints in the context of reviews. For information, write Andrews McMeel Publishing, LLC, an Andrews McMeel Universal company, 1130 Walnut Street, Kansas City, Missouri 64106.

10 11 12 13 14 BBG 10 9 8 7 6 5 4 3 2 1

ISBN-13: 978-0-7407-9196-3
ISBN-10: 0-7407-9196-6

Library of Congress Control Number: 2009943088

www.andrewsmcmeel.com

DOONESBURY may be viewed on the Internet at:
www.doonesbury.com and www.GoComics.com

──────── **ATTENTION: SCHOOLS AND BUSINESSES** ────────

Andrews McMeel books are available at quantity discounts with bulk purchase for educational, business, or sales promotional use. For information, please write to: Special Sales Department, Andrews McMeel Publishing, LLC, 1130 Walnut Street, Kansas City, Missouri 64106.

War does not determine who is right—only who is left.

—Bertrand Russell

Foreword
by General Peter Pace, U.S. Marine Corps (Retired),
Sixteenth Chairman of the Joint Chiefs of Staff

This book contains important lessons about life in the Armed Forces. The lessons are disguised, as familiar comic strip personalities come to grips with real injuries, seen and unseen, from service in a time of war.

We watch Toggle stammer and stutter his way to a New Normal, living with aphasia, memory loss, and other devastating symptoms of traumatic brain injury (TBI)—truly the "signature wound" of duty in Iraq and Afghanistan.

We see his mom and his extended family—a network of battle buddies, caregivers, and counselors—as they try to understand how best to support Toggle along this difficult journey.

As a nation, we owe an incredible debt of gratitude to all who have stepped forward and volunteered to protect the freedoms we hold dear. Their steadfast dedication is an inspiration to us all! Garry Trudeau helps us recognize the tremendous sacrifice and amazing resilience of America's service members and their devoted families. He captures the very essence of the military ethos in a manner that those in and out of uniform can appreciate. The camaraderie, sense of service, and gallows humor are familiar territory.

To his credit, Trudeau offers the unairbrushed truth of a painful and unpredictable path to recovery, and reveals the broader perspective of TBI's impact on families and friends as they struggle to act "normal"—and eventually learn how to live with *their* New Normal. None of it is easy, but all of it is made easier by the wry smiles and shared experiences we find among these pages.

Countless Toggles and B.D.s will recognize themselves sketched in these frames, and perhaps they will breathe a little easier, comforted by the realization that they are not alone.

SIGNATURE WOUND

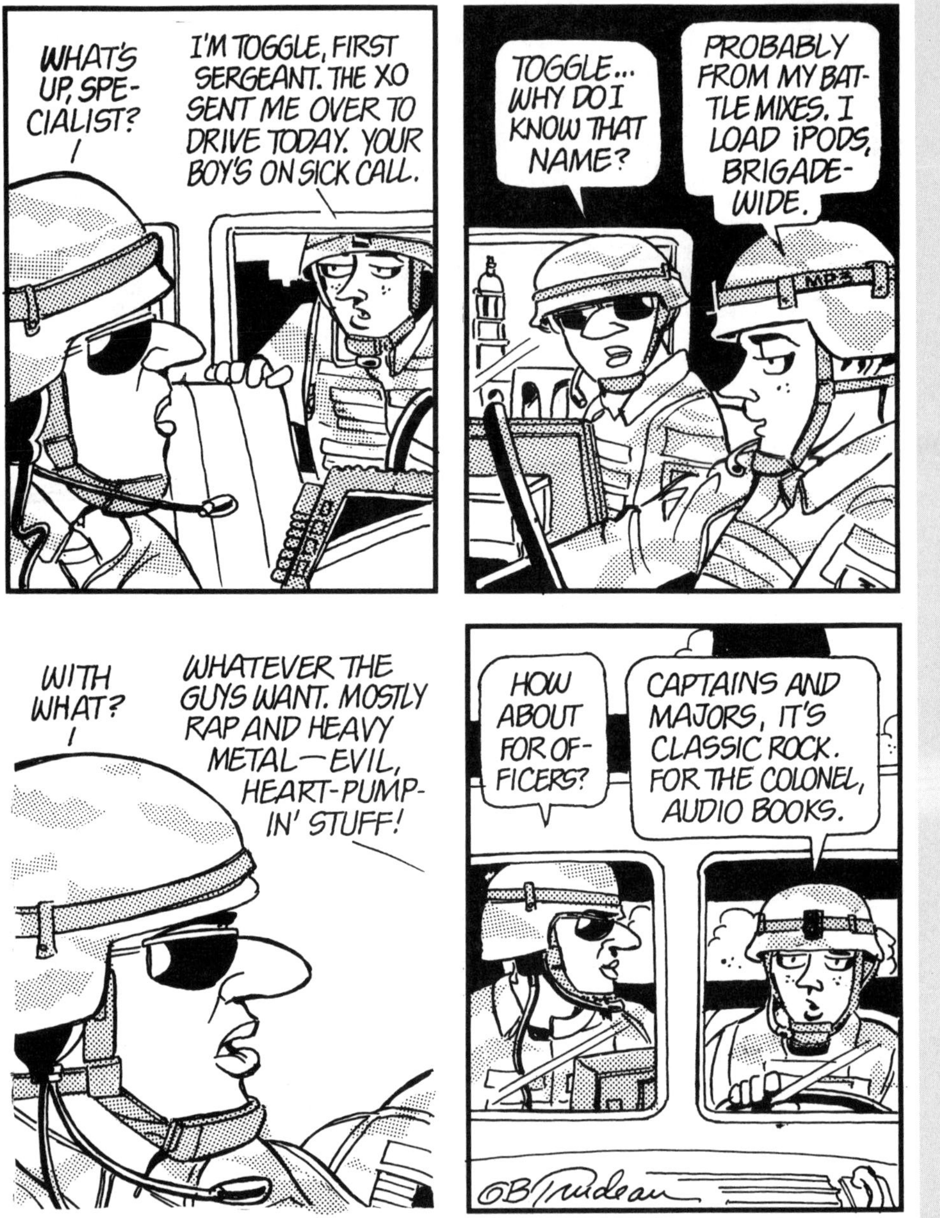
WHAT'S UP, SPECIALIST?
I'M TOGGLE, FIRST SERGEANT. THE XO SENT ME OVER TO DRIVE TODAY. YOUR BOY'S ON SICK CALL.
TOGGLE... WHY DO I KNOW THAT NAME?
PROBABLY FROM MY BATTLE MIXES. I LOAD iPODS, BRIGADE-WIDE.
WITH WHAT?
WHATEVER THE GUYS WANT. MOSTLY RAP AND HEAVY METAL—EVIL, HEART-PUMPIN' STUFF!
HOW ABOUT FOR OFFICERS?
CAPTAINS AND MAJORS, IT'S CLASSIC ROCK. FOR THE COLONEL, AUDIO BOOKS.
©B Trudeau

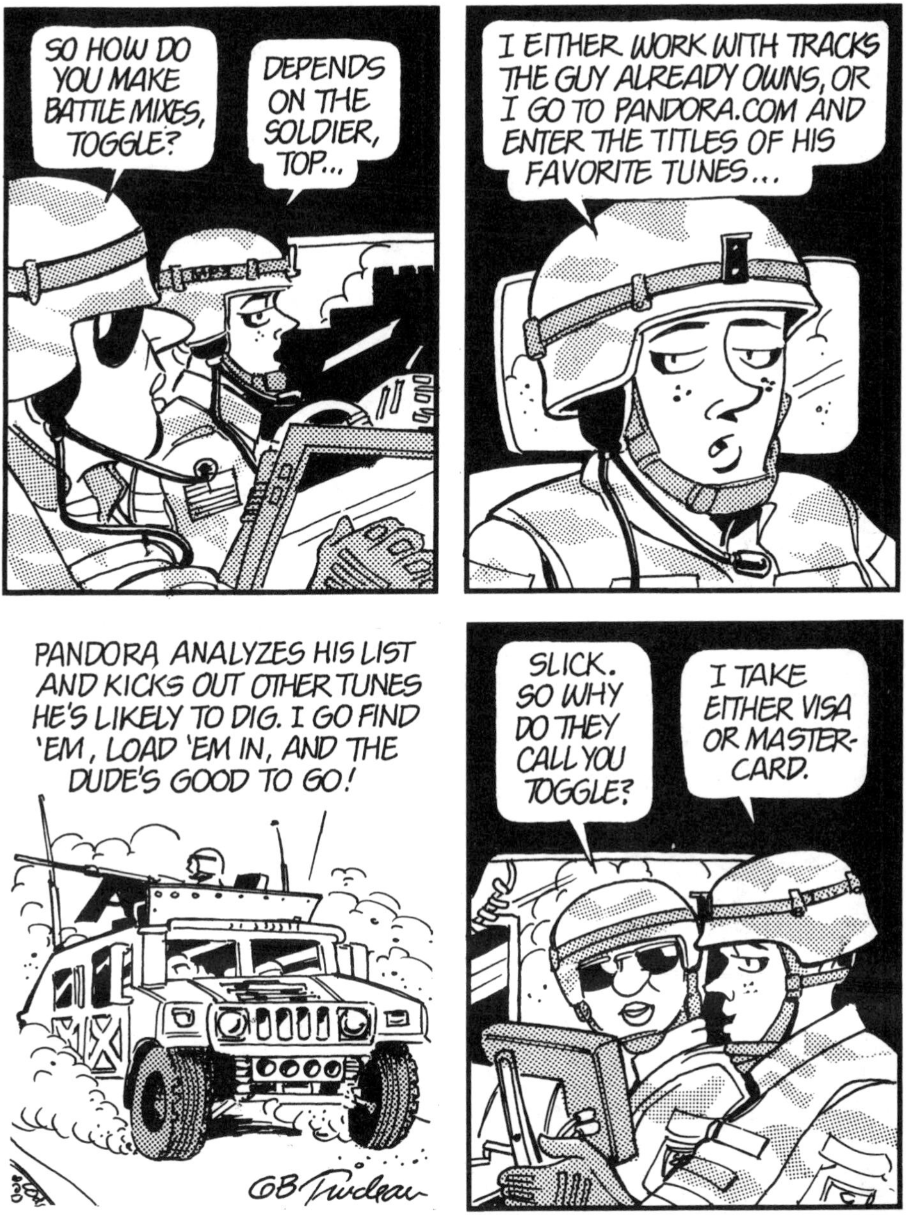
SO HOW DO YOU MAKE BATTLE MIXES, TOGGLE?
DEPENDS ON THE SOLDIER, TOP...
I EITHER WORK WITH TRACKS THE GUY ALREADY OWNS, OR I GO TO PANDORA.COM AND ENTER THE TITLES OF HIS FAVORITE TUNES...
PANDORA ANALYZES HIS LIST AND KICKS OUT OTHER TUNES HE'S LIKELY TO DIG. I GO FIND 'EM, LOAD 'EM IN, AND THE DUDE'S GOOD TO GO!
GB Trudeau
SLICK. SO WHY DO THEY CALL YOU TOGGLE?
I TAKE EITHER VISA OR MASTER-CARD.

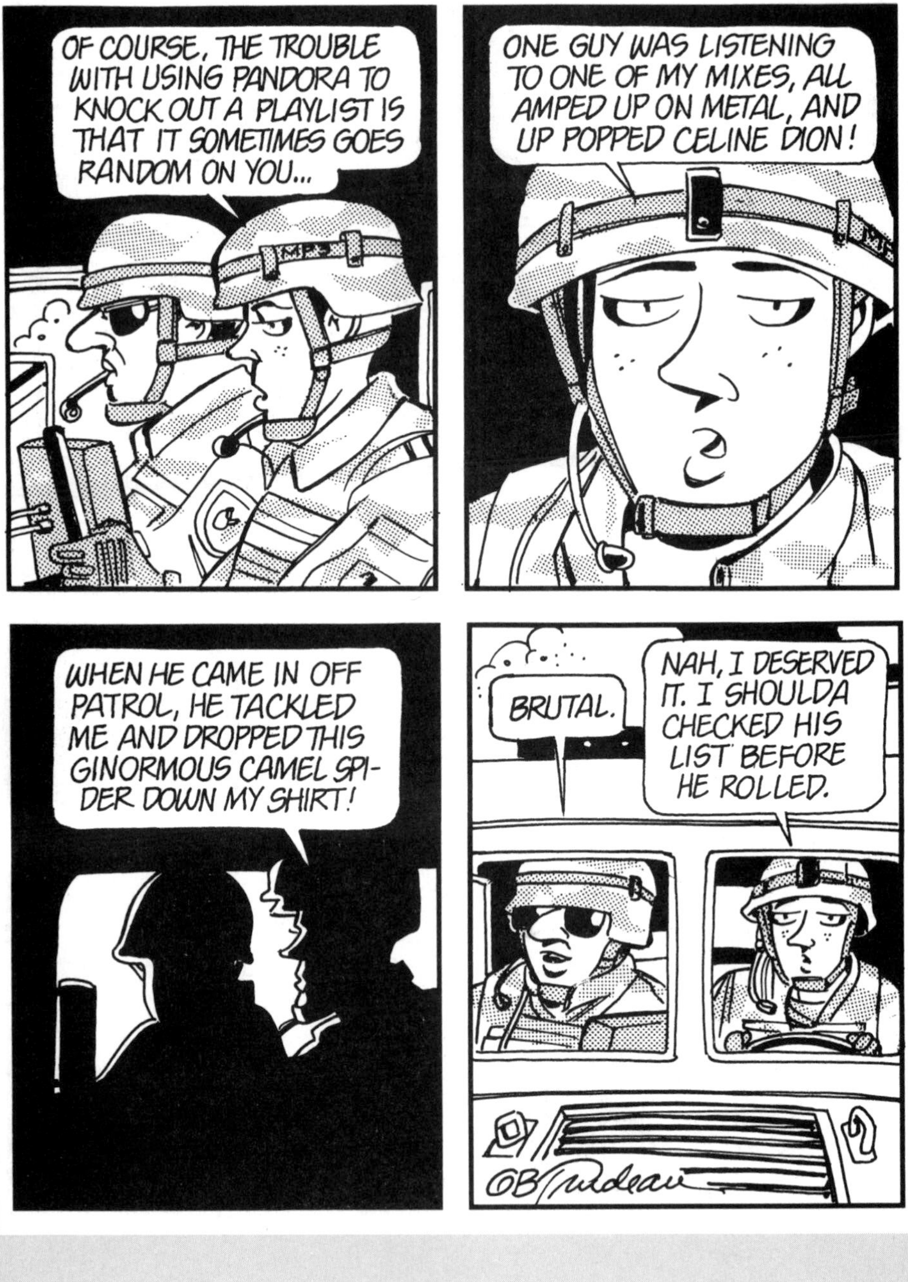
OF COURSE, THE TROUBLE WITH USING PANDORA TO KNOCK OUT A PLAYLIST IS THAT IT SOMETIMES GOES RANDOM ON YOU...
ONE GUY WAS LISTENING TO ONE OF MY MIXES, ALL AMPED UP ON METAL, AND UP POPPED CELINE DION!
WHEN HE CAME IN OFF PATROL, HE TACKLED ME AND DROPPED THIS GINORMOUS CAMEL SPIDER DOWN MY SHIRT!
BRUTAL.
NAH, I DESERVED IT. I SHOULDA CHECKED HIS LIST BEFORE HE ROLLED.
©B Trudeau

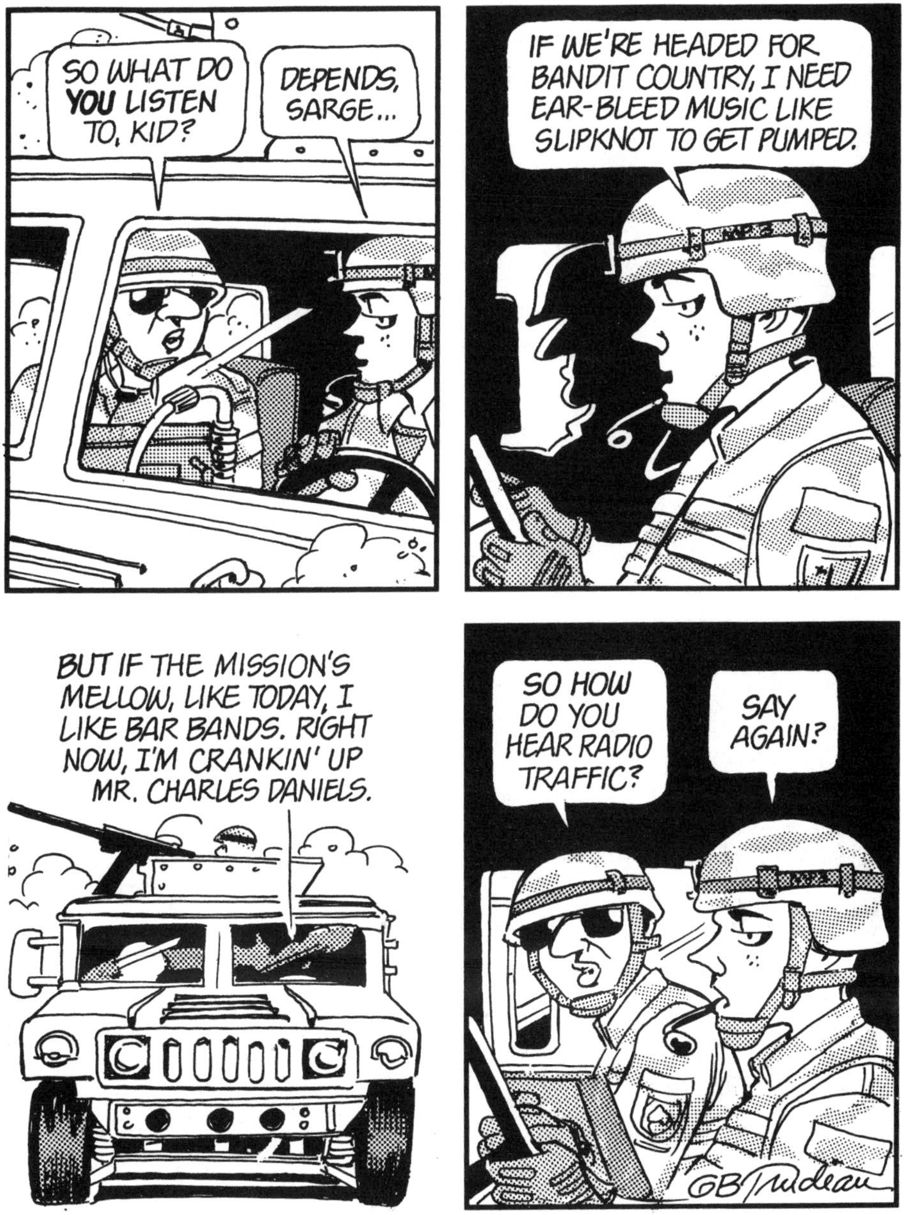
SO WHAT DO **YOU** LISTEN TO, KID?
DEPENDS, SARGE...
IF WE'RE HEADED FOR BANDIT COUNTRY, I NEED EAR-BLEED MUSIC LIKE SLIPKNOT TO GET PUMPED.
BUT IF THE MISSION'S MELLOW, LIKE TODAY, I LIKE BAR BANDS. RIGHT NOW, I'M CRANKIN' UP MR. CHARLES DANIELS.
SO HOW DO YOU HEAR RADIO TRAFFIC?
SAY AGAIN?
GB Trudeau

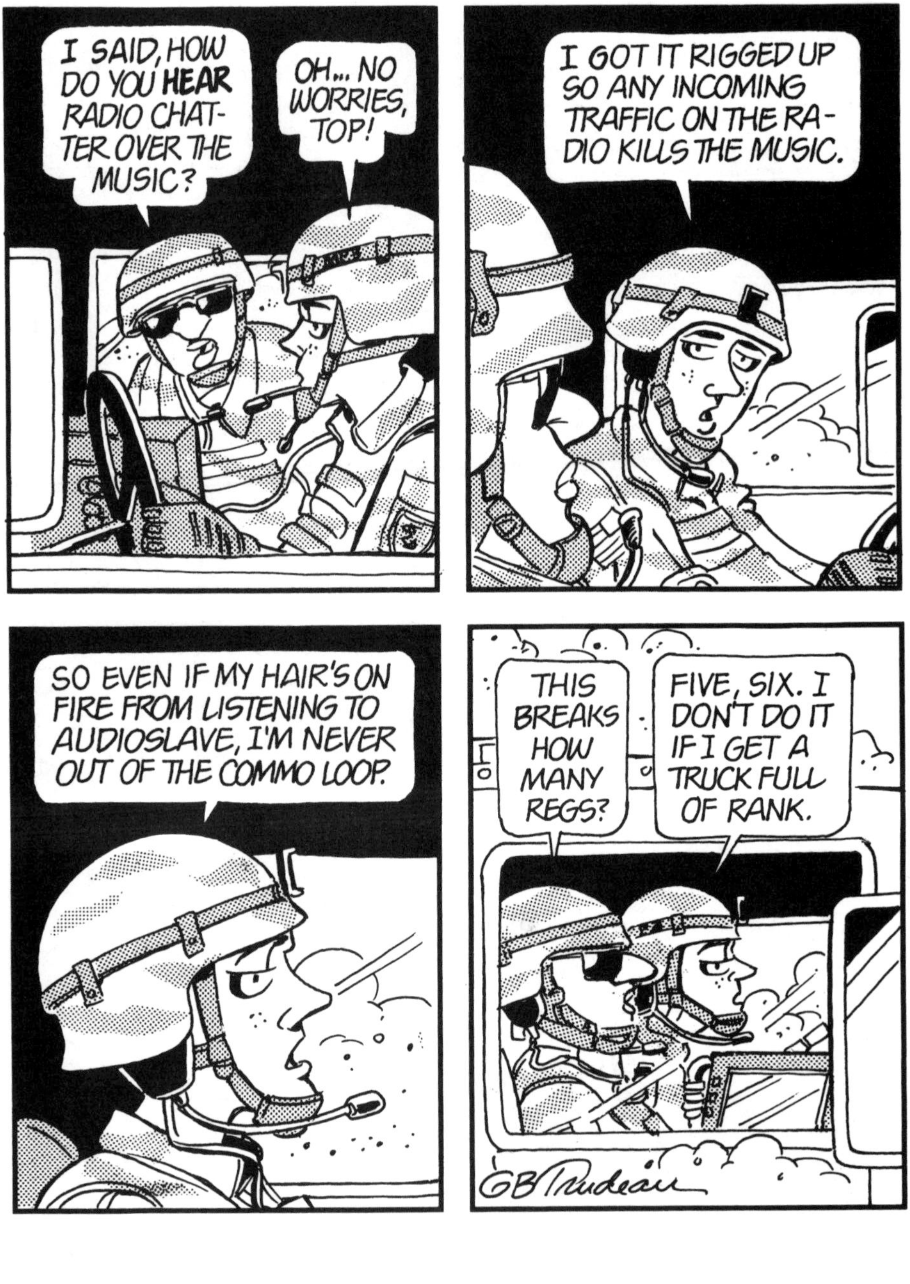
I SAID, HOW DO YOU HEAR RADIO CHATTER OVER THE MUSIC?
OH... NO WORRIES, TOP!
I GOT IT RIGGED UP SO ANY INCOMING TRAFFIC ON THE RADIO KILLS THE MUSIC.
SO EVEN IF MY HAIR'S ON FIRE FROM LISTENING TO AUDIOSLAVE, I'M NEVER OUT OF THE COMMO LOOP.
THIS BREAKS HOW MANY REGS?
FIVE, SIX. I DON'T DO IT IF I GET A TRUCK FULL OF RANK.
GB Trudeau

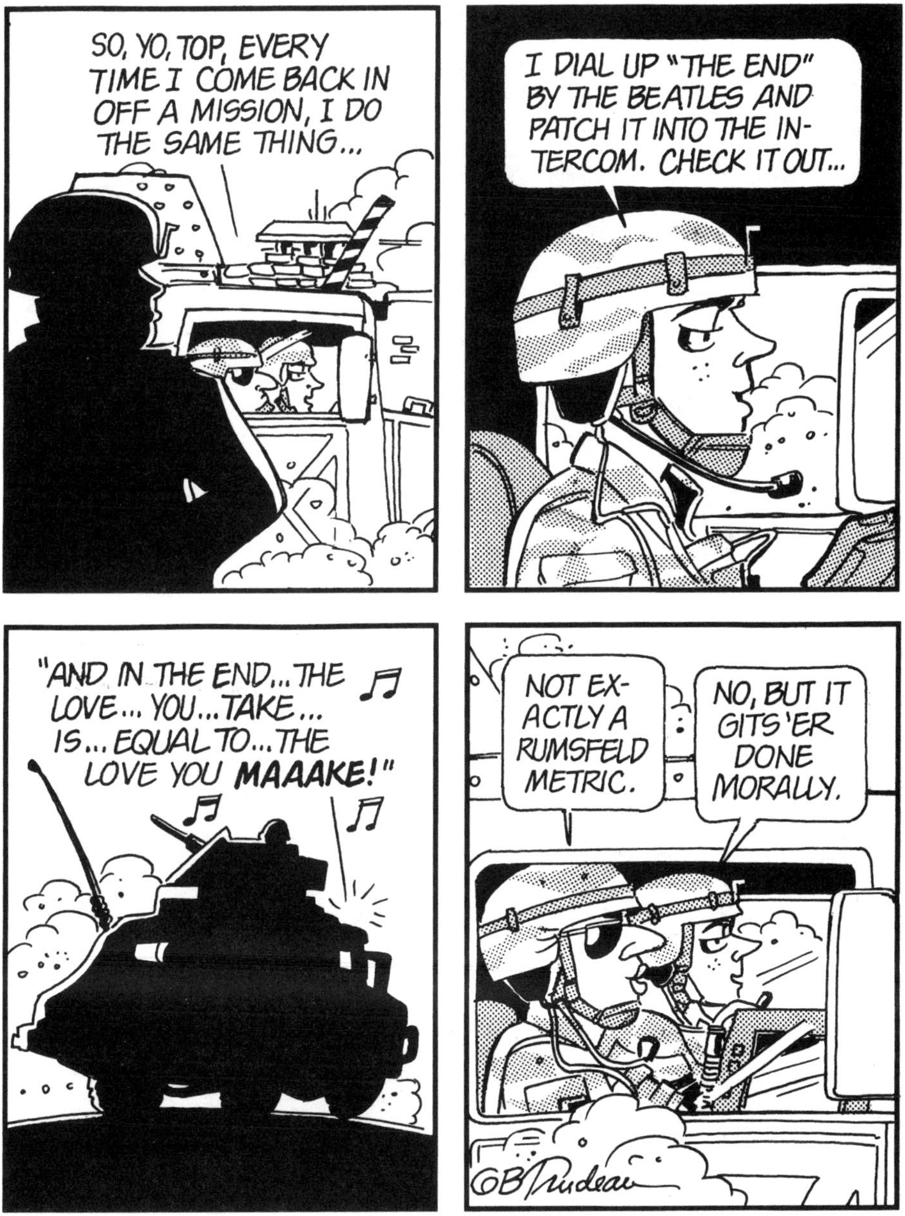
SO, YO, TOP, EVERY TIME I COME BACK IN OFF A MISSION, I DO THE SAME THING...
I DIAL UP "THE END" BY THE BEATLES AND PATCH IT INTO THE INTERCOM. CHECK IT OUT...
"AND IN THE END... THE LOVE... YOU... TAKE... IS... EQUAL TO... THE LOVE YOU MAAAKE!"
NOT EXACTLY A RUMSFELD METRIC.
NO, BUT IT GITS 'ER DONE MORALLY.
©B Trudeau

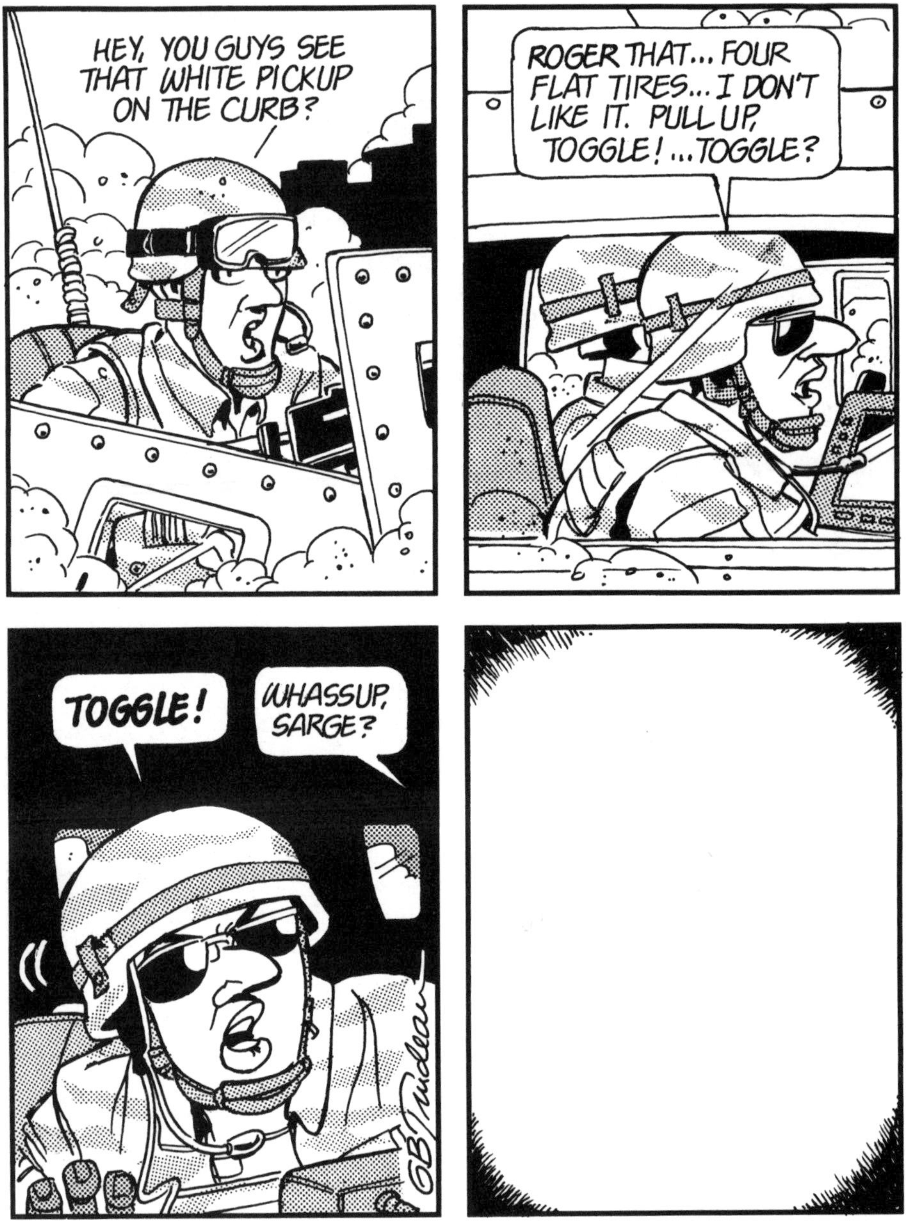
HEY, YOU GUYS SEE THAT WHITE PICKUP ON THE CURB?
ROGER THAT... FOUR FLAT TIRES... I DON'T LIKE IT. PULL UP, TOGGLE! ...TOGGLE?
TOGGLE!
WHASSUP, SARGE?
GBTrudeau

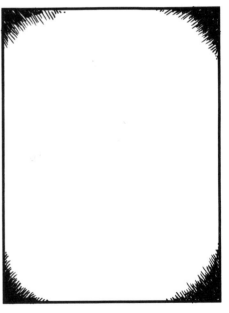

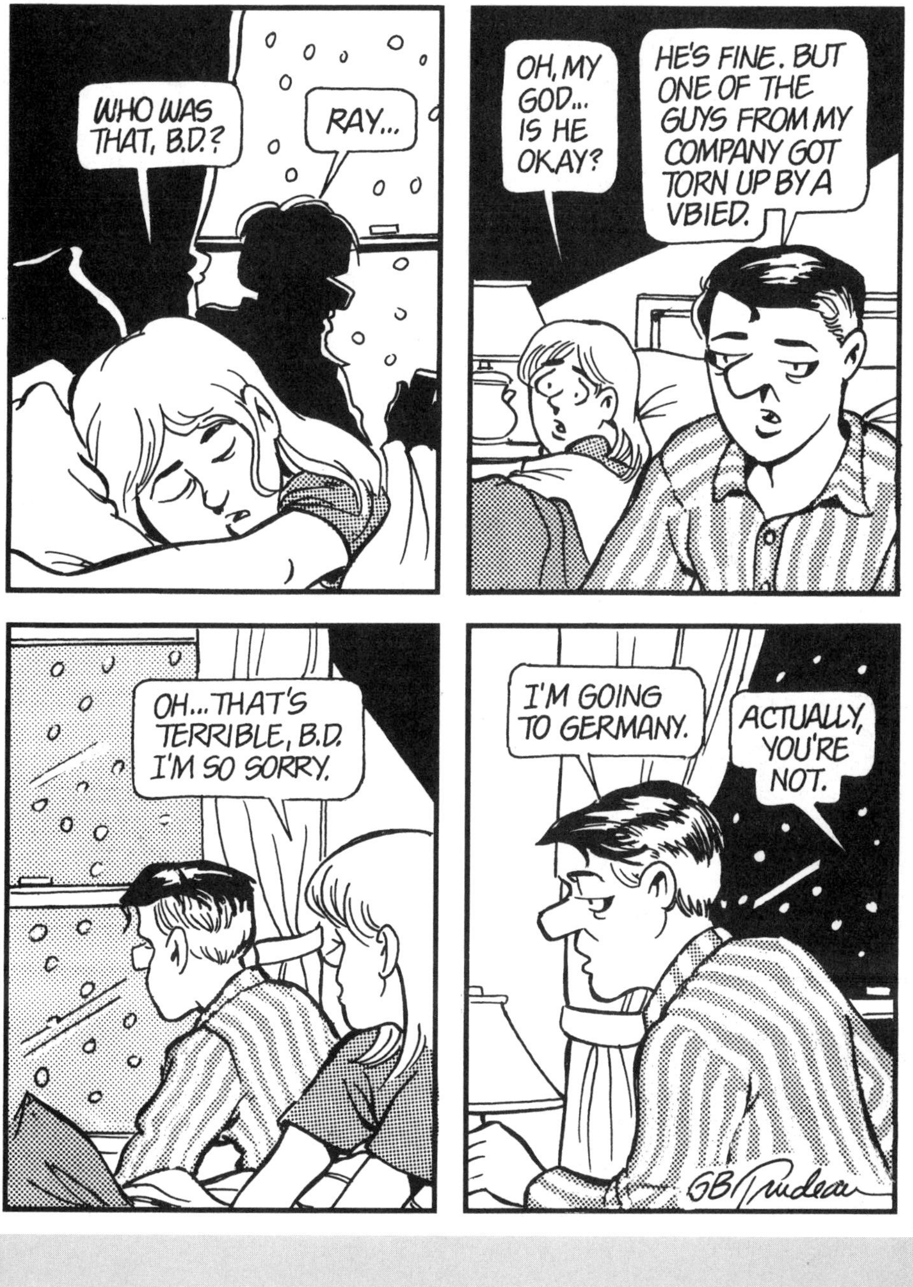
WHO WAS THAT, B.D.?
RAY...
OH, MY GOD... IS HE OKAY?
HE'S FINE. BUT ONE OF THE GUYS FROM MY COMPANY GOT TORN UP BY A VBIED.
OH... THAT'S TERRIBLE, B.D. I'M SO SORRY.
I'M GOING TO GERMANY.
ACTUALLY, YOU'RE NOT.
GB Trudeau

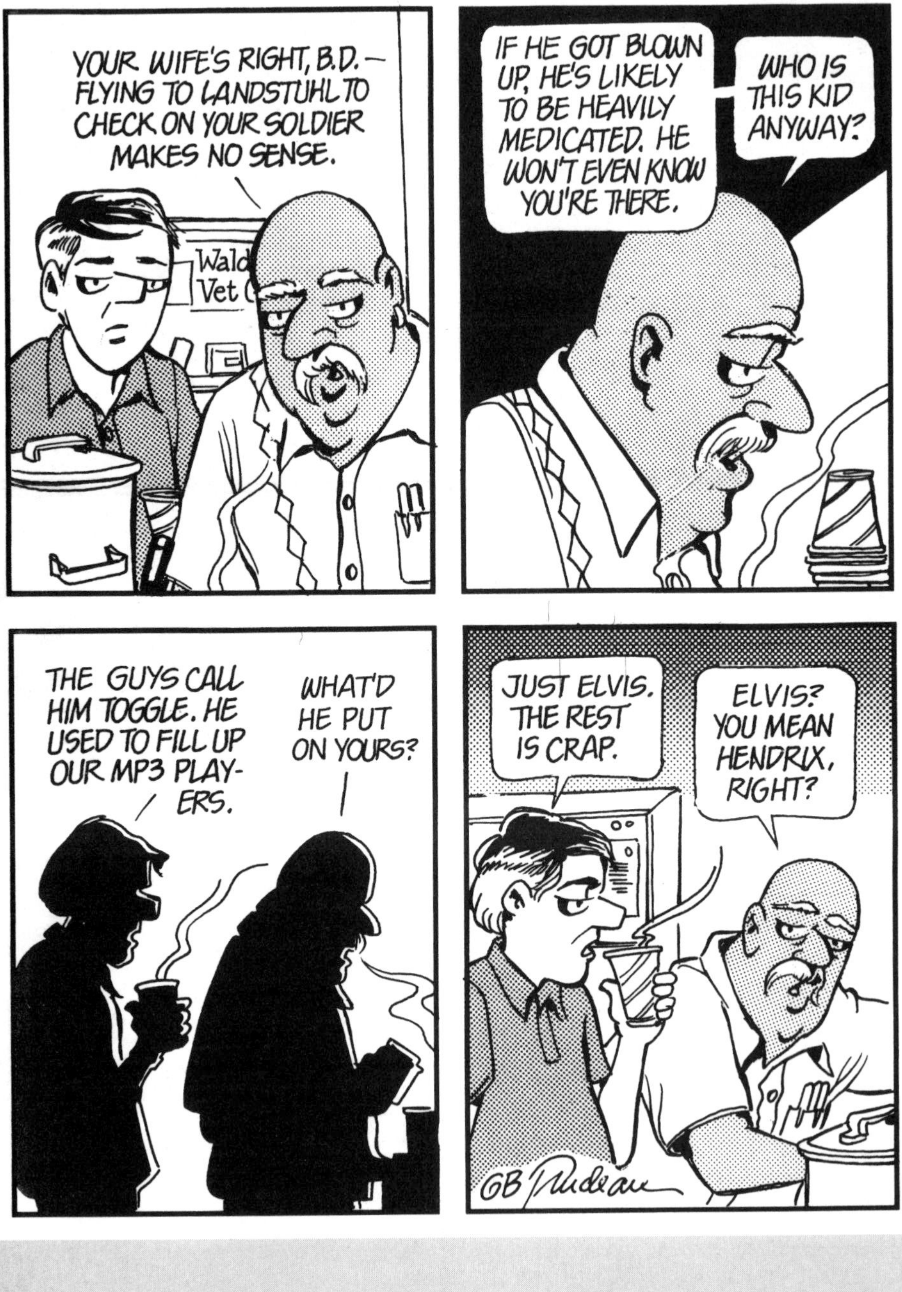
YOUR WIFE'S RIGHT, B.D.— FLYING TO LANDSTUHL TO CHECK ON YOUR SOLDIER MAKES NO SENSE.
Wald Vet
IF HE GOT BLOWN UP, HE'S LIKELY TO BE HEAVILY MEDICATED. HE WON'T EVEN KNOW YOU'RE THERE.
WHO IS THIS KID ANYWAY?
THE GUYS CALL HIM TOGGLE. HE USED TO FILL UP OUR MP3 PLAYERS.
WHAT'D HE PUT ON YOURS?
JUST ELVIS. THE REST IS CRAP.
ELVIS? YOU MEAN HENDRIX, RIGHT?
GB Trudeau

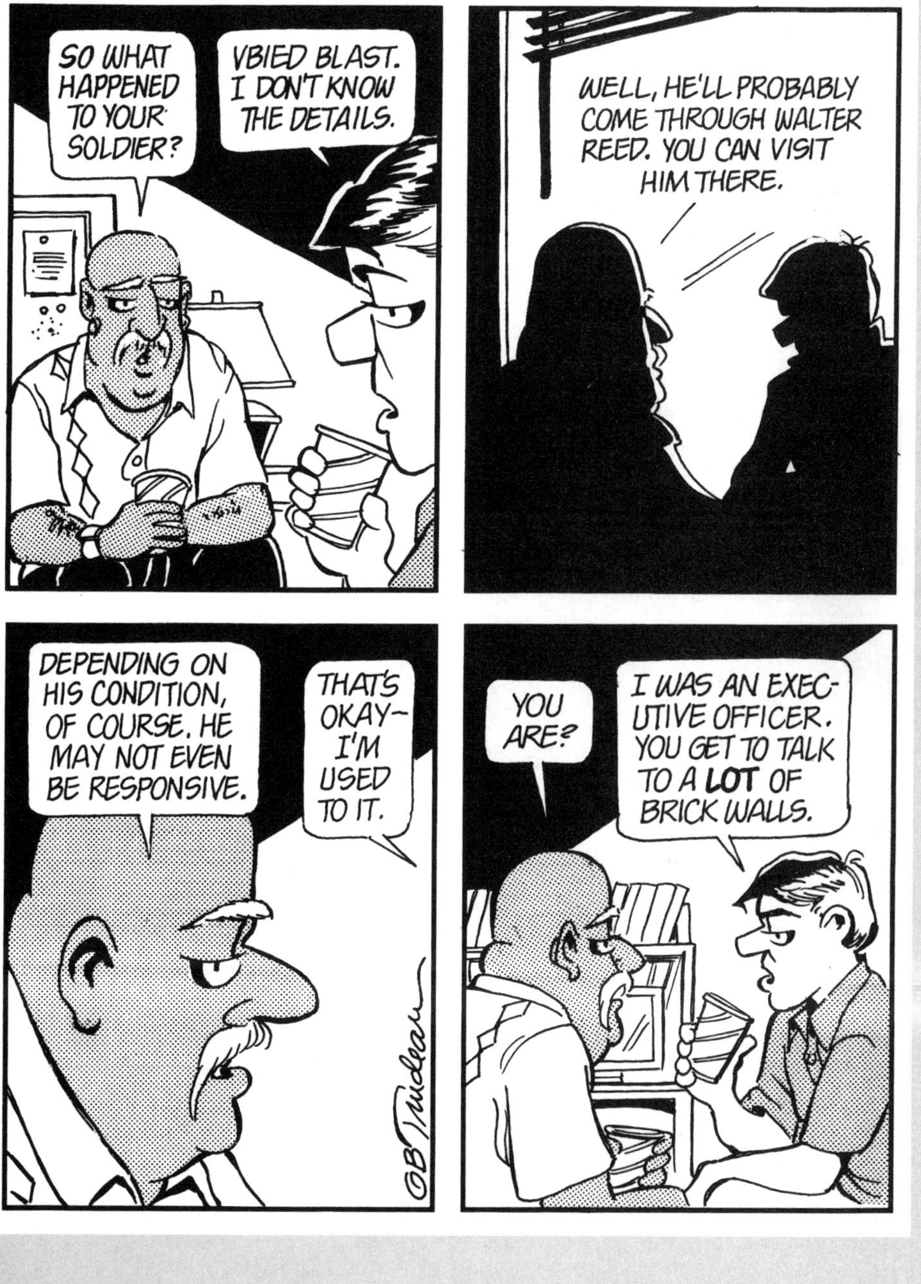
SO WHAT HAPPENED TO YOUR SOLDIER?
VBIED BLAST. I DON'T KNOW THE DETAILS.
WELL, HE'LL PROBABLY COME THROUGH WALTER REED. YOU CAN VISIT HIM THERE.
DEPENDING ON HIS CONDITION, OF COURSE. HE MAY NOT EVEN BE RESPONSIVE.
THAT'S OKAY— I'M USED TO IT.
YOU ARE?
I WAS AN EXECUTIVE OFFICER. YOU GET TO TALK TO A **LOT** OF BRICK WALLS.
GBTrudeau

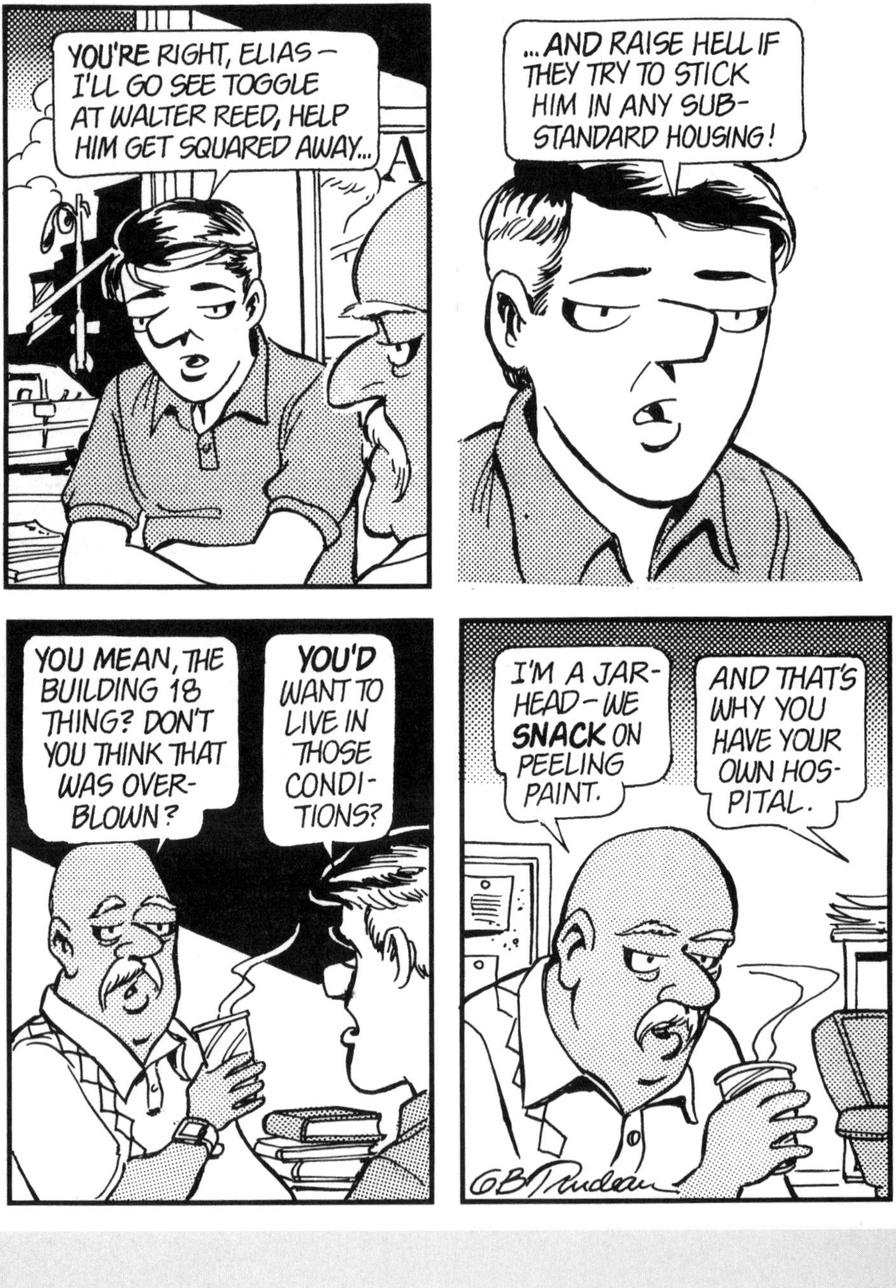
YOU'RE RIGHT, ELIAS – I'LL GO SEE TOGGLE AT WALTER REED, HELP HIM GET SQUARED AWAY...
...AND RAISE HELL IF THEY TRY TO STICK HIM IN ANY SUB-STANDARD HOUSING!
YOU MEAN, THE BUILDING 18 THING? DON'T YOU THINK THAT WAS OVER-BLOWN?
YOU'D WANT TO LIVE IN THOSE CONDI-TIONS?
I'M A JAR-HEAD – WE **SNACK** ON PEELING PAINT.
AND THAT'S WHY YOU HAVE YOUR OWN HOS-PITAL.
GB Trudeau

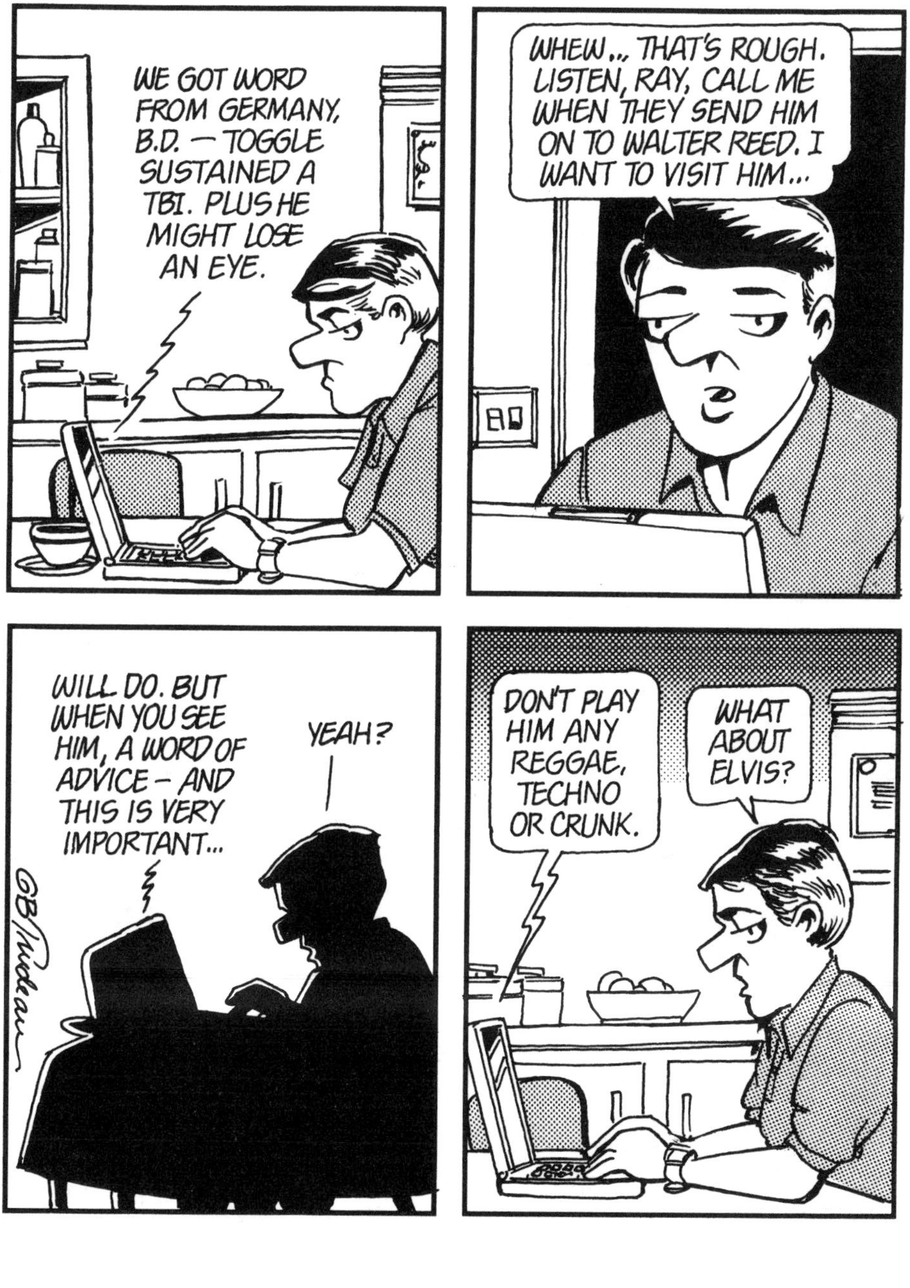
WE GOT WORD FROM GERMANY, B.D. — TOGGLE SUSTAINED A TBI. PLUS HE MIGHT LOSE AN EYE.
WHEW... THAT'S ROUGH. LISTEN, RAY, CALL ME WHEN THEY SEND HIM ON TO WALTER REED. I WANT TO VISIT HIM...
WILL DO. BUT WHEN YOU SEE HIM, A WORD OF ADVICE - AND THIS IS VERY IMPORTANT...
YEAH?
GB Trudeau
DON'T PLAY HIM ANY REGGAE, TECHNO OR CRUNK.
WHAT ABOUT ELVIS?

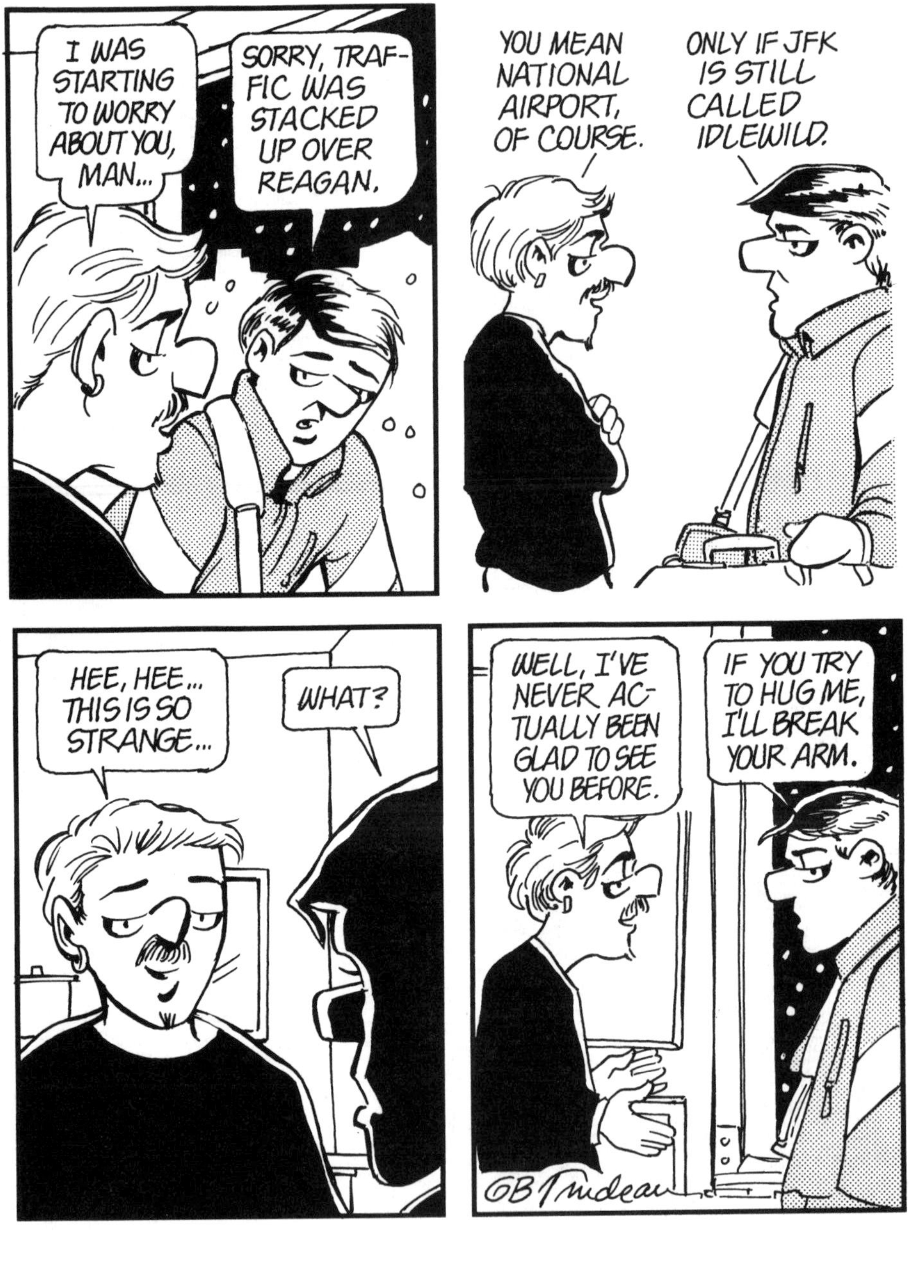
I WAS STARTING TO WORRY ABOUT YOU, MAN...
SORRY, TRAFFIC WAS STACKED UP OVER REAGAN.
YOU MEAN NATIONAL AIRPORT, OF COURSE.
ONLY IF JFK IS STILL CALLED IDLEWILD.
HEE, HEE... THIS IS SO STRANGE...
WHAT?
WELL, I'VE NEVER ACTUALLY BEEN GLAD TO SEE YOU BEFORE.
IF YOU TRY TO HUG ME, I'LL BREAK YOUR ARM.
GB Trudeau

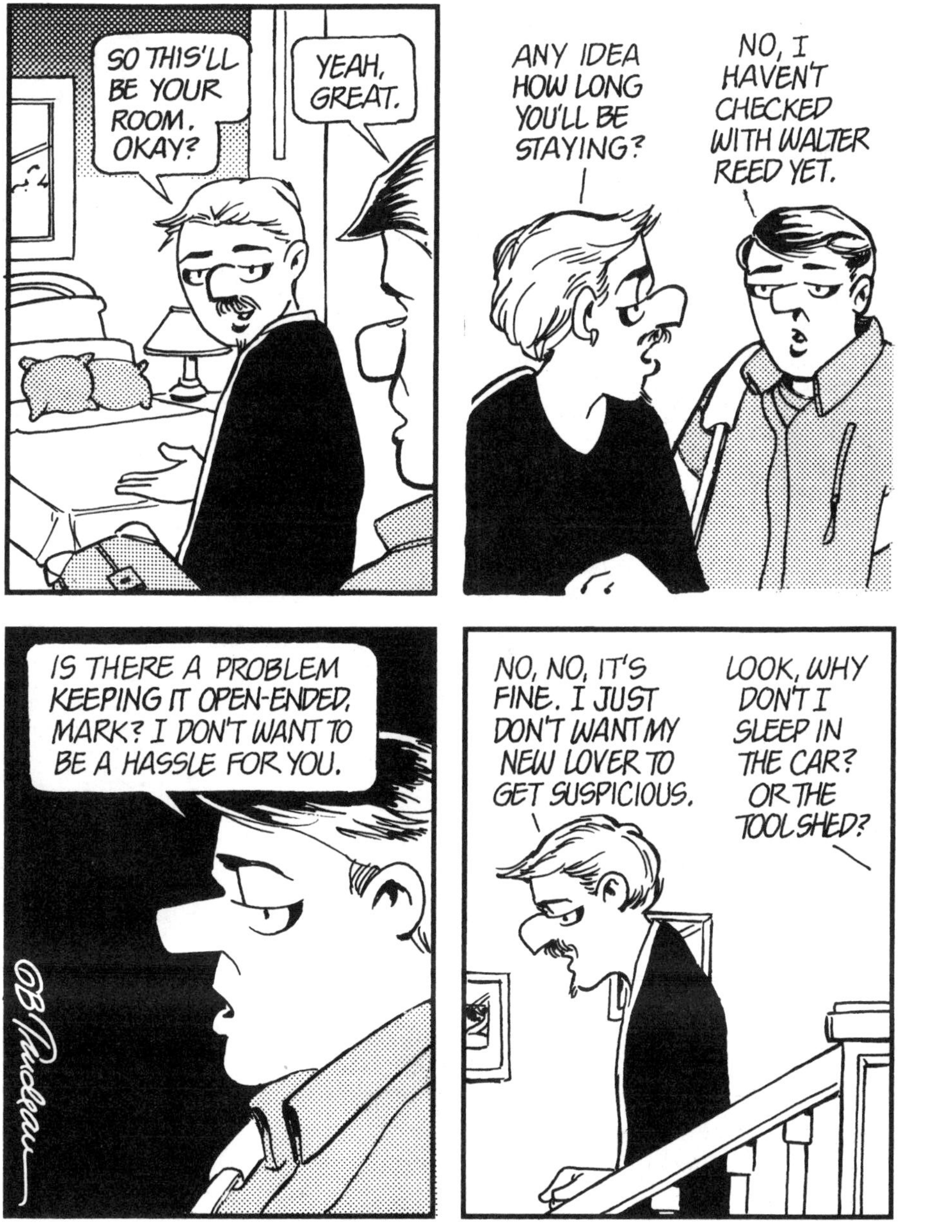
SO THIS'LL BE YOUR ROOM. OKAY?
YEAH, GREAT.
ANY IDEA HOW LONG YOU'LL BE STAYING?
NO, I HAVEN'T CHECKED WITH WALTER REED YET.
IS THERE A PROBLEM KEEPING IT OPEN-ENDED, MARK? I DON'T WANT TO BE A HASSLE FOR YOU.
NO, NO, IT'S FINE. I JUST DON'T WANT MY NEW LOVER TO GET SUSPICIOUS.
LOOK, WHY DON'T I SLEEP IN THE CAR? OR THE TOOLSHED?

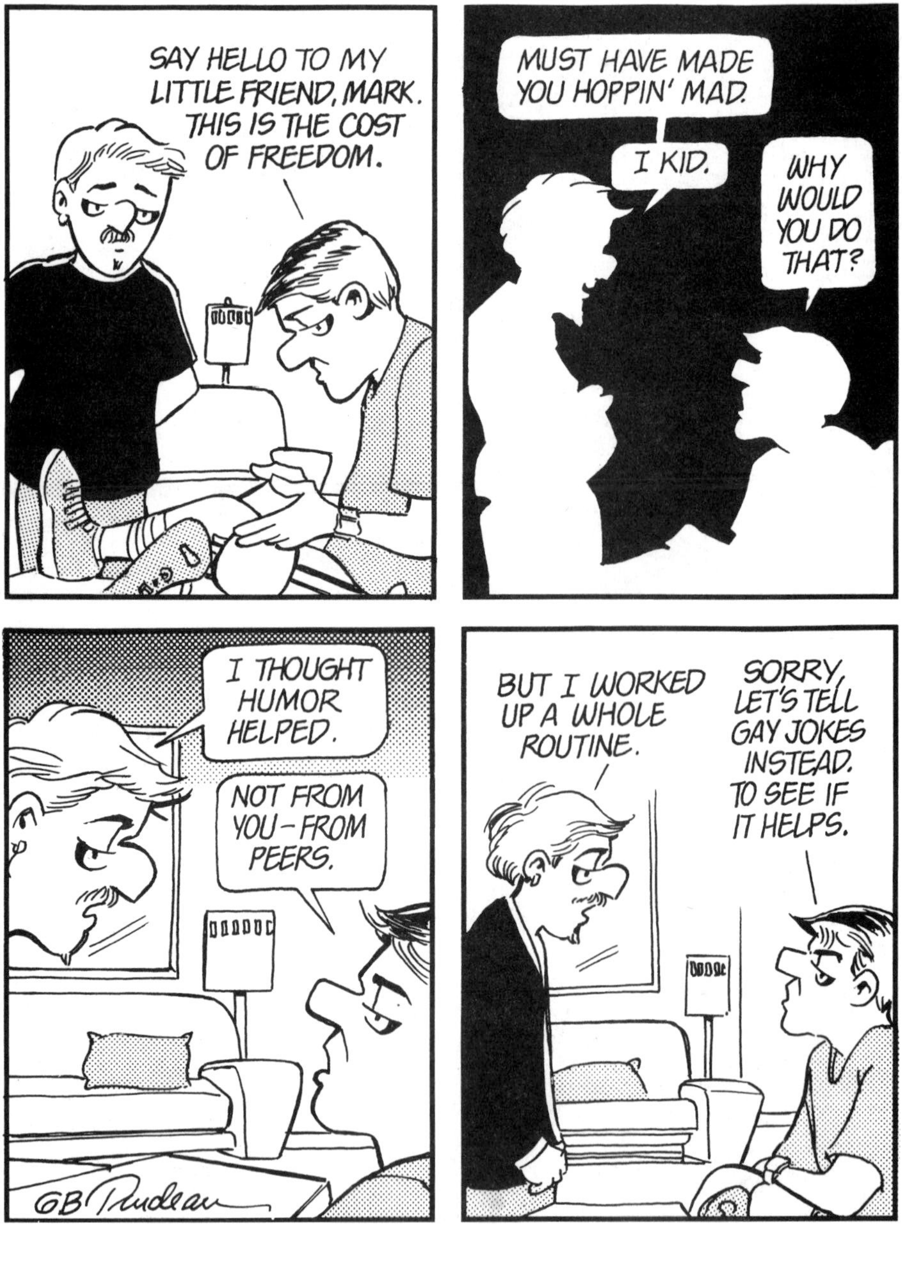
SAY HELLO TO MY LITTLE FRIEND, MARK. THIS IS THE COST OF FREEDOM.
MUST HAVE MADE YOU HOPPIN' MAD.
I KID.
WHY WOULD YOU DO THAT?
I THOUGHT HUMOR HELPED.
NOT FROM YOU-FROM PEERS.
GB Trudeau
BUT I WORKED UP A WHOLE ROUTINE.
SORRY, LET'S TELL GAY JOKES INSTEAD. TO SEE IF IT HELPS.

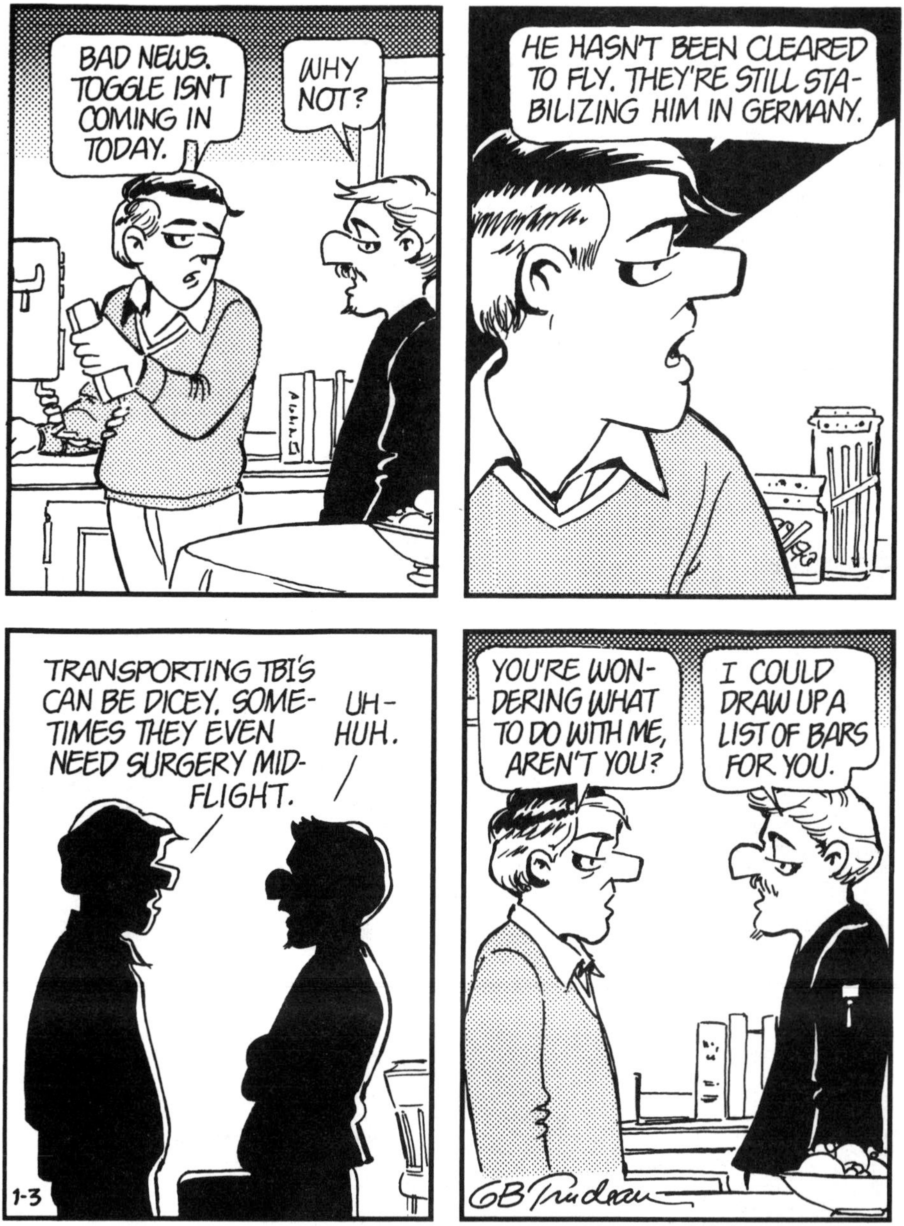

BAD NEWS. TOGGLE ISN'T COMING IN TODAY.
WHY NOT?
HE HASN'T BEEN CLEARED TO FLY. THEY'RE STILL STABILIZING HIM IN GERMANY.
TRANSPORTING TBI'S CAN BE DICEY. SOMETIMES THEY EVEN NEED SURGERY MIDFLIGHT.
UH-HUH.
YOU'RE WONDERING WHAT TO DO WITH ME, AREN'T YOU?
I COULD DRAW UP A LIST OF BARS FOR YOU.
1-3
GB Trudeau

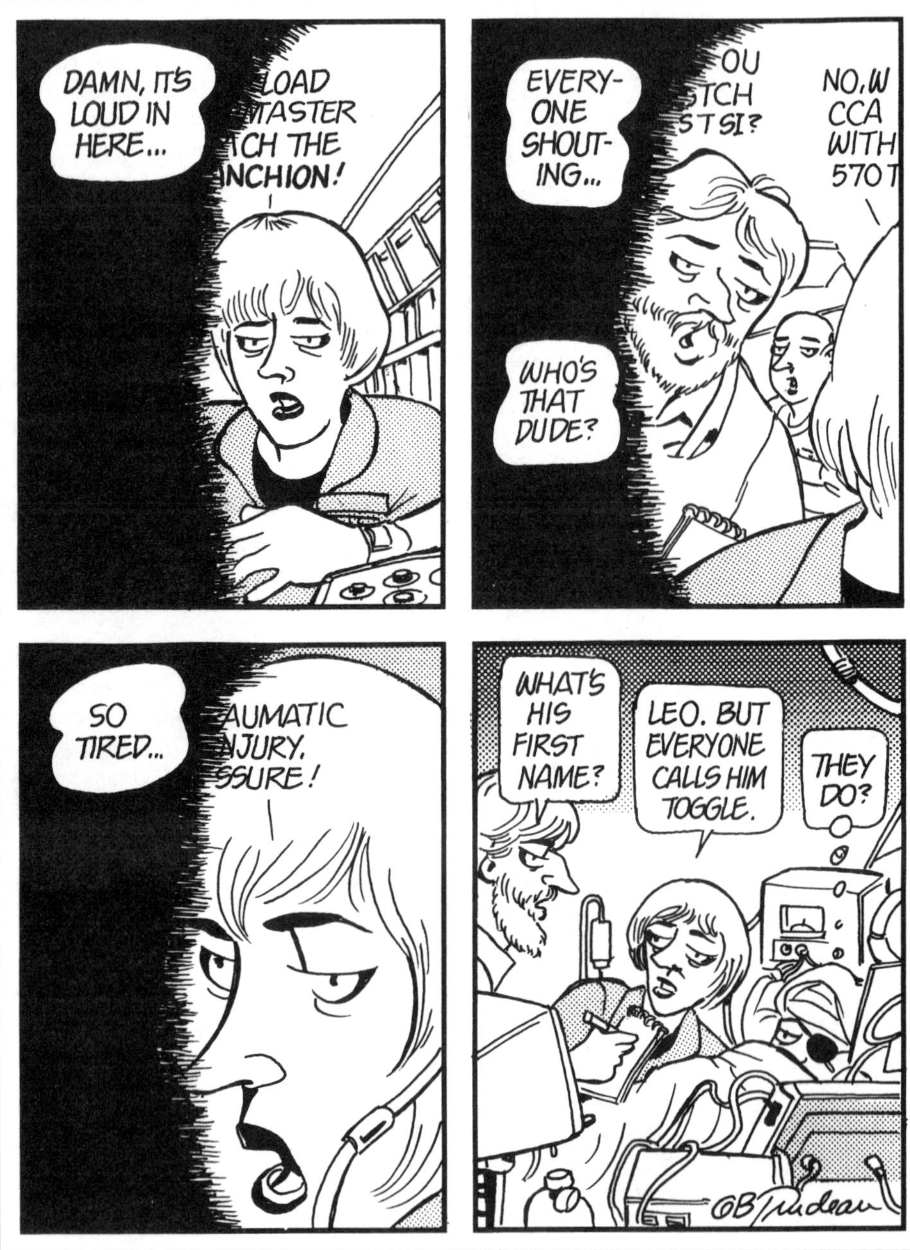

DAMN, IT'S LOUD IN HERE...
LOAD MASTER TCH THE NCHION!
EVERY-ONE SHOUT-ING...
OU TCH ST SI?
NO, W CCA WITH 570 T
WHO'S THAT DUDE?
SO TIRED...
AUMATIC NJURY. SSURE!
WHAT'S HIS FIRST NAME?
LEO. BUT EVERYONE CALLS HIM TOGGLE.
THEY DO?
©B Trudeau

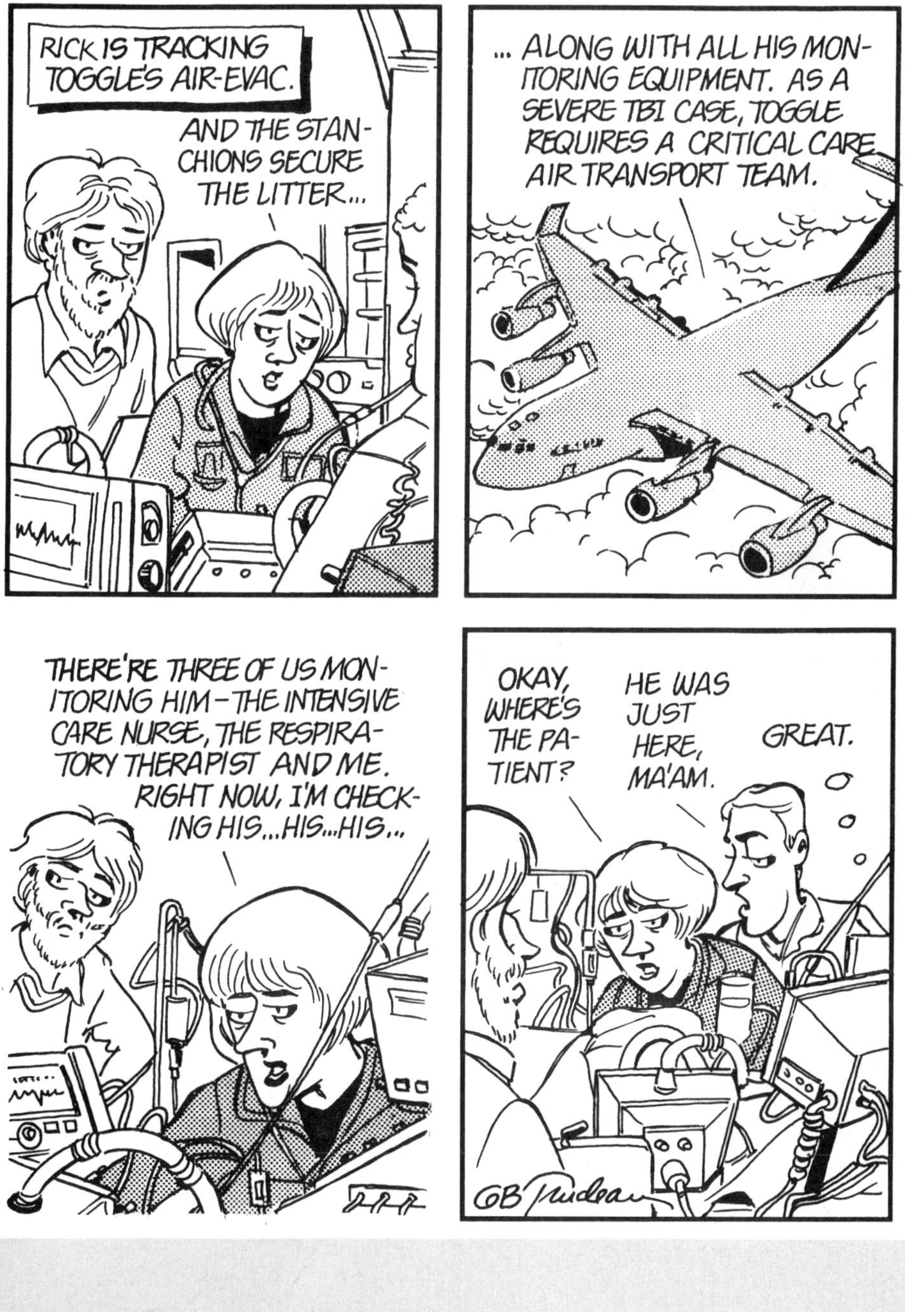
RICK IS TRACKING TOGGLE'S AIR-EVAC.
AND THE STANCHIONS SECURE THE LITTER...
... ALONG WITH ALL HIS MONITORING EQUIPMENT. AS A SEVERE TBI CASE, TOGGLE REQUIRES A CRITICAL CARE AIR TRANSPORT TEAM.
THERE'RE THREE OF US MONITORING HIM – THE INTENSIVE CARE NURSE, THE RESPIRATORY THERAPIST AND ME.
RIGHT NOW, I'M CHECKING HIS...HIS...HIS...
OKAY, WHERE'S THE PATIENT?
HE WAS JUST HERE, MA'AM.
GREAT.
GB Trudeau

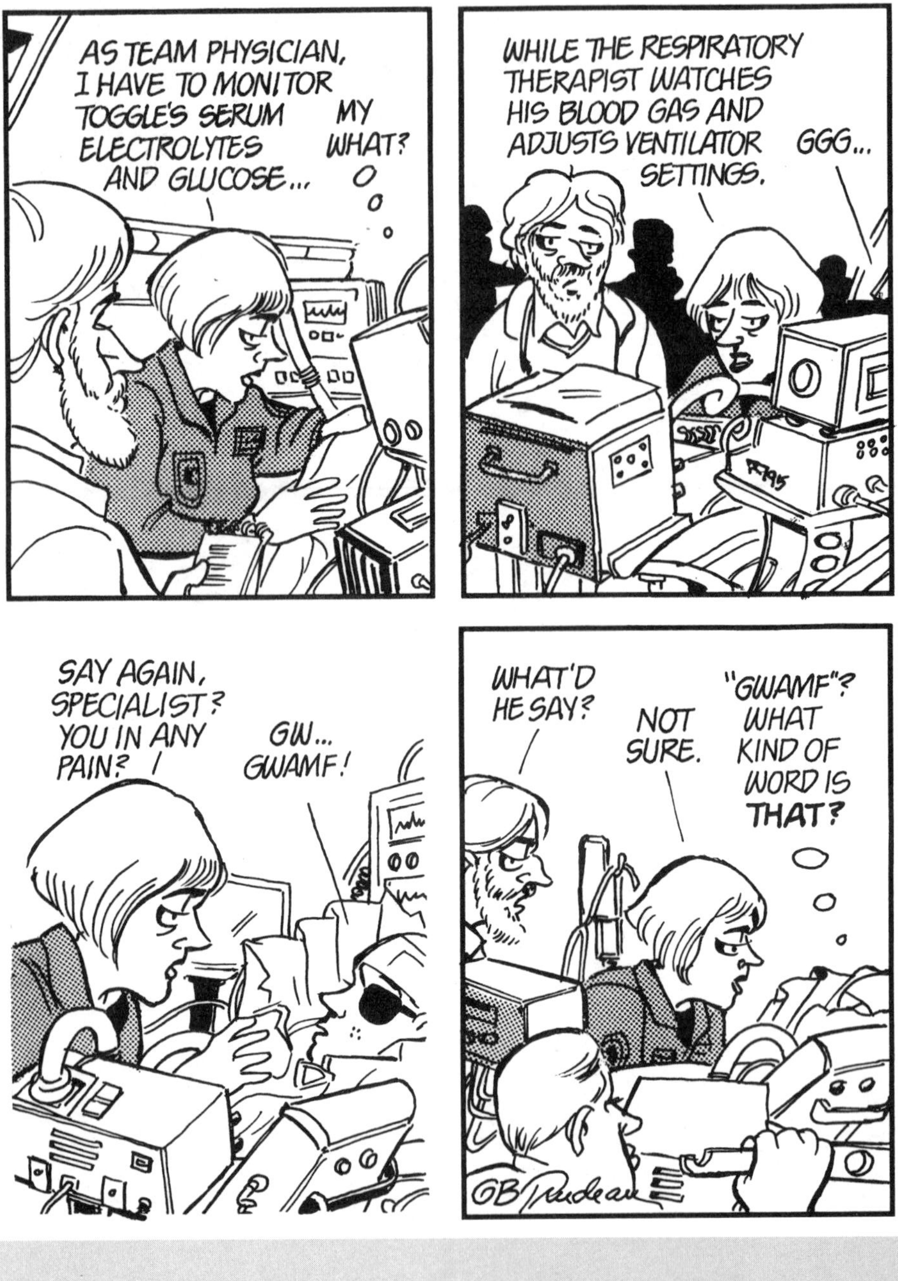
AS TEAM PHYSICIAN, I HAVE TO MONITOR TOGGLE'S SERUM ELECTROLYTES AND GLUCOSE...
MY WHAT?
WHILE THE RESPIRATORY THERAPIST WATCHES HIS BLOOD GAS AND ADJUSTS VENTILATOR SETTINGS.
GGG...
SAY AGAIN, SPECIALIST? YOU IN ANY PAIN?
GW... GWAMF!
WHAT'D HE SAY?
NOT SURE.
"GWAMF"? WHAT KIND OF WORD IS THAT?
GBTrudeau

WITH A TBI LIKE TOGGLE'S, WE HAVE TO BE PARTICULARLY VIGILANT ABOUT SWELLING...

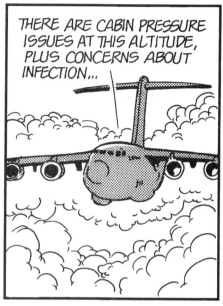

THERE ARE CABIN PRESSURE ISSUES AT THIS ALTITUDE, PLUS CONCERNS ABOUT INFECTION...

HE'S STILL CARRYING DEBRIS THAT BREACHED HIS SKULL DURING THE BLAST.

SHRAPNEL?

NO, AN iPOD EARBUD.

SO *THAT'S* WHERE IT IS!

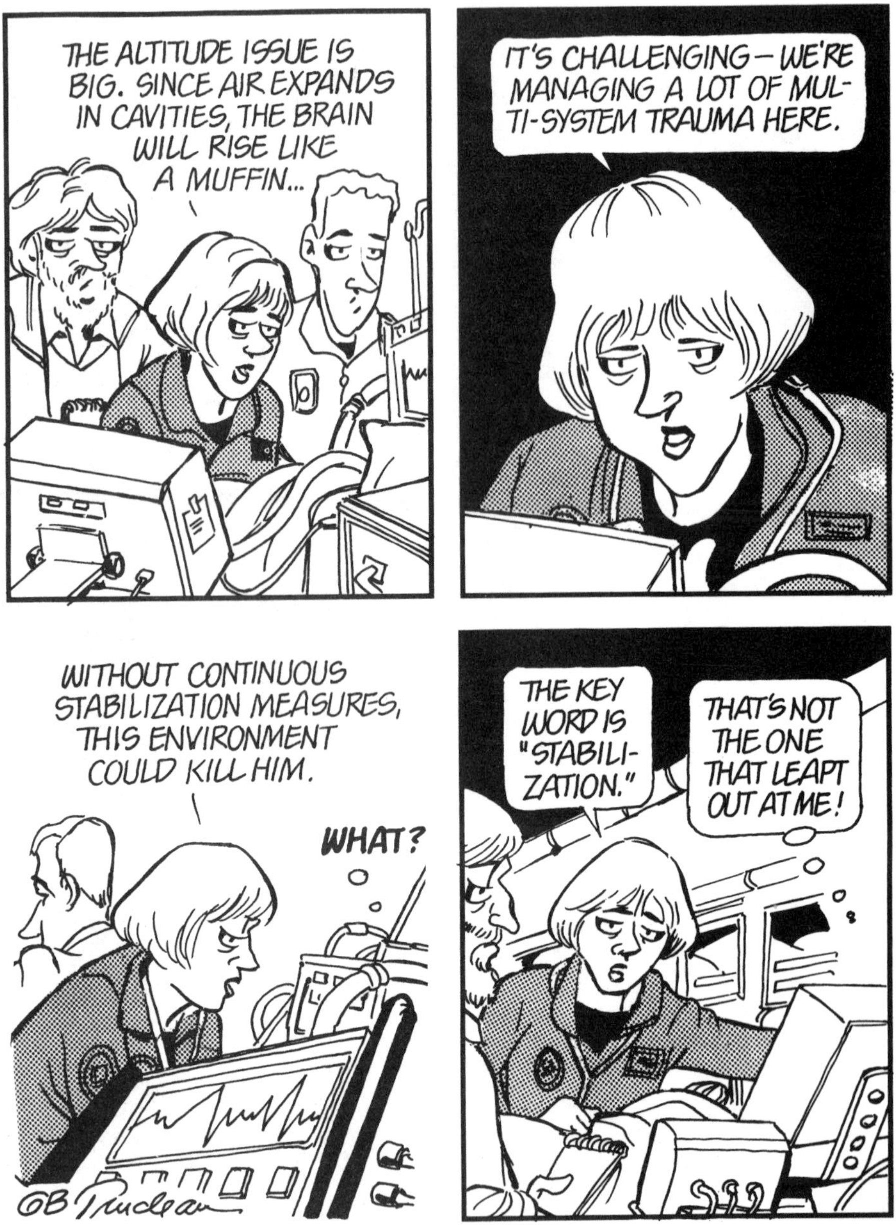
THE ALTITUDE ISSUE IS BIG. SINCE AIR EXPANDS IN CAVITIES, THE BRAIN WILL RISE LIKE A MUFFIN...
IT'S CHALLENGING—WE'RE MANAGING A LOT OF MULTI-SYSTEM TRAUMA HERE.
WITHOUT CONTINUOUS STABILIZATION MEASURES, THIS ENVIRONMENT COULD KILL HIM.
WHAT?
THE KEY WORD IS "STABILIZATION."
THAT'S NOT THE ONE THAT LEAPT OUT AT ME!
©B Trudeau

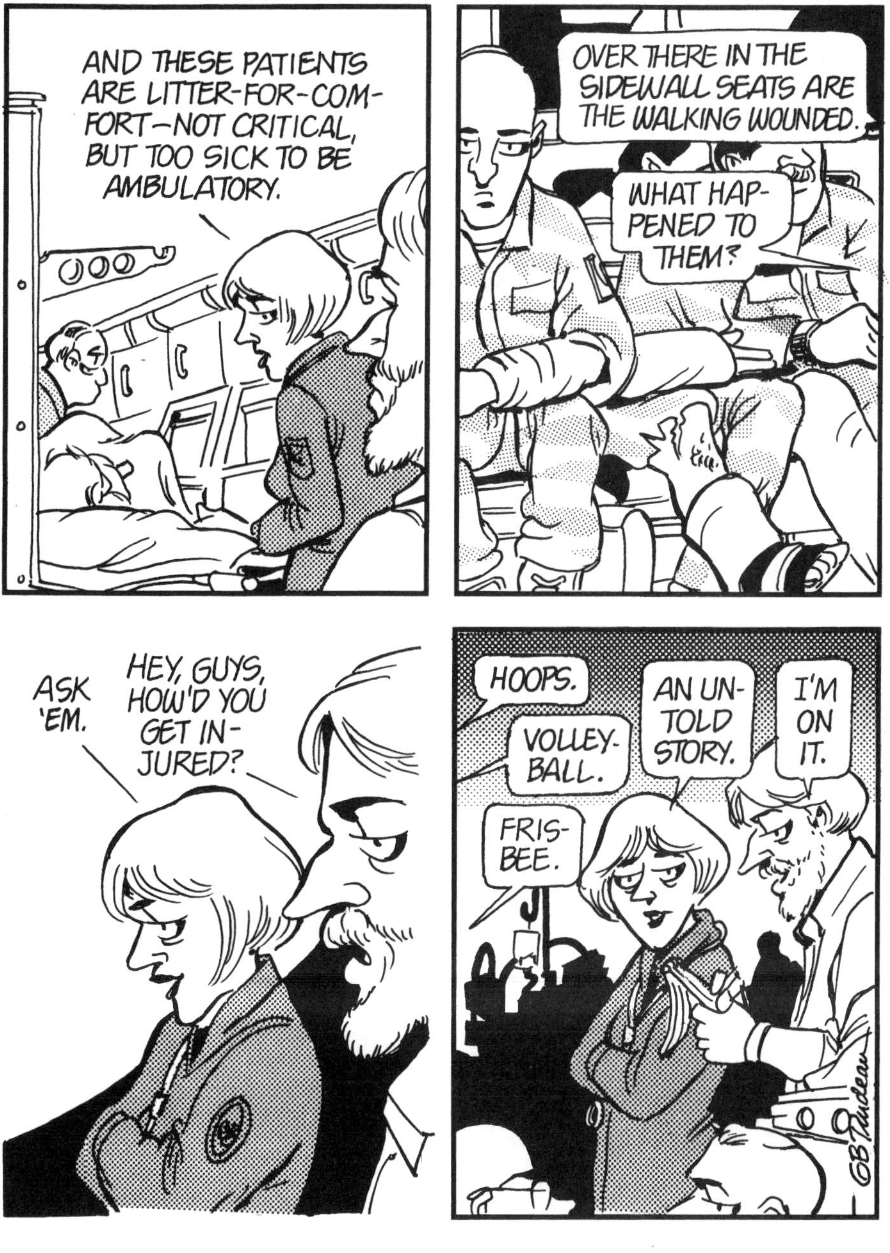
AND THESE PATIENTS ARE LITTER-FOR-COMFORT—NOT CRITICAL, BUT TOO SICK TO BE AMBULATORY.
OVER THERE IN THE SIDEWALL SEATS ARE THE WALKING WOUNDED.
WHAT HAPPENED TO THEM?
ASK 'EM.
HEY, GUYS, HOW'D YOU GET INJURED?
HOOPS.
VOLLEYBALL.
FRISBEE.
AN UNTOLD STORY.
I'M ON IT.
©GBTrudeau

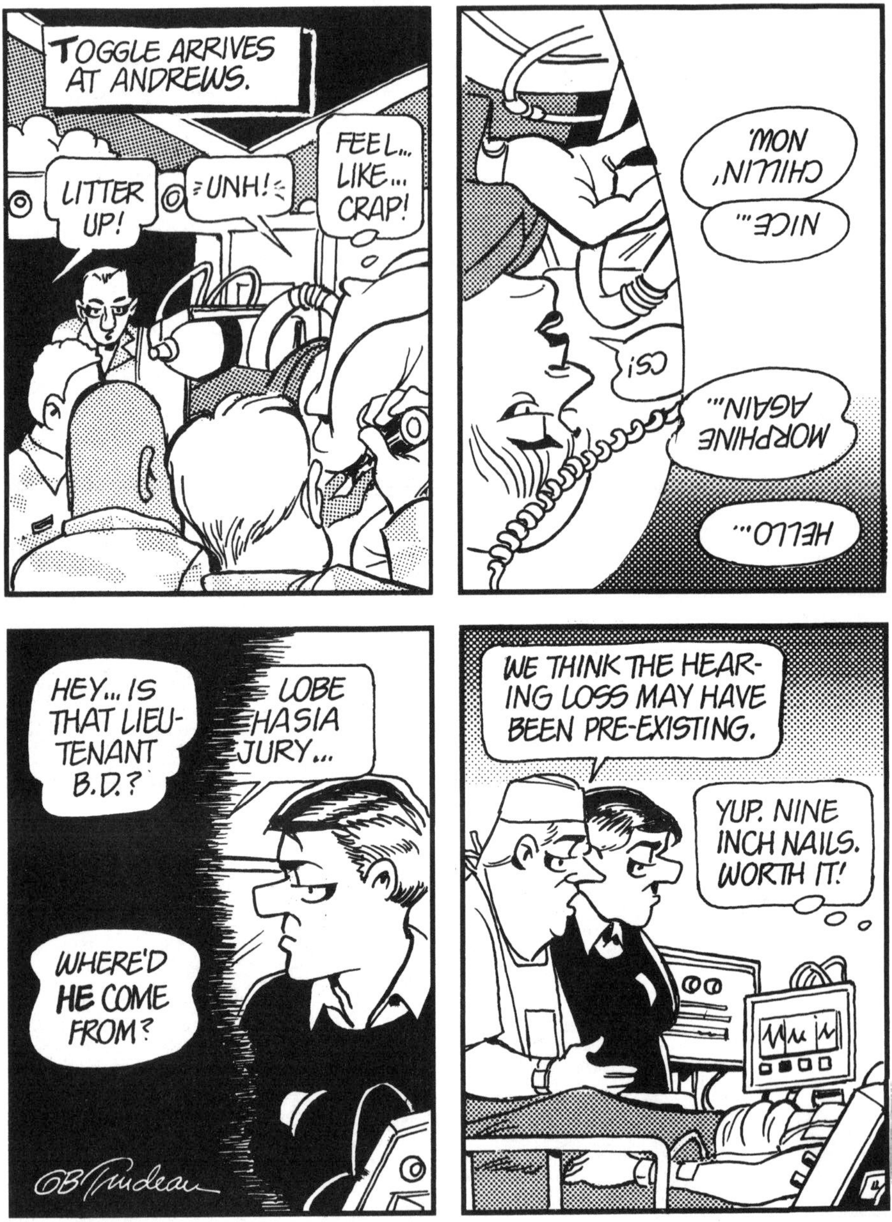
TOGGLE ARRIVES AT ANDREWS.
LITTER UP!
UNH!
FEEL... LIKE... CRAP!
HELLO...
MORPHINE AGAIN...
CS!
NICE...
CHILLIN', NOW.
HEY... IS THAT LIEU-TENANT B.D.?
LOBE HASIA JURY...
WHERE'D **HE** COME FROM?
WE THINK THE HEAR-ING LOSS MAY HAVE BEEN PRE-EXISTING.
YUP. NINE INCH NAILS. WORTH IT!
GB Trudeau

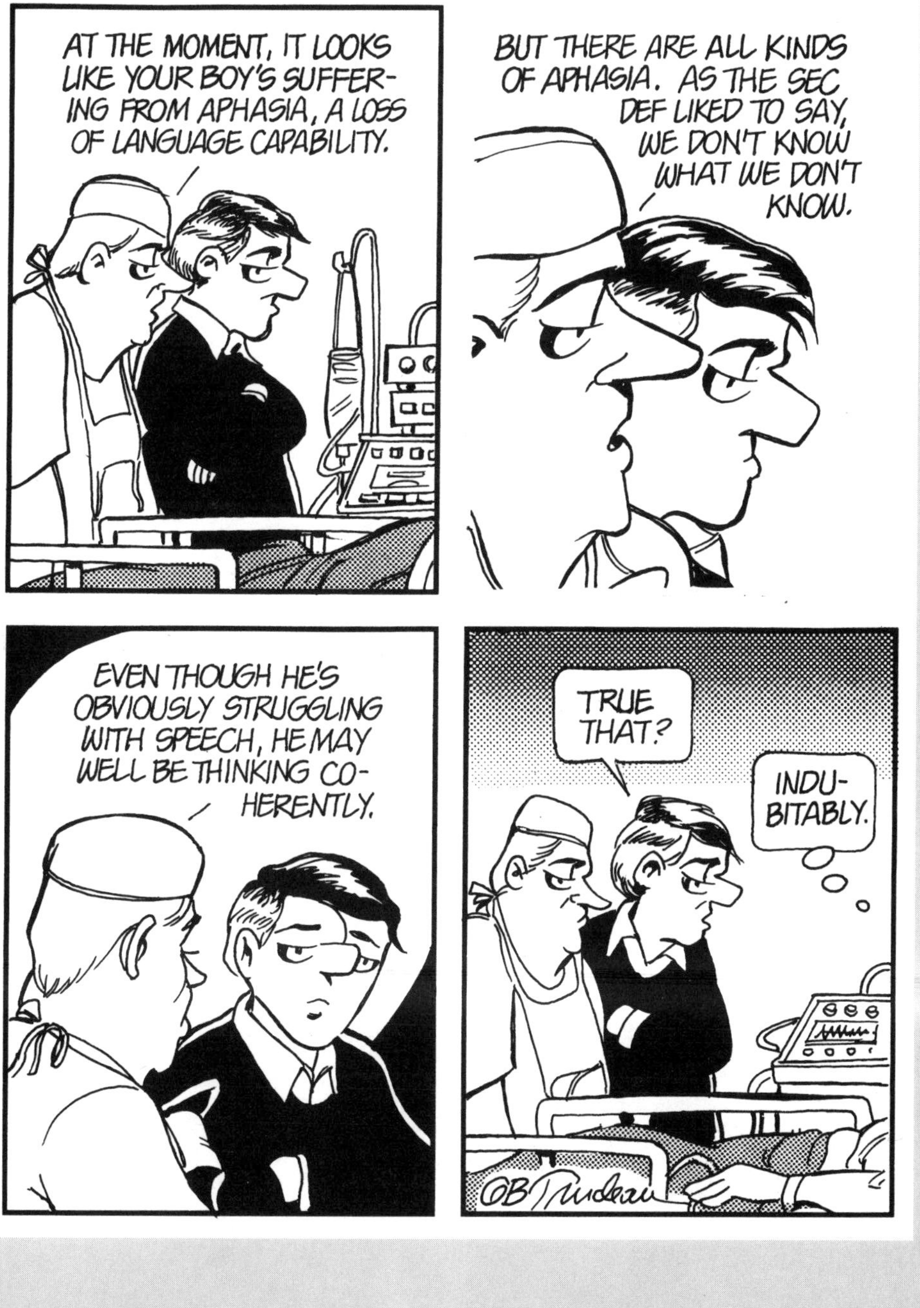
AT THE MOMENT, IT LOOKS LIKE YOUR BOY'S SUFFERING FROM APHASIA, A LOSS OF LANGUAGE CAPABILITY.
BUT THERE ARE ALL KINDS OF APHASIA. AS THE SEC DEF LIKED TO SAY, WE DON'T KNOW WHAT WE DON'T KNOW.
EVEN THOUGH HE'S OBVIOUSLY STRUGGLING WITH SPEECH, HE MAY WELL BE THINKING COHERENTLY.
TRUE THAT?
INDUBITABLY.
©B Trudeau

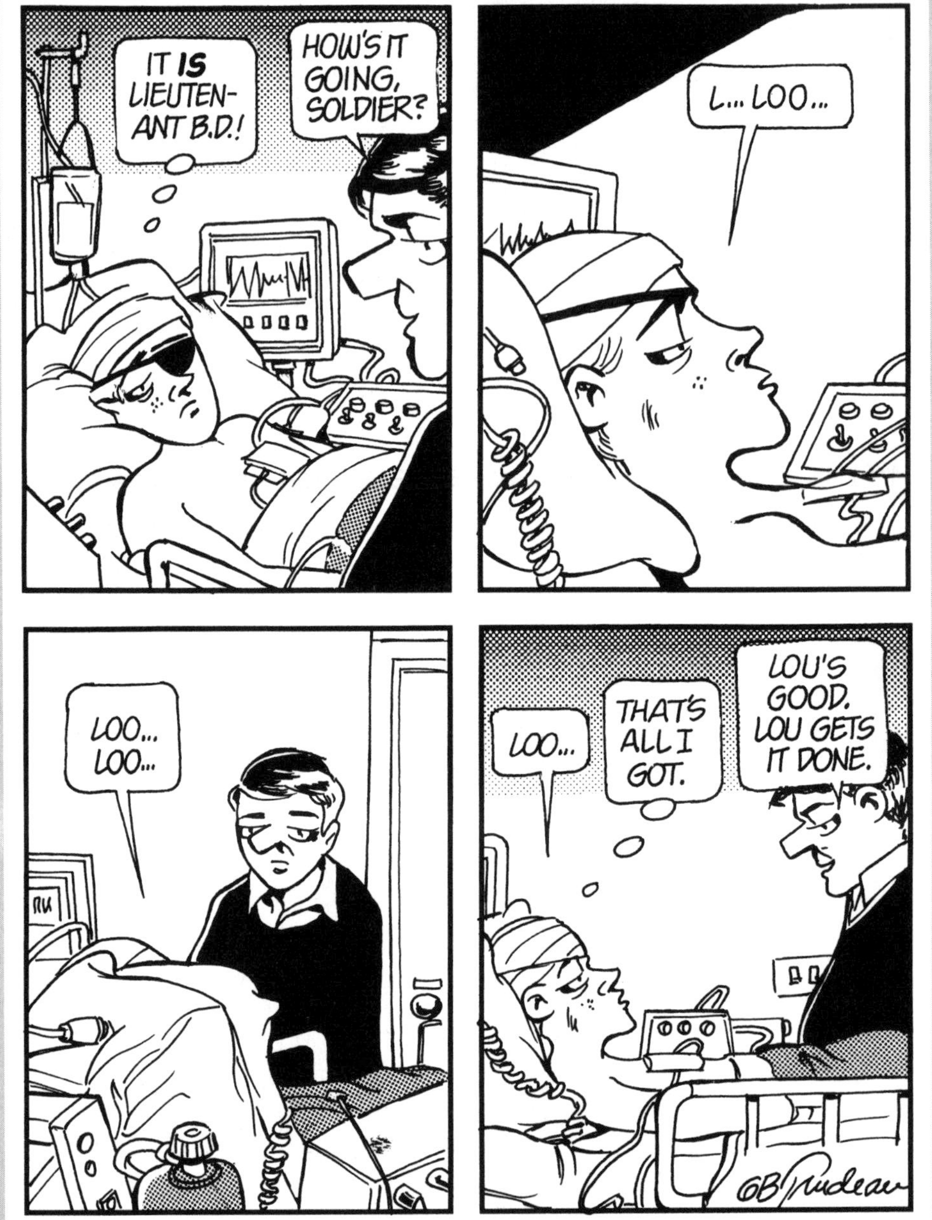
IT **IS** LIEUTEN-ANT B.D.!
HOW'S IT GOING, SOLDIER?
L... LOO...
LOO... LOO...
LOO...
THAT'S ALL I GOT.
LOU'S GOOD. LOU GETS IT DONE.
GB Trudeau

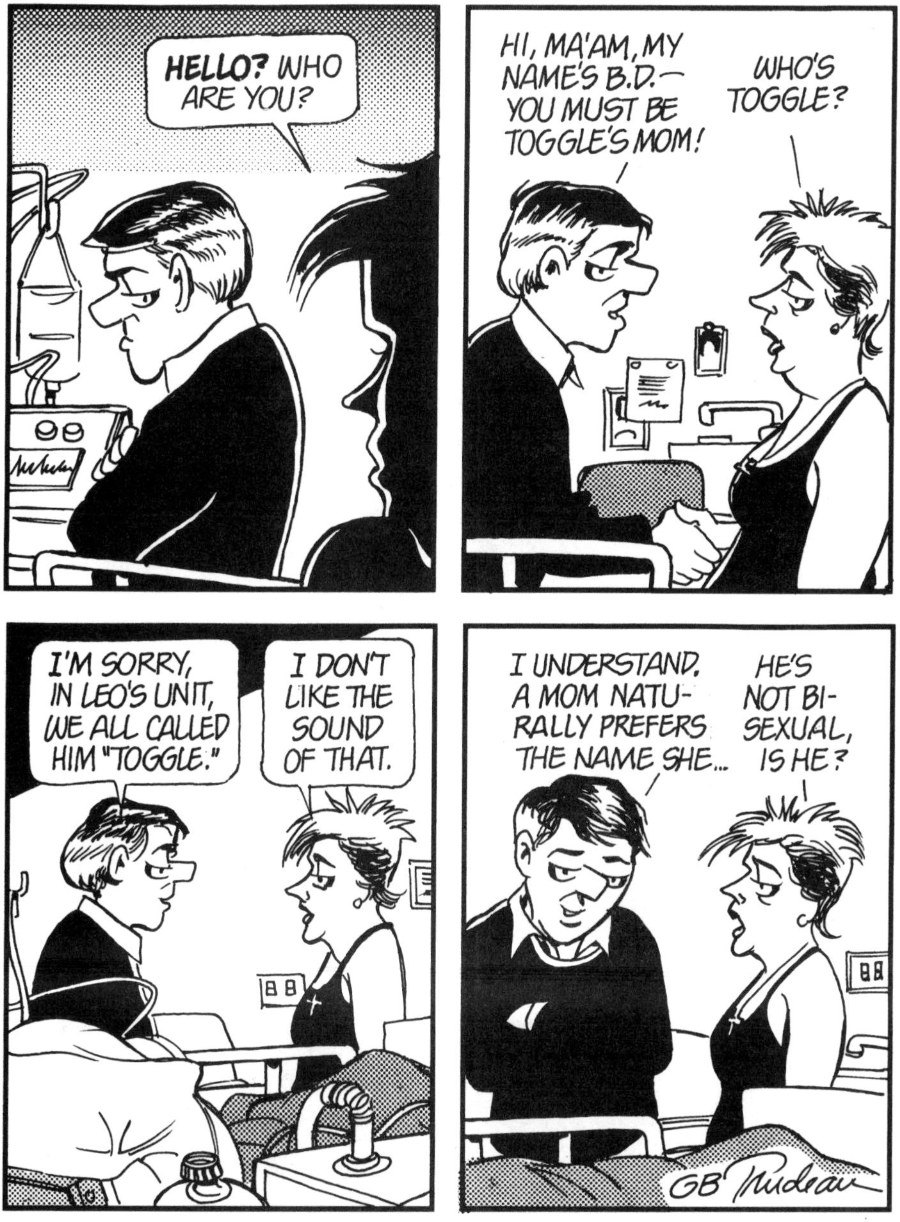
HELLO? WHO ARE YOU?
HI, MA'AM, MY NAME'S B.D.— YOU MUST BE TOGGLE'S MOM!
WHO'S TOGGLE?
I'M SORRY, IN LEO'S UNIT, WE ALL CALLED HIM "TOGGLE."
I DON'T LIKE THE SOUND OF THAT.
I UNDERSTAND. A MOM NATU-RALLY PREFERS THE NAME SHE...
HE'S NOT BI-SEXUAL, IS HE?
GB Trudeau

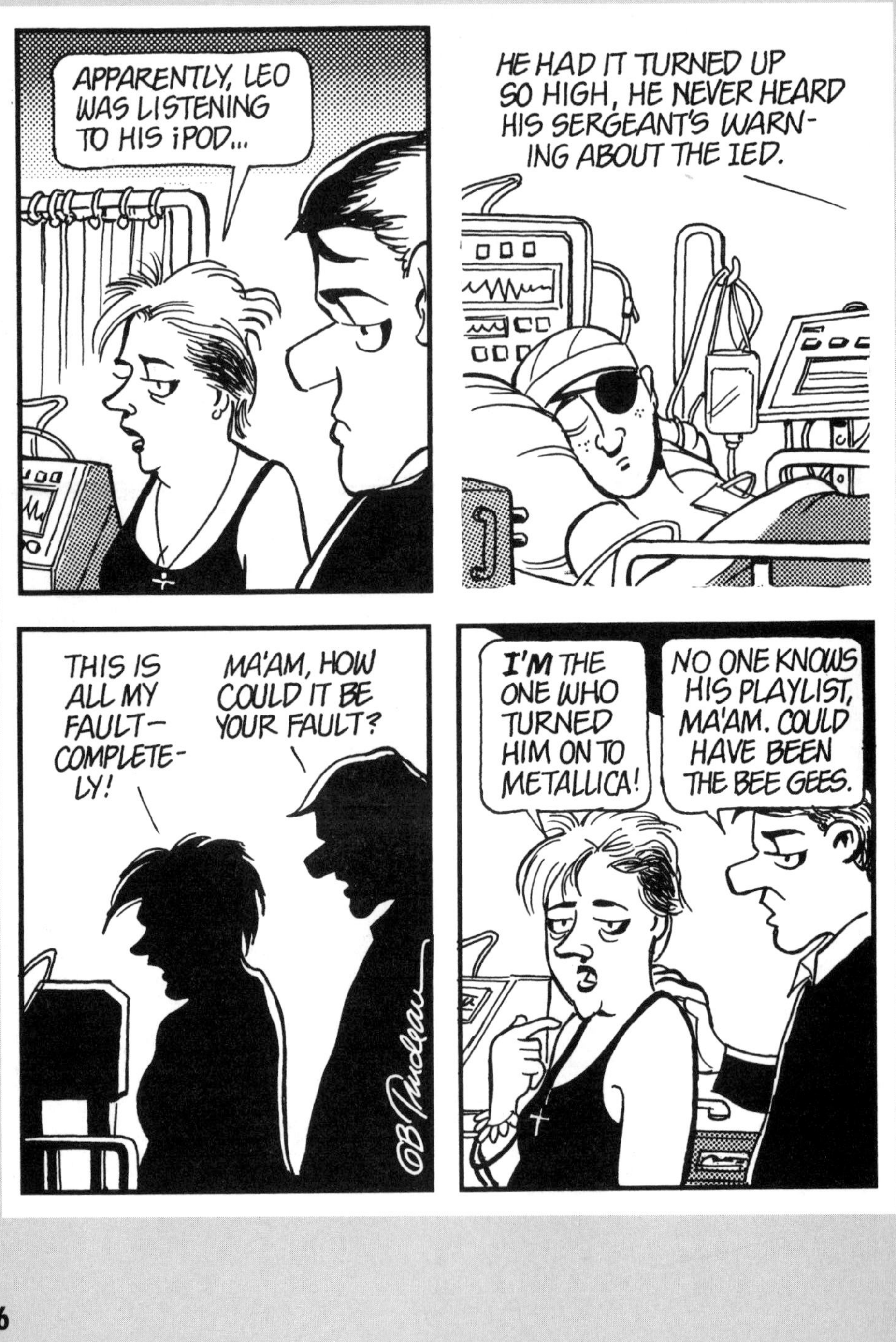

APPARENTLY, LEO WAS LISTENING TO HIS iPOD...
HE HAD IT TURNED UP SO HIGH, HE NEVER HEARD HIS SERGEANT'S WARNING ABOUT THE IED.
THIS IS ALL MY FAULT— COMPLETELY!
MA'AM, HOW COULD IT BE YOUR FAULT?
I'M THE ONE WHO TURNED HIM ON TO METALLICA!
NO ONE KNOWS HIS PLAYLIST, MA'AM. COULD HAVE BEEN THE BEE GEES.
©B Trudeau

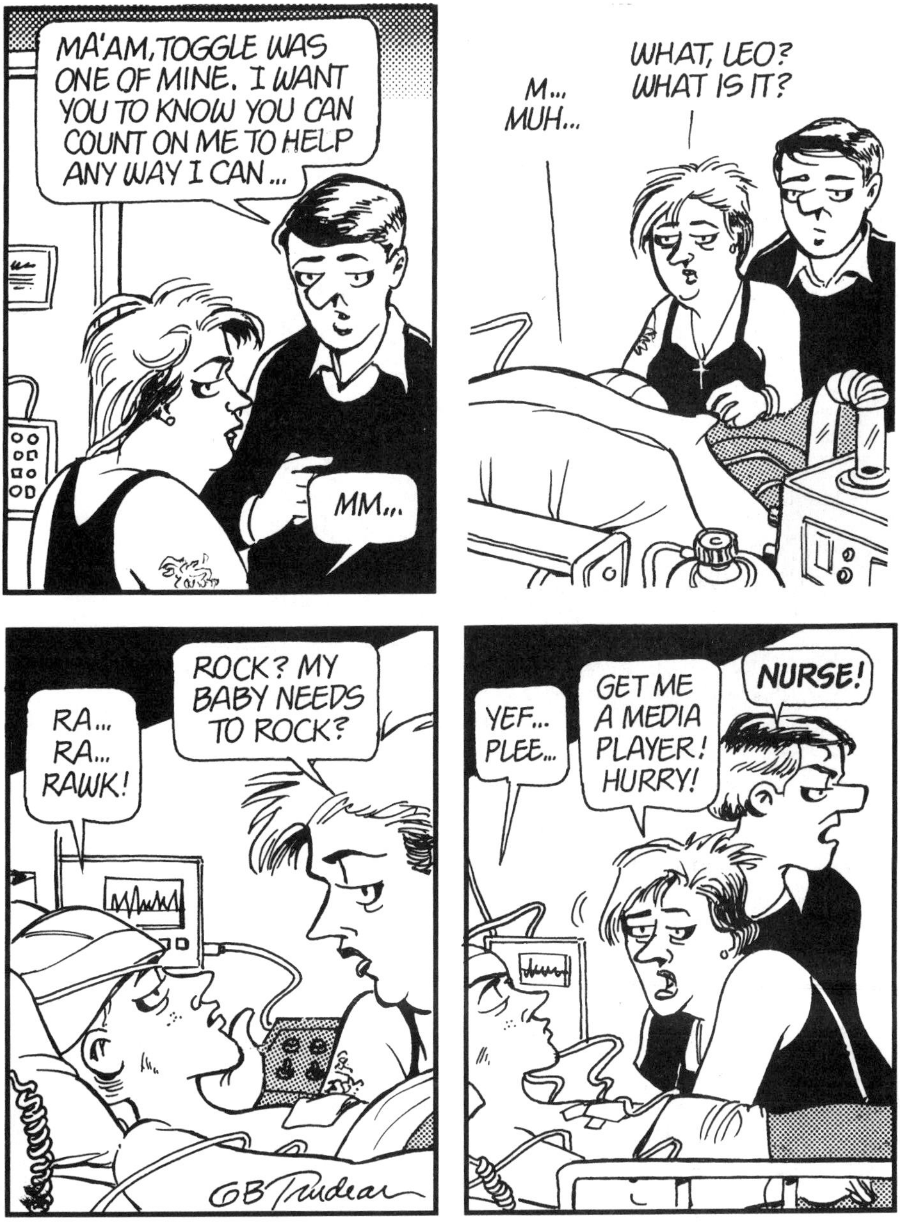
MA'AM, TOGGLE WAS ONE OF MINE. I WANT YOU TO KNOW YOU CAN COUNT ON ME TO HELP ANY WAY I CAN...
MM...
M... MUH...
WHAT, LEO? WHAT IS IT?
RA... RA... RAWK!
ROCK? MY BABY NEEDS TO ROCK?
YEF... PLEE...
GET ME A MEDIA PLAYER! HURRY!
NURSE!
GB Trudeau

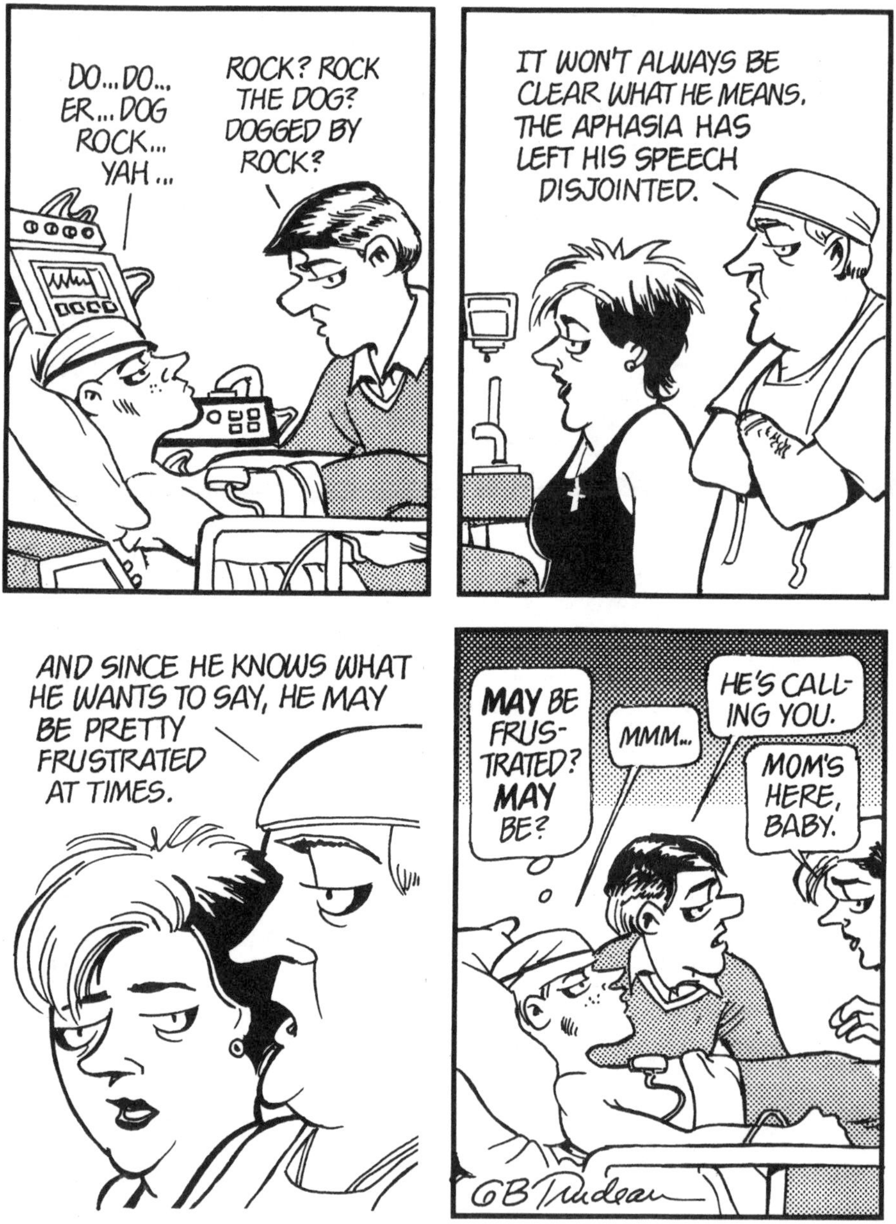
DO...DO... ER...DOG ROCK... YAH...
ROCK? ROCK THE DOG? DOGGED BY ROCK?
IT WON'T ALWAYS BE CLEAR WHAT HE MEANS. THE APHASIA HAS LEFT HIS SPEECH DISJOINTED.
AND SINCE HE KNOWS WHAT HE WANTS TO SAY, HE MAY BE PRETTY FRUSTRATED AT TIMES.
MAY BE FRUS-TRATED? MAY BE?
MMM...
HE'S CALL-ING YOU.
MOM'S HERE, BABY.
GB Trudeau

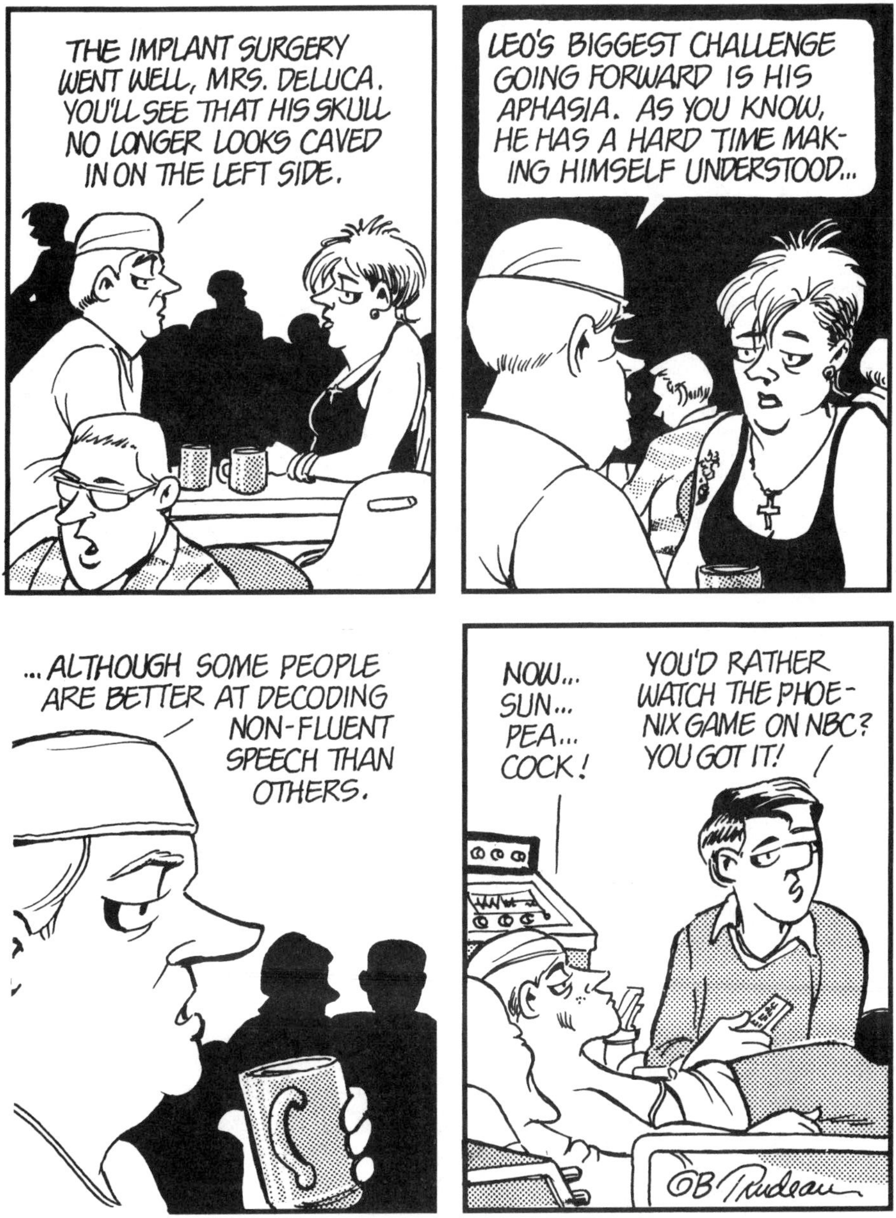
THE IMPLANT SURGERY WENT WELL, MRS. DELUCA. YOU'LL SEE THAT HIS SKULL NO LONGER LOOKS CAVED IN ON THE LEFT SIDE.
LEO'S BIGGEST CHALLENGE GOING FORWARD IS HIS APHASIA. AS YOU KNOW, HE HAS A HARD TIME MAKING HIMSELF UNDERSTOOD...
...ALTHOUGH SOME PEOPLE ARE BETTER AT DECODING NON-FLUENT SPEECH THAN OTHERS.
NOW... SUN... PEA... COCK!
YOU'D RATHER WATCH THE PHOENIX GAME ON NBC? YOU GOT IT!
©B. Trudeau

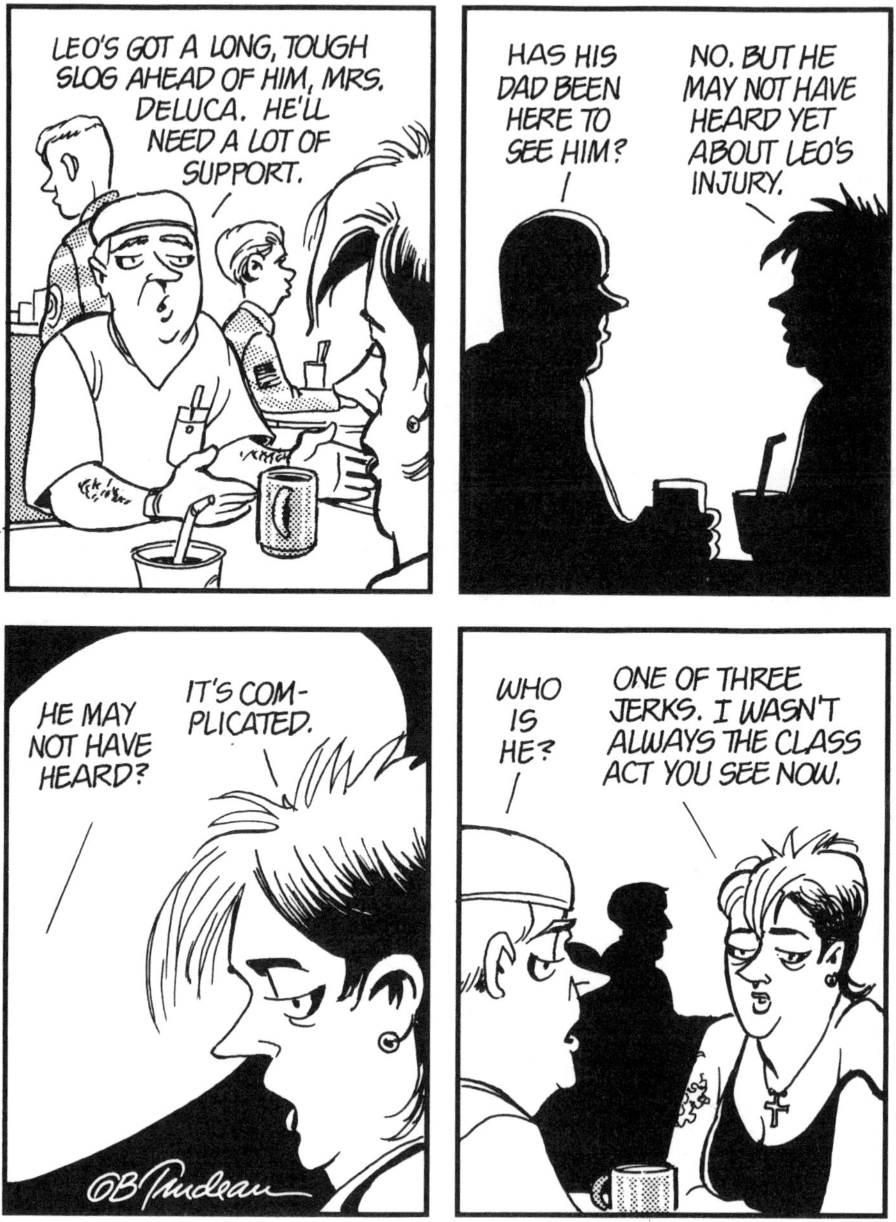
LEO'S GOT A LONG, TOUGH SLOG AHEAD OF HIM, MRS. DELUCA. HE'LL NEED A LOT OF SUPPORT.
HAS HIS DAD BEEN HERE TO SEE HIM?
NO. BUT HE MAY NOT HAVE HEARD YET ABOUT LEO'S INJURY.
HE MAY NOT HAVE HEARD?
IT'S COM-PLICATED.
©B Trudeau
WHO IS HE?
ONE OF THREE JERKS. I WASN'T ALWAYS THE CLASS ACT YOU SEE NOW.

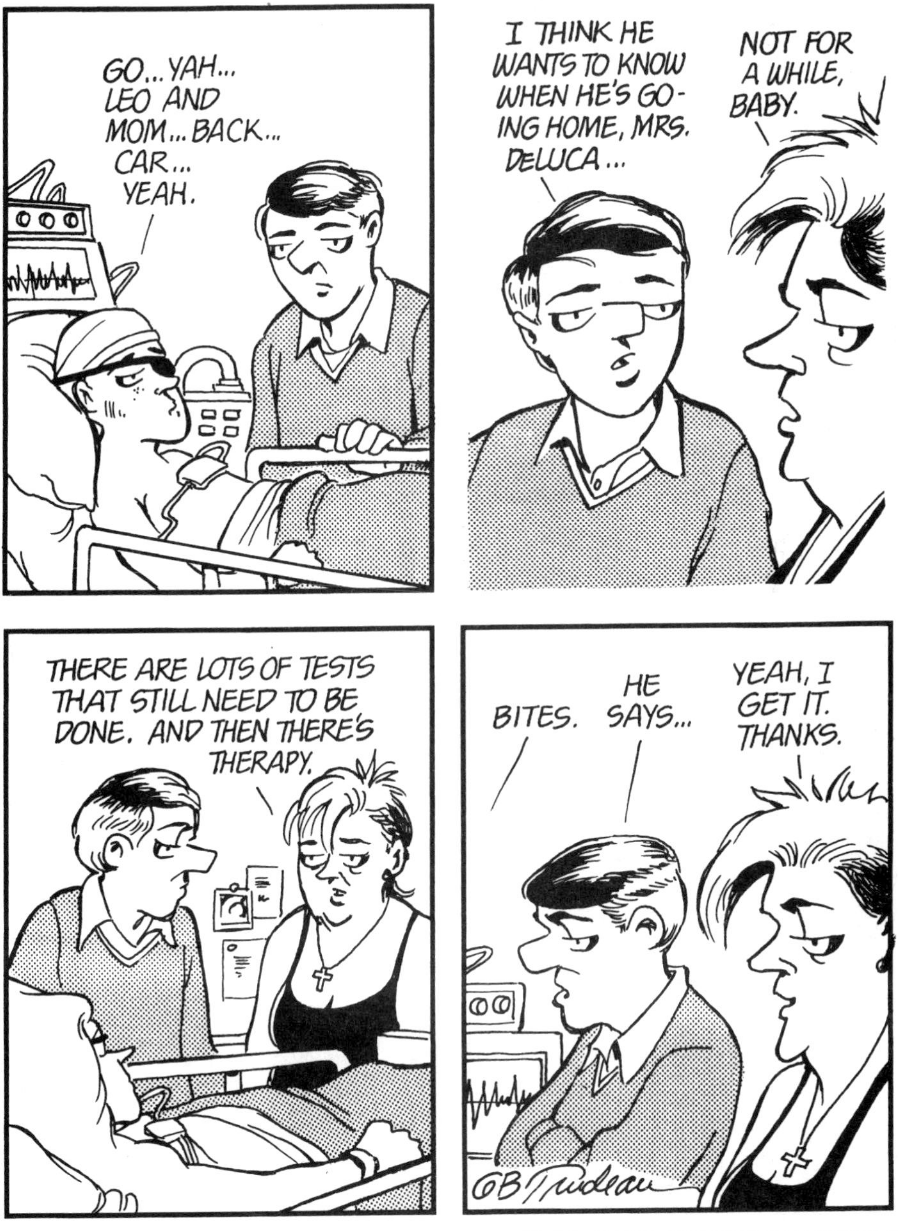
GO... YAH... LEO AND MOM... BACK... CAR... YEAH.
I THINK HE WANTS TO KNOW WHEN HE'S GO-ING HOME, MRS. DELUCA...
NOT FOR A WHILE, BABY.
THERE ARE LOTS OF TESTS THAT STILL NEED TO BE DONE. AND THEN THERE'S THERAPY.
BITES.
HE SAYS...
YEAH, I GET IT. THANKS.
©B Trudeau

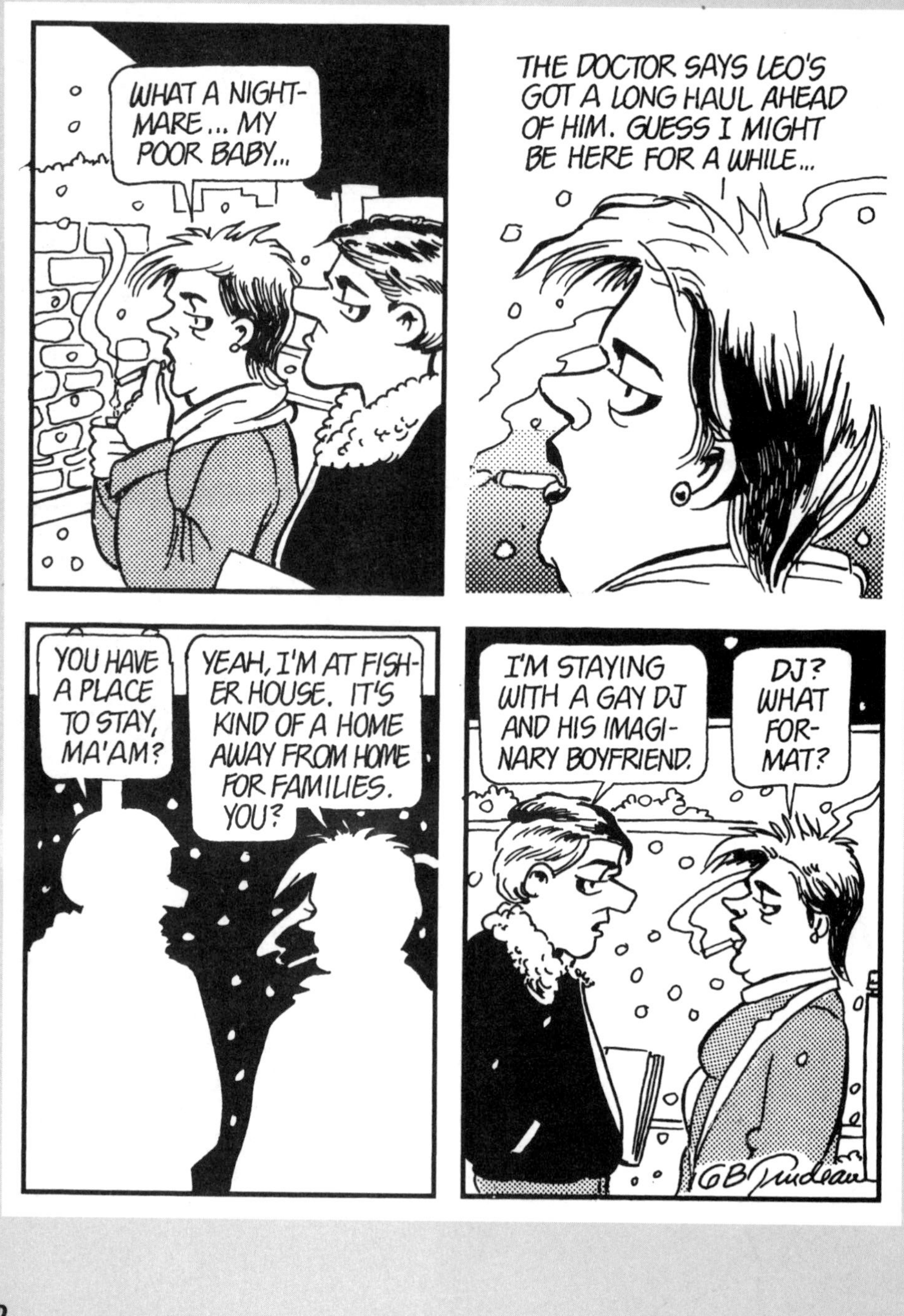
WHAT A NIGHT-MARE... MY POOR BABY...
THE DOCTOR SAYS LEO'S GOT A LONG HAUL AHEAD OF HIM. GUESS I MIGHT BE HERE FOR A WHILE...
YOU HAVE A PLACE TO STAY, MA'AM?
YEAH, I'M AT FISH-ER HOUSE. IT'S KIND OF A HOME AWAY FROM HOME FOR FAMILIES. YOU?
I'M STAYING WITH A GAY DJ AND HIS IMAGI-NARY BOYFRIEND.
DJ? WHAT FOR-MAT?
GB Trudeau

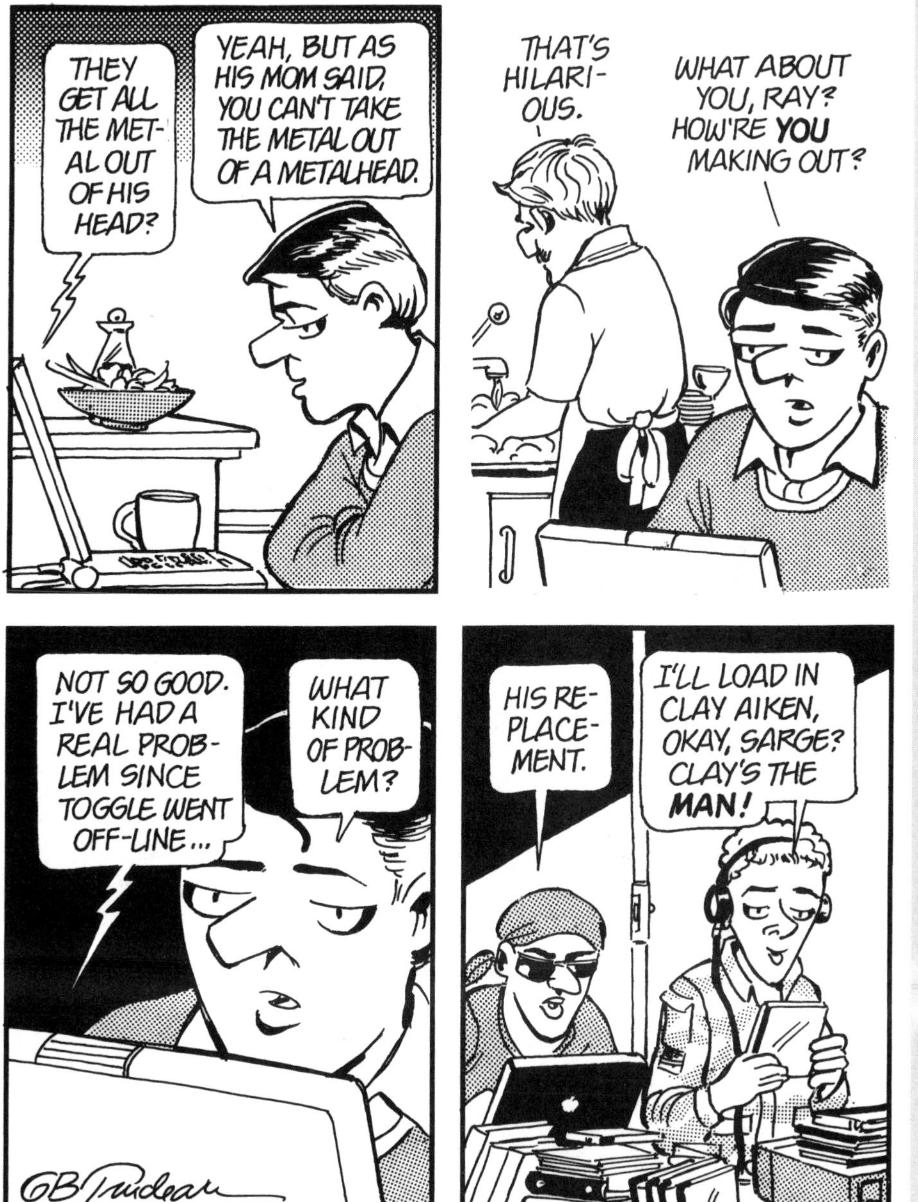
THEY GET ALL THE MET-AL OUT OF HIS HEAD?
YEAH, BUT AS HIS MOM SAID, YOU CAN'T TAKE THE METAL OUT OF A METALHEAD.
THAT'S HILARI-OUS.
WHAT ABOUT YOU, RAY? HOW'RE **YOU** MAKING OUT?
NOT SO GOOD. I'VE HAD A REAL PROB-LEM SINCE TOGGLE WENT OFF-LINE...
WHAT KIND OF PROB-LEM?
HIS RE-PLACE-MENT.
I'LL LOAD IN CLAY AIKEN, OKAY, SARGE? CLAY'S THE **MAN**!
GB Trudeau

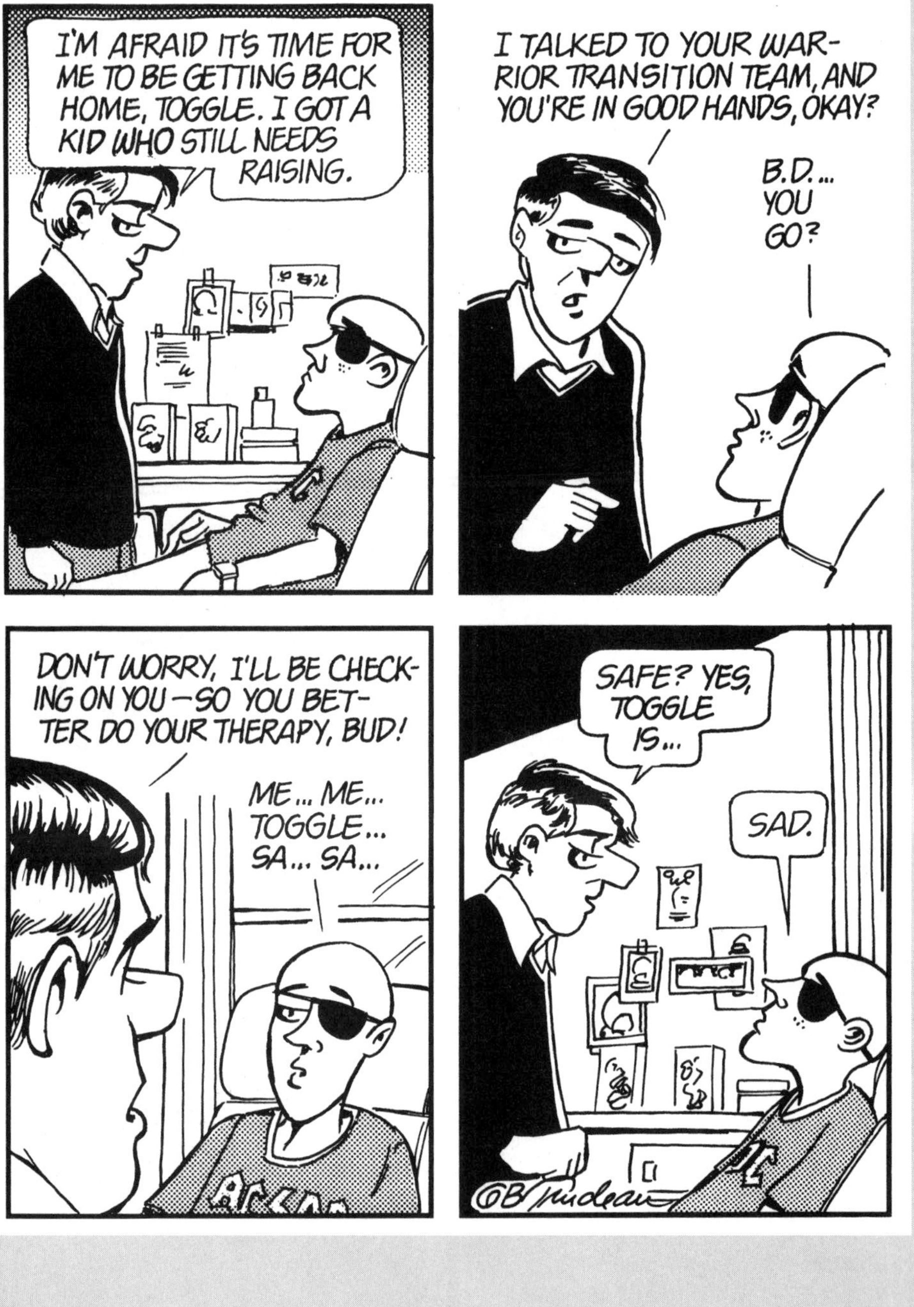
I'M AFRAID IT'S TIME FOR ME TO BE GETTING BACK HOME, TOGGLE. I GOT A KID WHO STILL NEEDS RAISING.
I TALKED TO YOUR WARRIOR TRANSITION TEAM, AND YOU'RE IN GOOD HANDS, OKAY?
B.D.... YOU GO?
DON'T WORRY, I'LL BE CHECKING ON YOU—SO YOU BETTER DO YOUR THERAPY, BUD!
ME... ME... TOGGLE... SA... SA...
SAFE? YES, TOGGLE IS...
SAD.
©B Trudeau

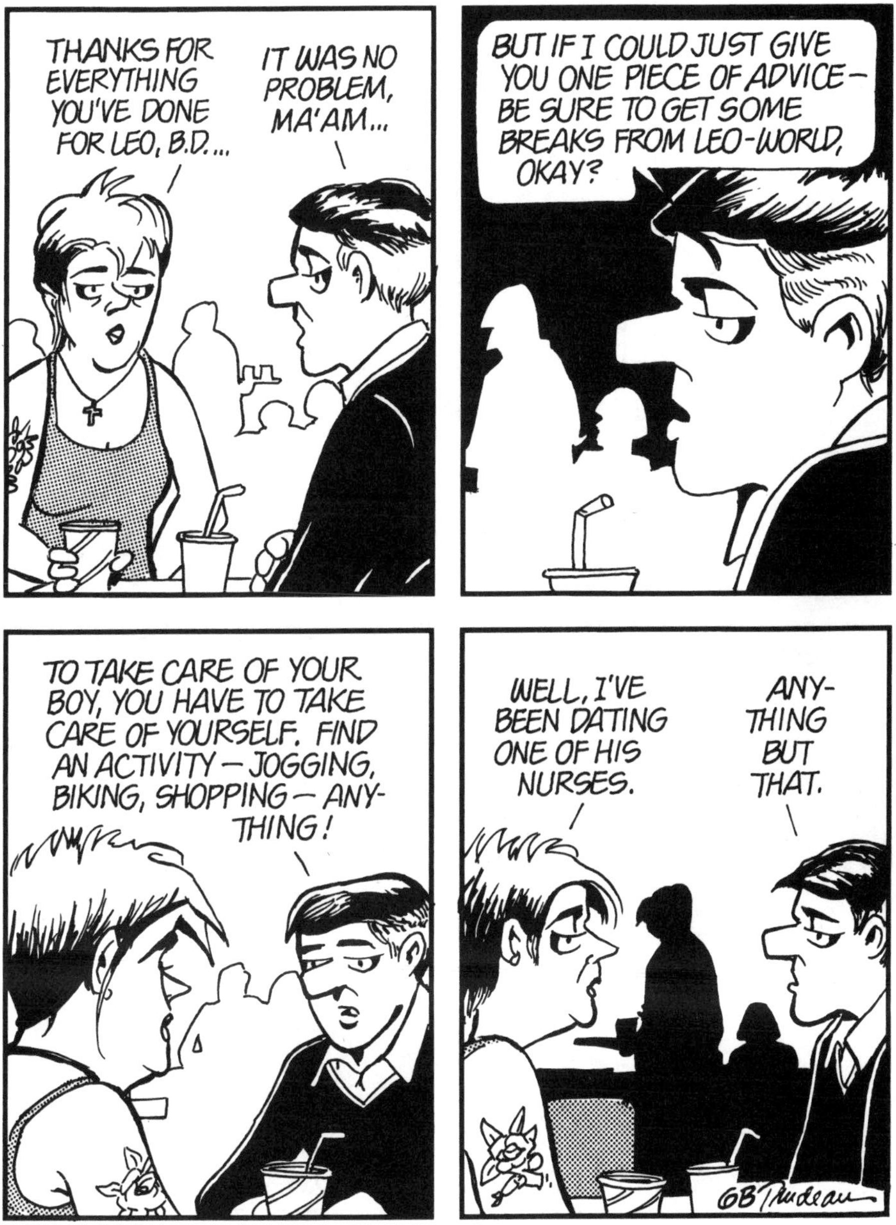
THANKS FOR EVERYTHING YOU'VE DONE FOR LEO, B.D....
IT WAS NO PROBLEM, MA'AM...
BUT IF I COULD JUST GIVE YOU ONE PIECE OF ADVICE— BE SURE TO GET SOME BREAKS FROM LEO-WORLD, OKAY?
TO TAKE CARE OF YOUR BOY, YOU HAVE TO TAKE CARE OF YOURSELF. FIND AN ACTIVITY — JOGGING, BIKING, SHOPPING — ANYTHING!
WELL, I'VE BEEN DATING ONE OF HIS NURSES.
ANYTHING BUT THAT.
GBTrudeau

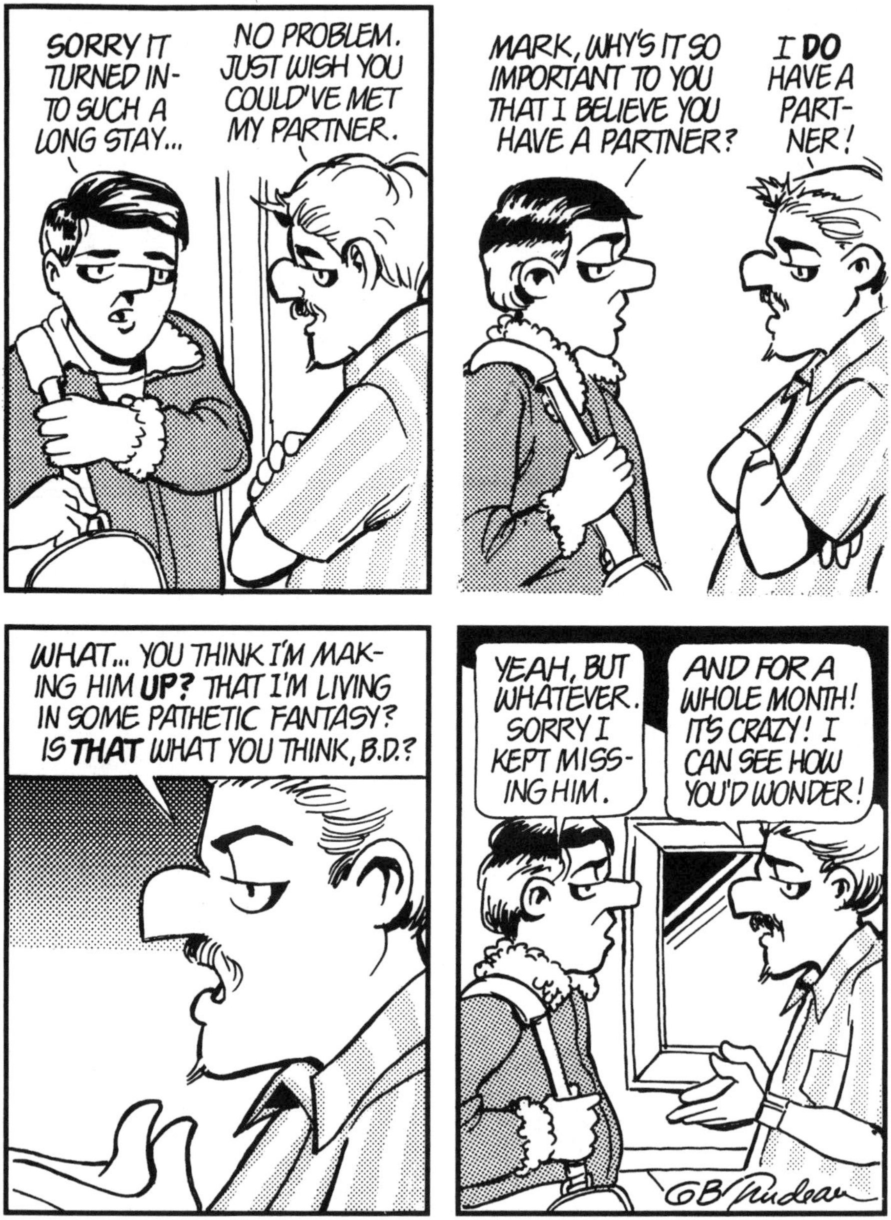
SORRY IT TURNED INTO SUCH A LONG STAY...
NO PROBLEM. JUST WISH YOU COULD'VE MET MY PARTNER.
MARK, WHY'S IT SO IMPORTANT TO YOU THAT I BELIEVE YOU HAVE A PARTNER?
I **DO** HAVE A PARTNER!
WHAT... YOU THINK I'M MAKING HIM **UP?** THAT I'M LIVING IN SOME PATHETIC FANTASY? IS **THAT** WHAT YOU THINK, B.D.?
YEAH, BUT WHATEVER. SORRY I KEPT MISSING HIM.
AND FOR A WHOLE MONTH! IT'S CRAZY! I CAN SEE HOW YOU'D WONDER!
GB Trudeau

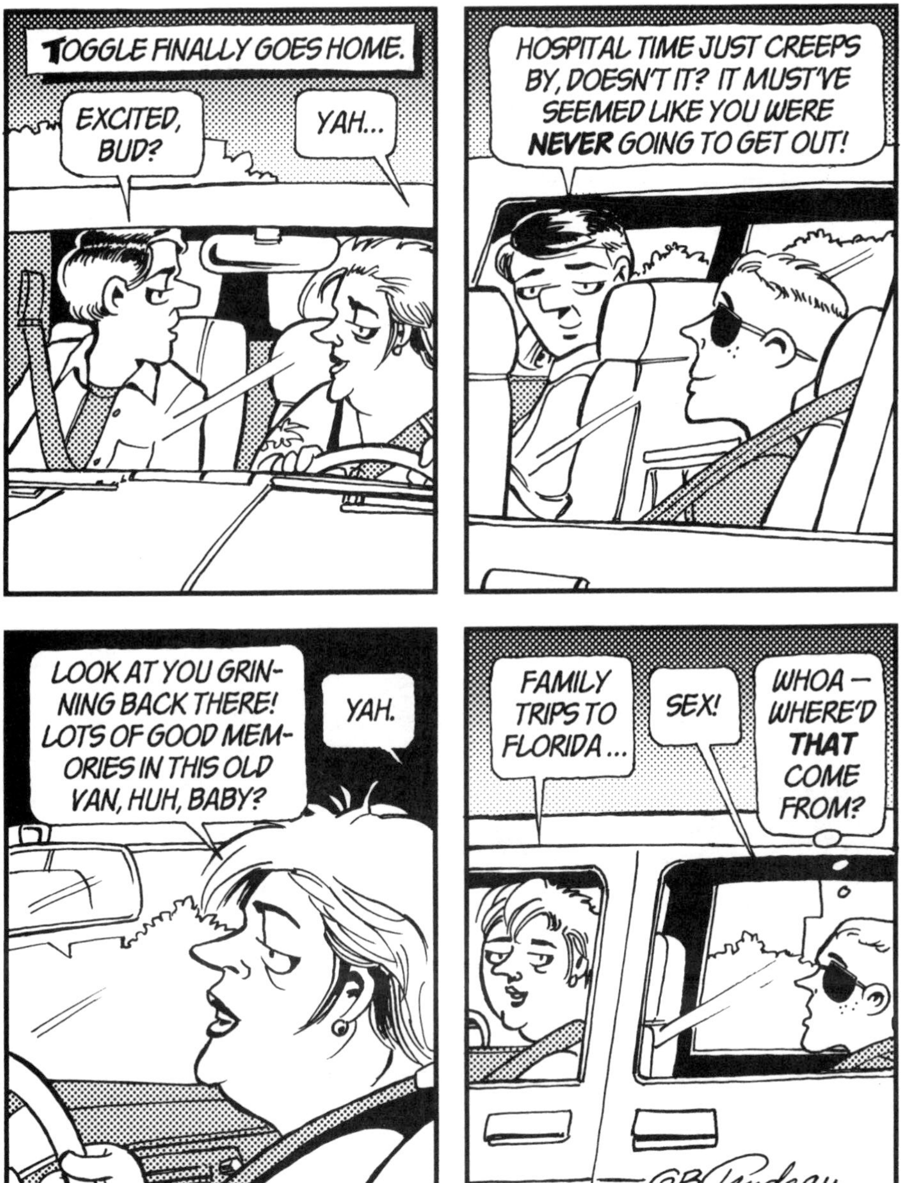
TOGGLE FINALLY GOES HOME.
EXCITED, BUD?
YAH...
HOSPITAL TIME JUST CREEPS BY, DOESN'T IT? IT MUST'VE SEEMED LIKE YOU WERE **NEVER** GOING TO GET OUT!
LOOK AT YOU GRINNING BACK THERE! LOTS OF GOOD MEMORIES IN THIS OLD VAN, HUH, BABY?
YAH.
FAMILY TRIPS TO FLORIDA...
SEX!
WHOA — WHERE'D **THAT** COME FROM?
GB Trudeau

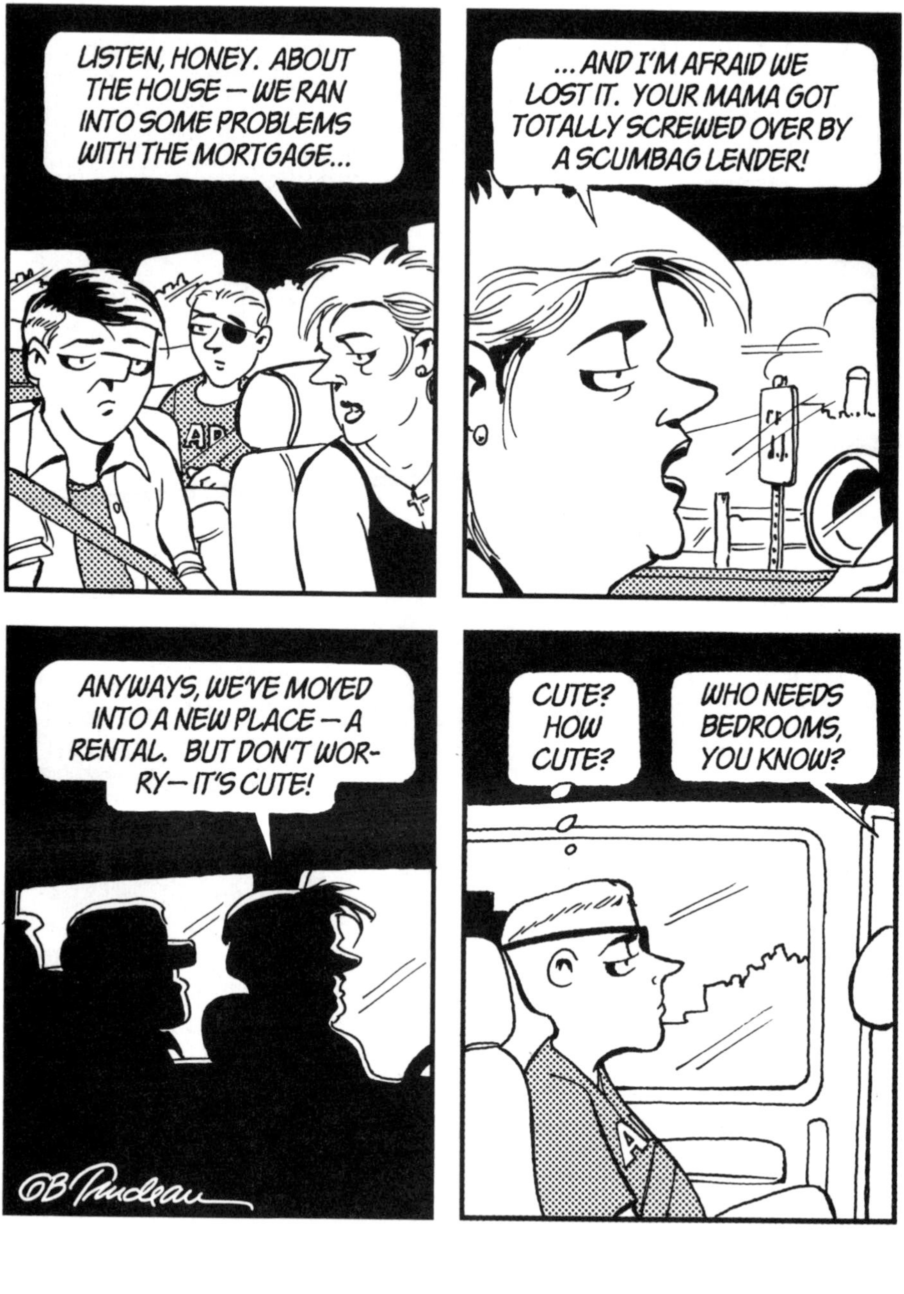
LISTEN, HONEY. ABOUT THE HOUSE — WE RAN INTO SOME PROBLEMS WITH THE MORTGAGE...
...AND I'M AFRAID WE LOST IT. YOUR MAMA GOT TOTALLY SCREWED OVER BY A SCUMBAG LENDER!
ANYWAYS, WE'VE MOVED INTO A NEW PLACE — A RENTAL. BUT DON'T WORRY— IT'S CUTE!
CUTE? HOW CUTE?
WHO NEEDS BEDROOMS, YOU KNOW?
©B Trudeau

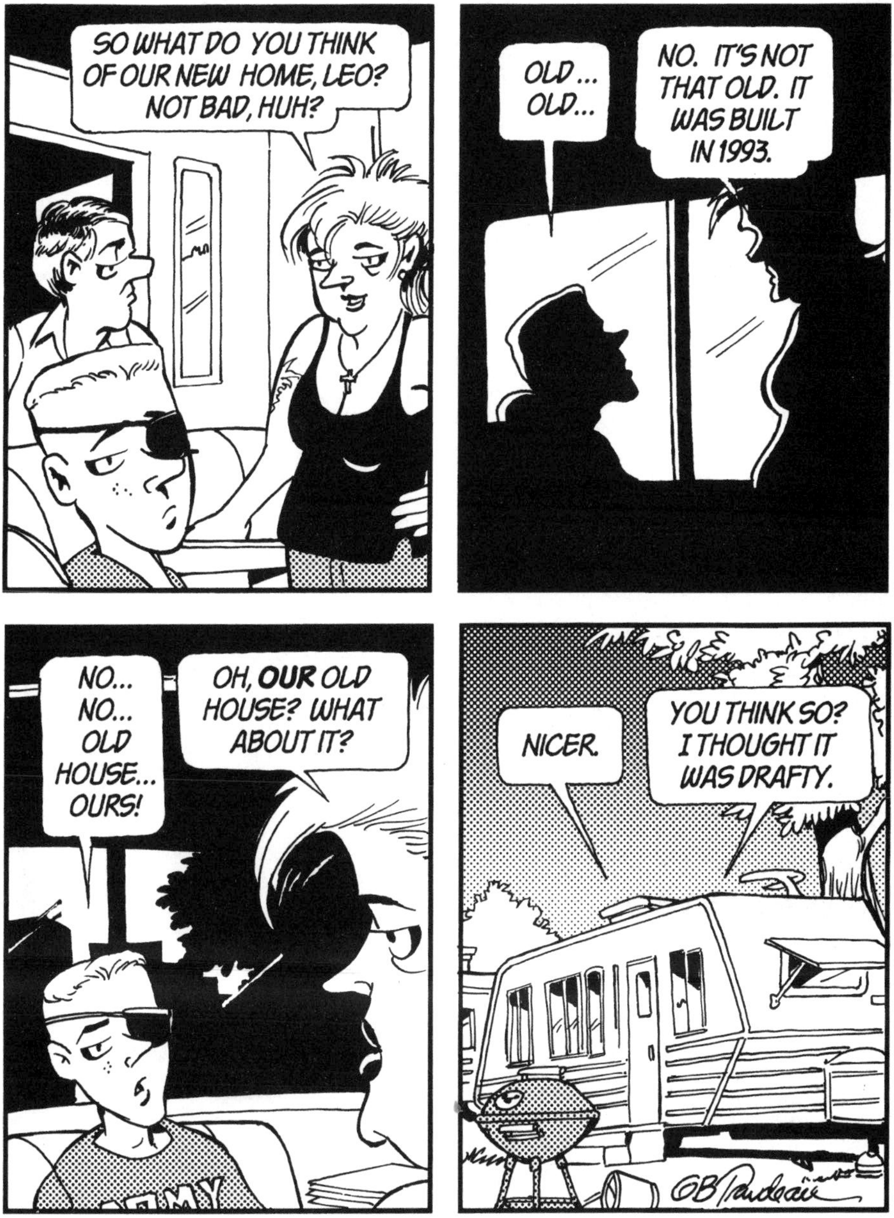
SO WHAT DO YOU THINK OF OUR NEW HOME, LEO? NOT BAD, HUH?
OLD ... OLD...
NO. IT'S NOT THAT OLD. IT WAS BUILT IN 1993.
NO... NO... OLD HOUSE... OURS!
OH, **OUR** OLD HOUSE? WHAT ABOUT IT?
NICER.
YOU THINK SO? I THOUGHT IT WAS DRAFTY.

SO IT WASN'T JUST YOUR GULLIBLE MOM, LEO. PEO- PLE GOT BURNED BY SUB- PRIME MORTGAGES ALL OVER THE COUNTRY!
COUN... COUNTRY!
RIGHT...
COUNTRY... HAND... HAND... HAND...
HAND WHAT, LEO?
HAND- BASKET!
SAY NO MORE.
TRUE THAT, BABY.
ARMY
©B Trudeau

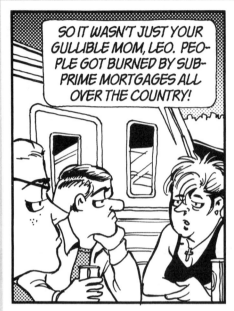

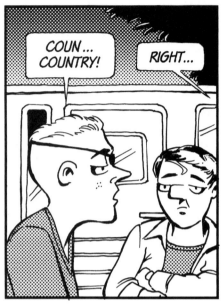

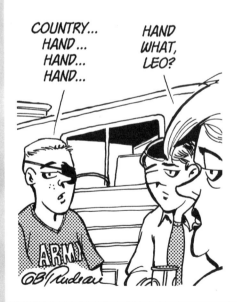

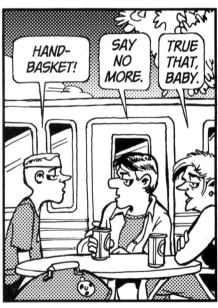

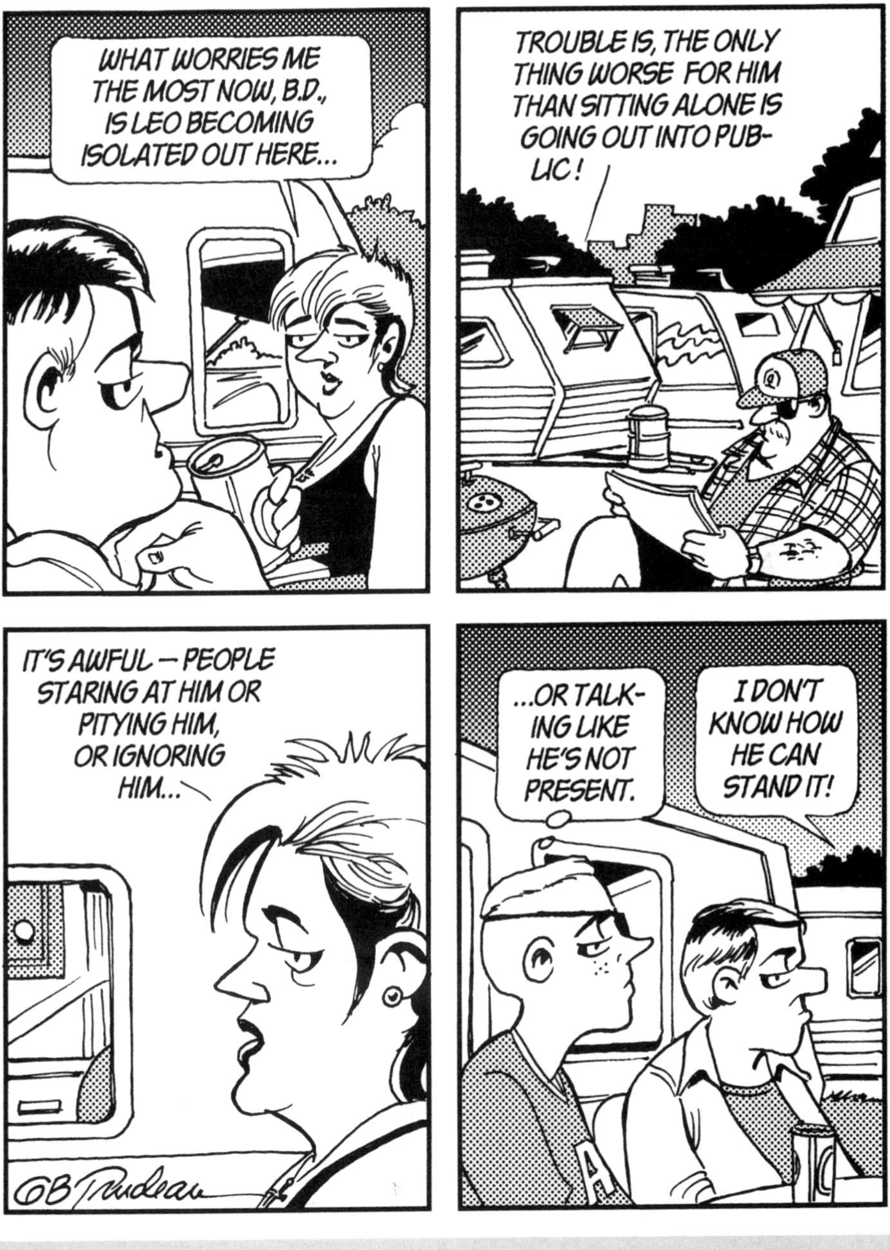
WHAT WORRIES ME THE MOST NOW, B.D., IS LEO BECOMING ISOLATED OUT HERE...
TROUBLE IS, THE ONLY THING WORSE FOR HIM THAN SITTING ALONE IS GOING OUT INTO PUB-LIC!
IT'S AWFUL — PEOPLE STARING AT HIM OR PITYING HIM, OR IGNORING HIM...
©B Trudeau
...OR TALK-ING LIKE HE'S NOT PRESENT.
I DON'T KNOW HOW HE CAN STAND IT!

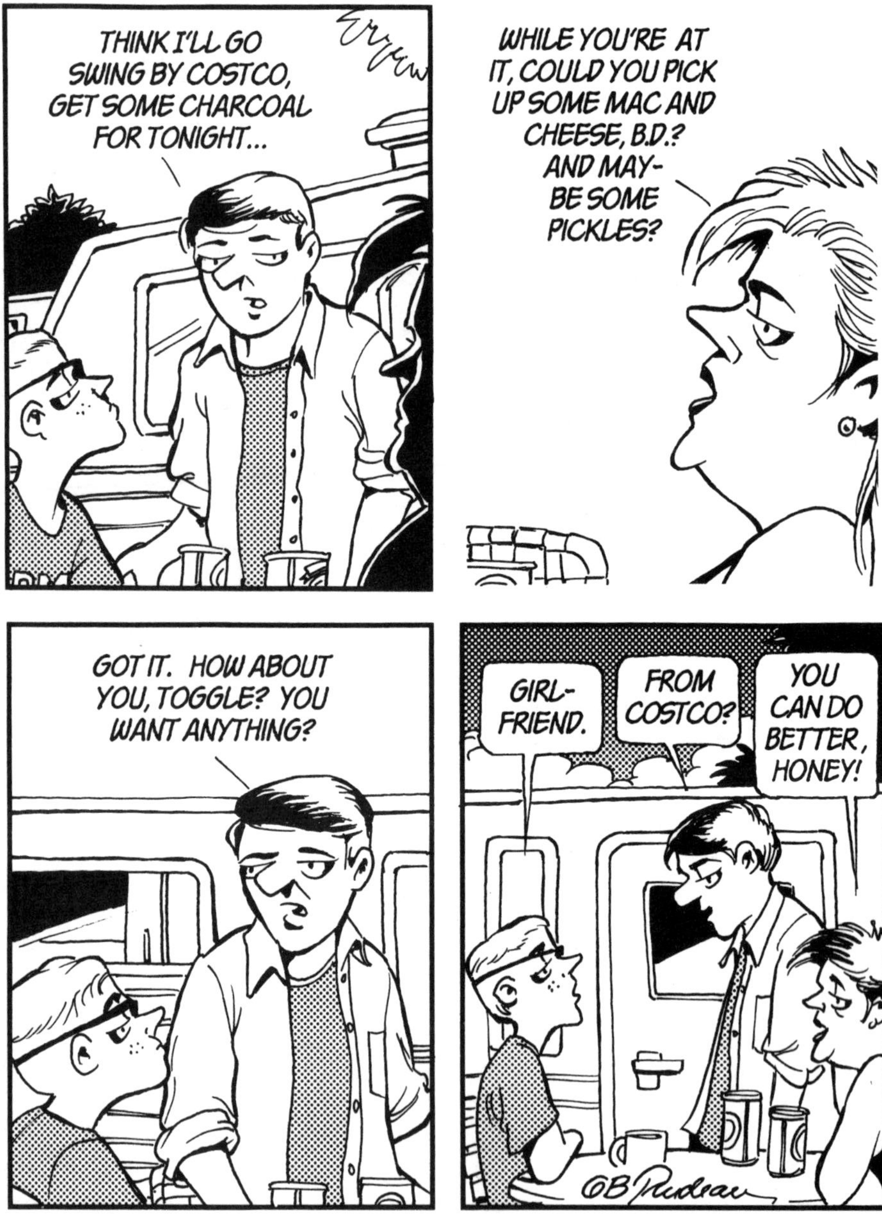
THINK I'LL GO SWING BY COSTCO, GET SOME CHARCOAL FOR TONIGHT...
WHILE YOU'RE AT IT, COULD YOU PICK UP SOME MAC AND CHEESE, B.D.? AND MAYBE SOME PICKLES?
GOT IT. HOW ABOUT YOU, TOGGLE? YOU WANT ANYTHING?
GIRL-FRIEND.
FROM COSTCO?
YOU CAN DO BETTER, HONEY!
GB Trudeau

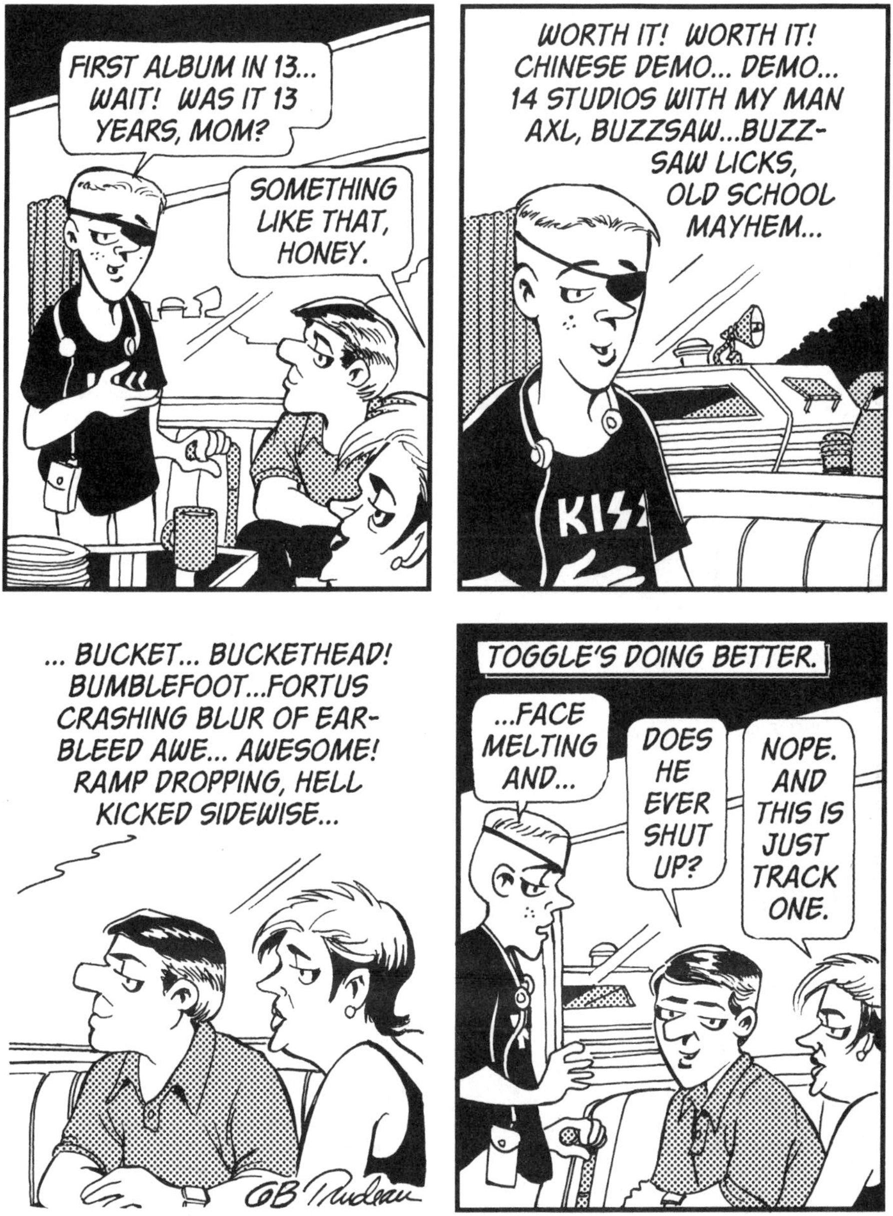
FIRST ALBUM IN 13... WAIT! WAS IT 13 YEARS, MOM?
SOMETHING LIKE THAT, HONEY.
WORTH IT! WORTH IT! CHINESE DEMO... DEMO... 14 STUDIOS WITH MY MAN AXL, BUZZSAW...BUZZ-SAW LICKS, OLD SCHOOL MAYHEM...
KISS
... BUCKET... BUCKETHEAD! BUMBLEFOOT...FORTUS CRASHING BLUR OF EAR-BLEED AWE... AWESOME! RAMP DROPPING, HELL KICKED SIDEWISE...
TOGGLE'S DOING BETTER.
...FACE MELTING AND...
DOES HE EVER SHUT UP?
NOPE. AND THIS IS JUST TRACK ONE.

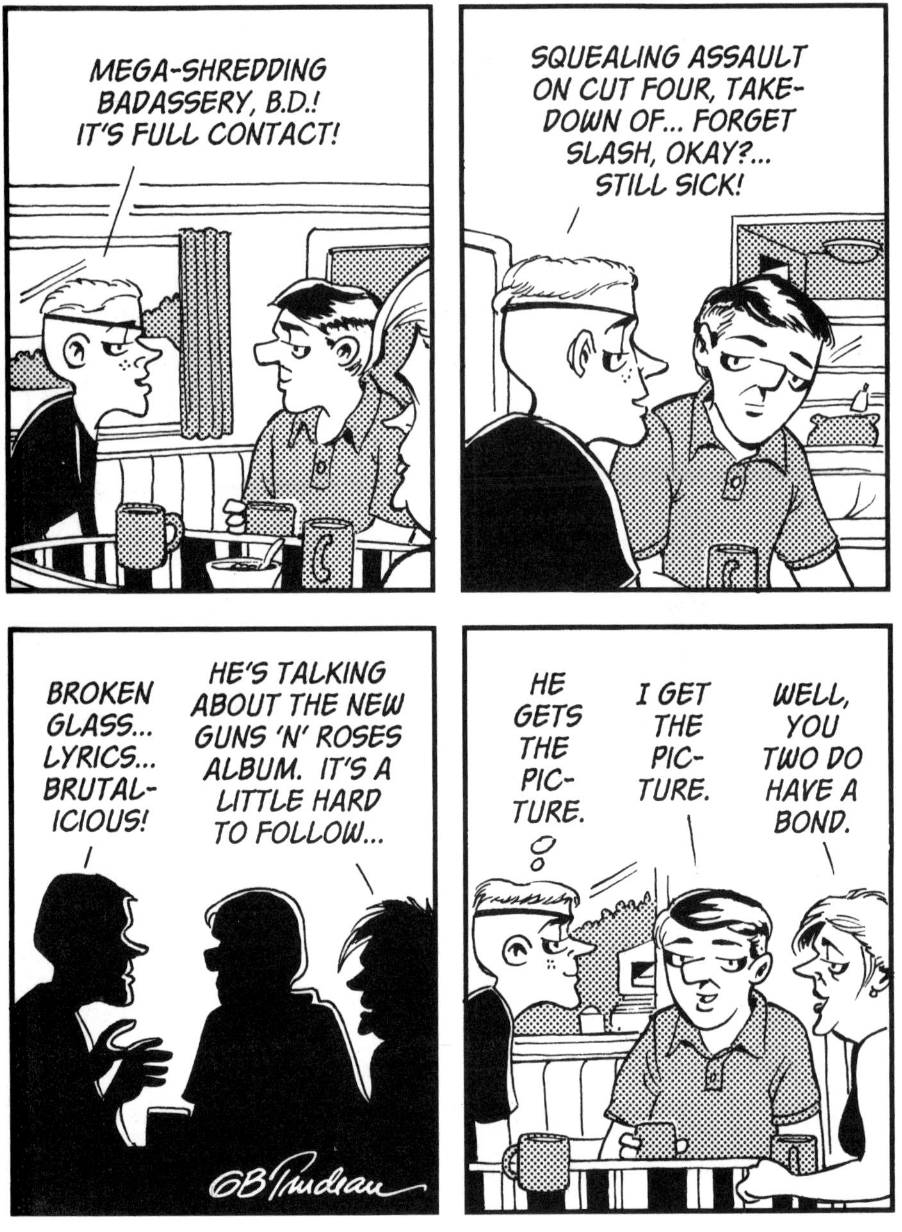
MEGA-SHREDDING BADASSERY, B.D.! IT'S FULL CONTACT!
SQUEALING ASSAULT ON CUT FOUR, TAKE-DOWN OF... FORGET SLASH, OKAY?... STILL SICK!
BROKEN GLASS... LYRICS... BRUTAL-ICIOUS!
HE'S TALKING ABOUT THE NEW GUNS 'N' ROSES ALBUM. IT'S A LITTLE HARD TO FOLLOW...
GB Trudeau
HE GETS THE PIC-TURE.
I GET THE PIC-TURE.
WELL, YOU TWO DO HAVE A BOND.

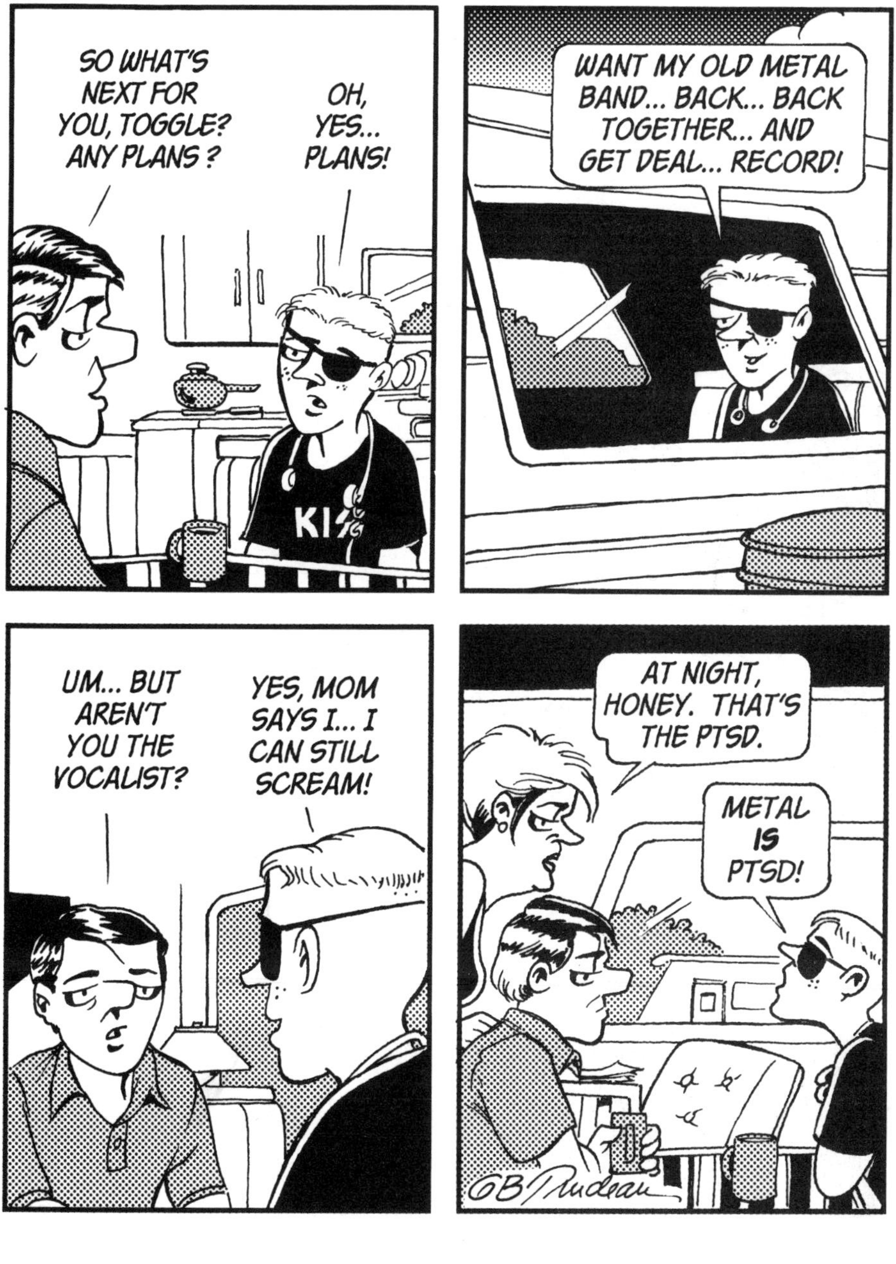
SO WHAT'S NEXT FOR YOU, TOGGLE? ANY PLANS ?
OH, YES... PLANS!
WANT MY OLD METAL BAND... BACK... BACK TOGETHER... AND GET DEAL... RECORD!
KI
UM... BUT AREN'T YOU THE VOCALIST?
YES, MOM SAYS I... I CAN STILL SCREAM!
AT NIGHT, HONEY. THAT'S THE PTSD.
METAL **IS** PTSD!
©B Trudeau

BAND... MY DREAM, SARGE!

WELL, DREAMS ARE GOOD, TOGGLE. BUT YOU'LL NEED A BACKUP DREAM.

HAVE BACKUP! UNTIL BAND... BAND TAKES OFF, I WANT TO GO TO... TO COLLEGE!

YOU WANT TO GO TO COLLEGE? REALLY?

THE APHASIA ONLY AFFECTS HIS SPEECH. THERE'S NOTHING WRONG WITH HIS MIND.

I'M THINKING HARVARD.

HAR... HAR...

YES, COLLEGE IS HARD. SO MAYBE WALDEN?

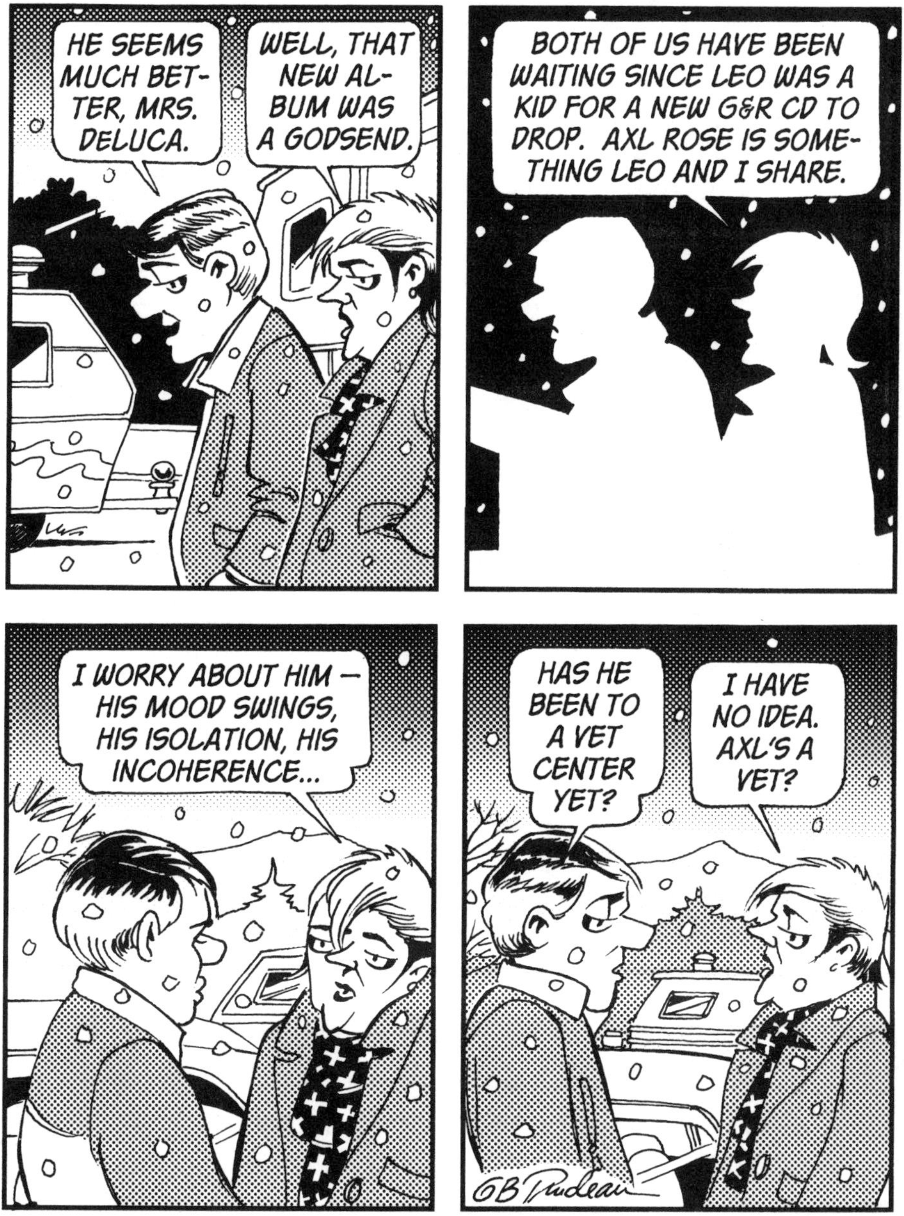
HE SEEMS MUCH BETTER, MRS. DELUCA.
WELL, THAT NEW ALBUM WAS A GODSEND.
BOTH OF US HAVE BEEN WAITING SINCE LEO WAS A KID FOR A NEW G&R CD TO DROP. AXL ROSE IS SOMETHING LEO AND I SHARE.
I WORRY ABOUT HIM — HIS MOOD SWINGS, HIS ISOLATION, HIS INCOHERENCE...
HAS HE BEEN TO A VET CENTER YET?
I HAVE NO IDEA. AXL'S A VET?
GB Trudeau

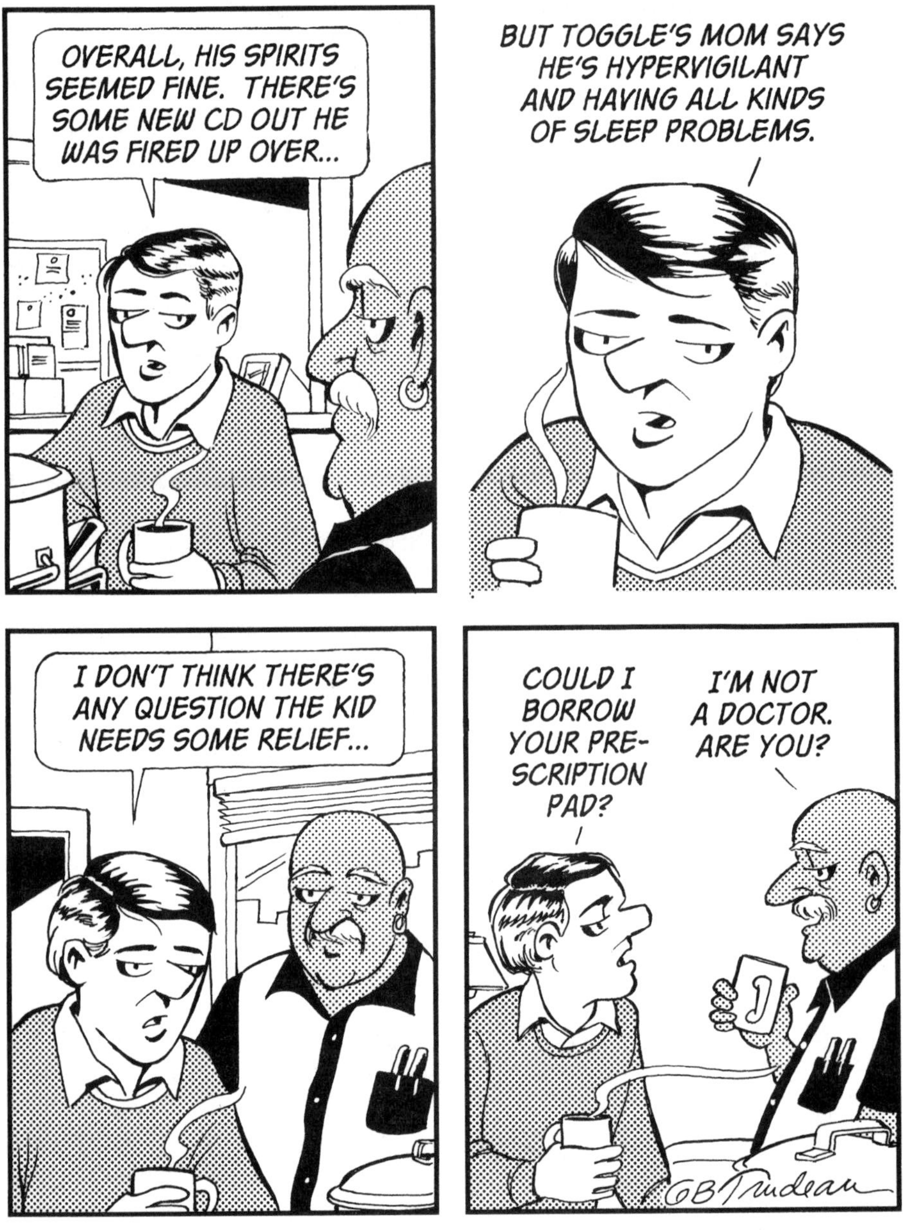

OVERALL, HIS SPIRITS SEEMED FINE. THERE'S SOME NEW CD OUT HE WAS FIRED UP OVER...
BUT TOGGLE'S MOM SAYS HE'S HYPERVIGILANT AND HAVING ALL KINDS OF SLEEP PROBLEMS.
I DON'T THINK THERE'S ANY QUESTION THE KID NEEDS SOME RELIEF...
COULD I BORROW YOUR PRE-SCRIPTION PAD?
I'M NOT A DOCTOR. ARE YOU?
GB Trudeau

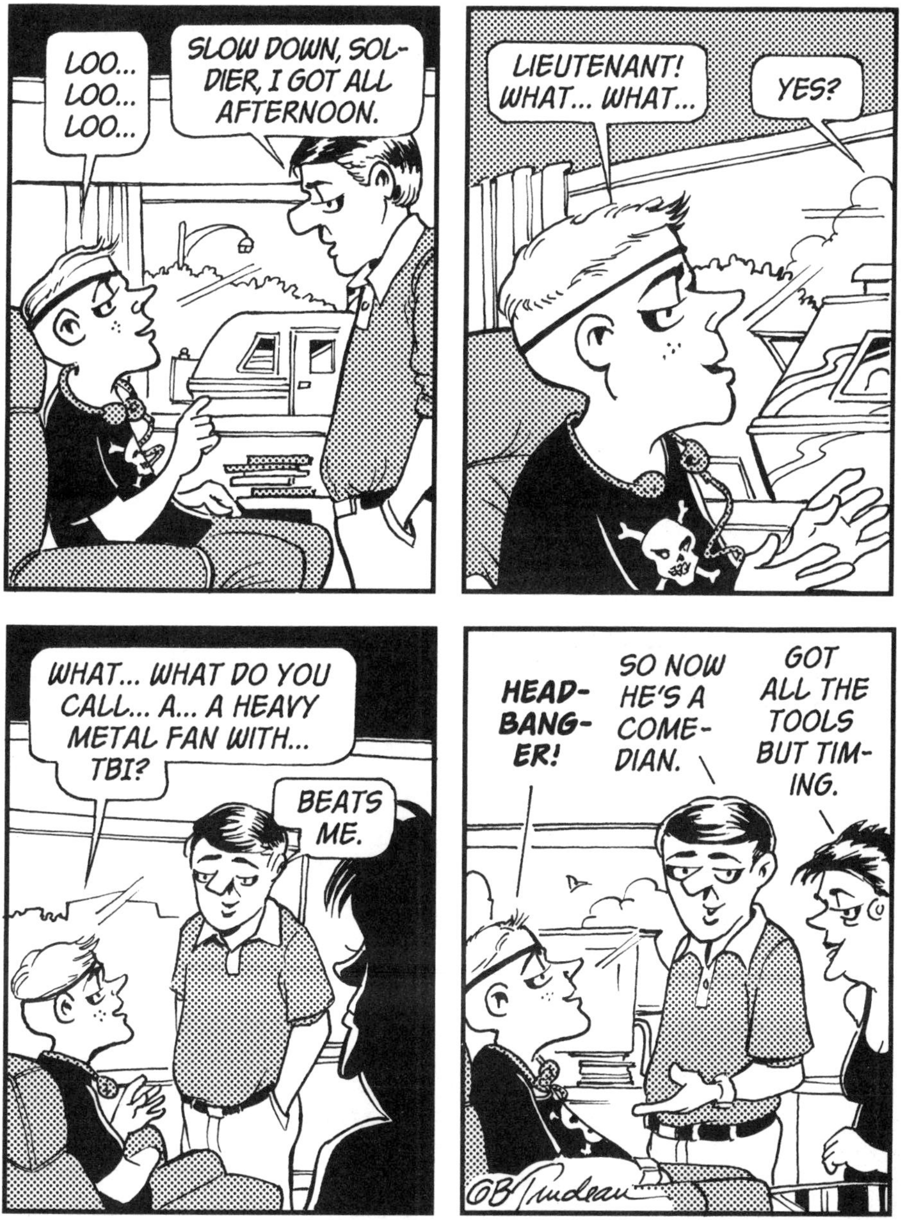
LOO... LOO... LOO...
SLOW DOWN, SOLDIER, I GOT ALL AFTERNOON.
LIEUTENANT! WHAT... WHAT...
YES?
WHAT... WHAT DO YOU CALL... A... A HEAVY METAL FAN WITH... TBI?
BEATS ME.
HEAD-BANGER!
SO NOW HE'S A COMEDIAN.
GOT ALL THE TOOLS BUT TIMING.
©B Trudeau

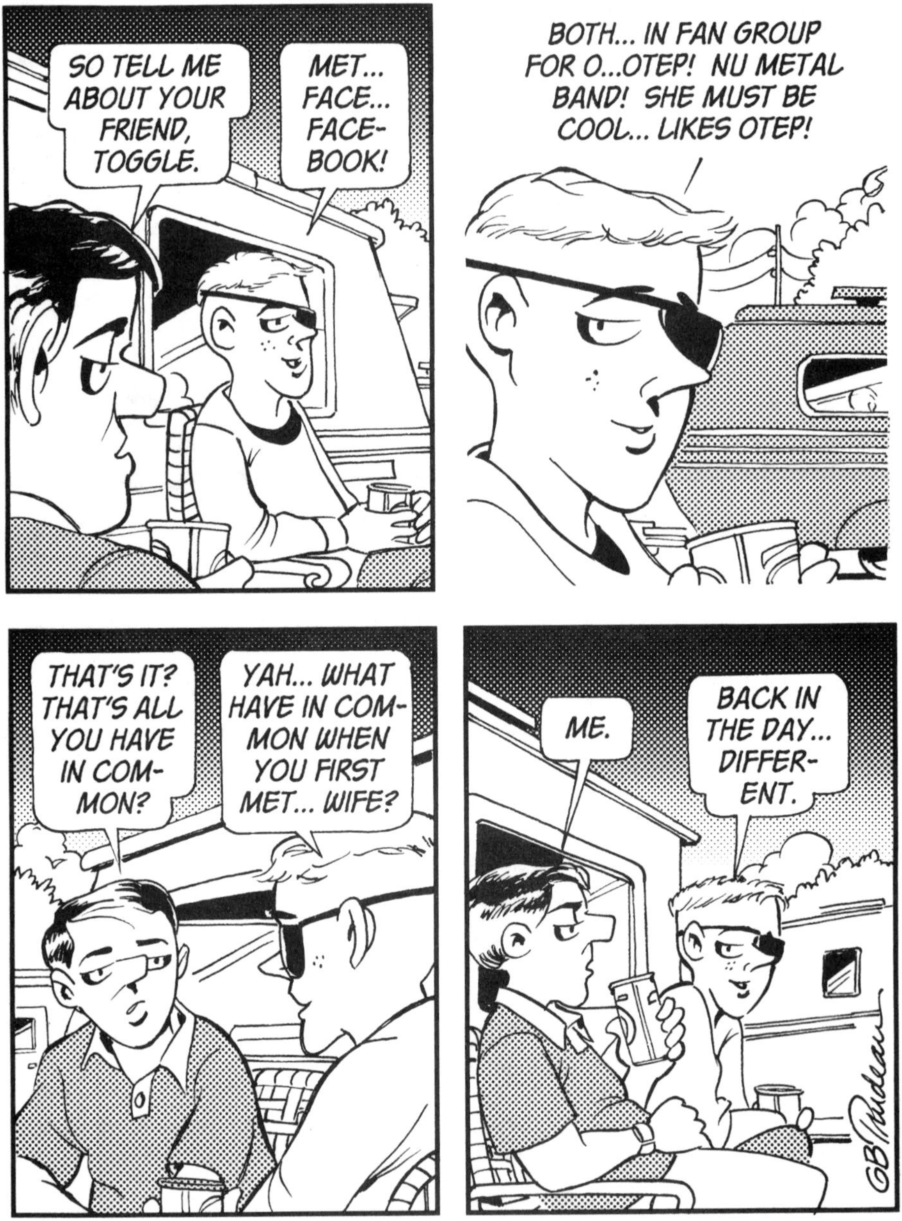
SO TELL ME ABOUT YOUR FRIEND, TOGGLE.
MET... FACE... FACE-BOOK!
BOTH... IN FAN GROUP FOR O...OTEP! NU METAL BAND! SHE MUST BE COOL... LIKES OTEP!
THAT'S IT? THAT'S ALL YOU HAVE IN COM-MON?
YAH... WHAT HAVE IN COM-MON WHEN YOU FIRST MET... WIFE?
ME.
BACK IN THE DAY... DIFFER-ENT.
GB Trudeau

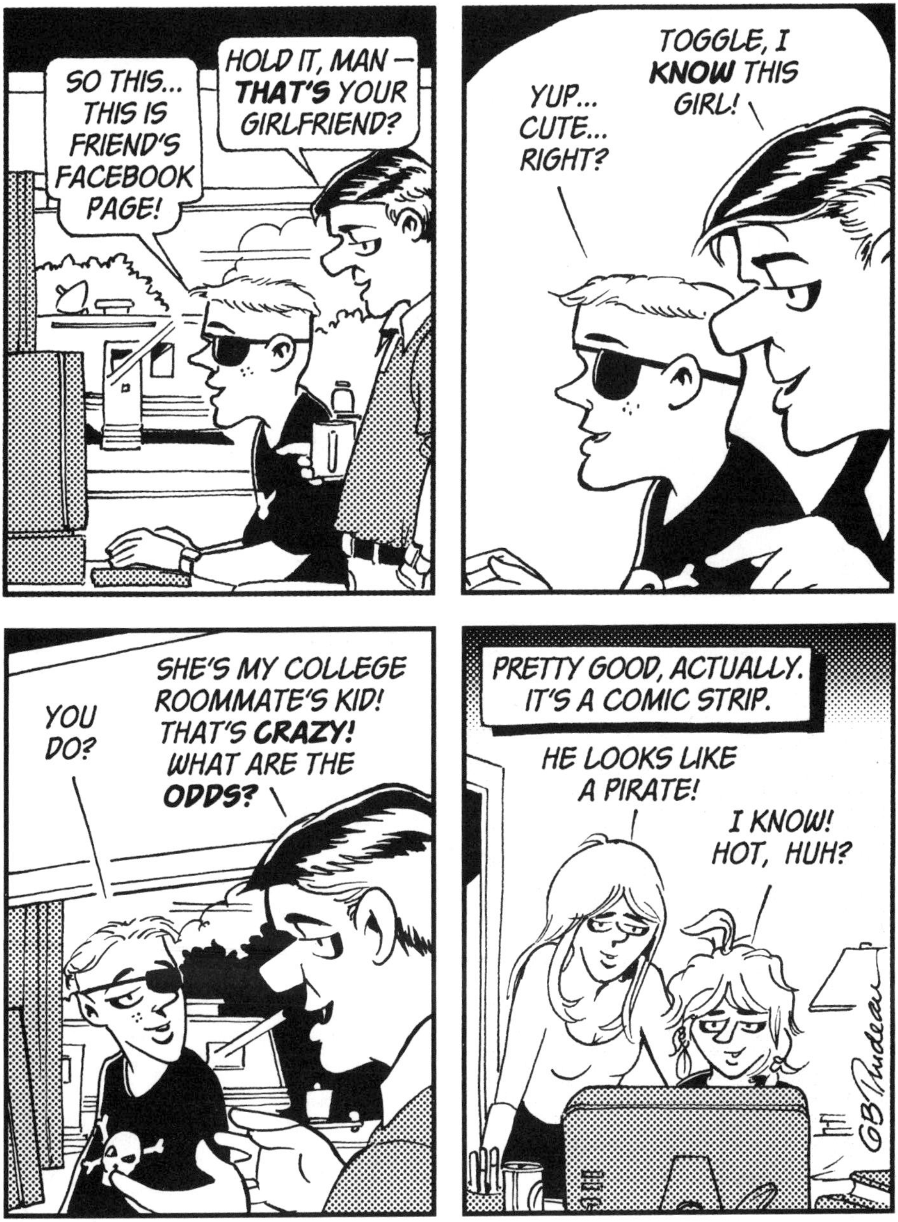
SO THIS... THIS IS FRIEND'S FACEBOOK PAGE!
HOLD IT, MAN — THAT'S YOUR GIRLFRIEND?
YUP... CUTE... RIGHT?
TOGGLE, I KNOW THIS GIRL!
YOU DO?
SHE'S MY COLLEGE ROOMMATE'S KID! THAT'S CRAZY! WHAT ARE THE ODDS?
PRETTY GOOD, ACTUALLY. IT'S A COMIC STRIP.
HE LOOKS LIKE A PIRATE!
I KNOW! HOT, HUH?
GBTrudeau

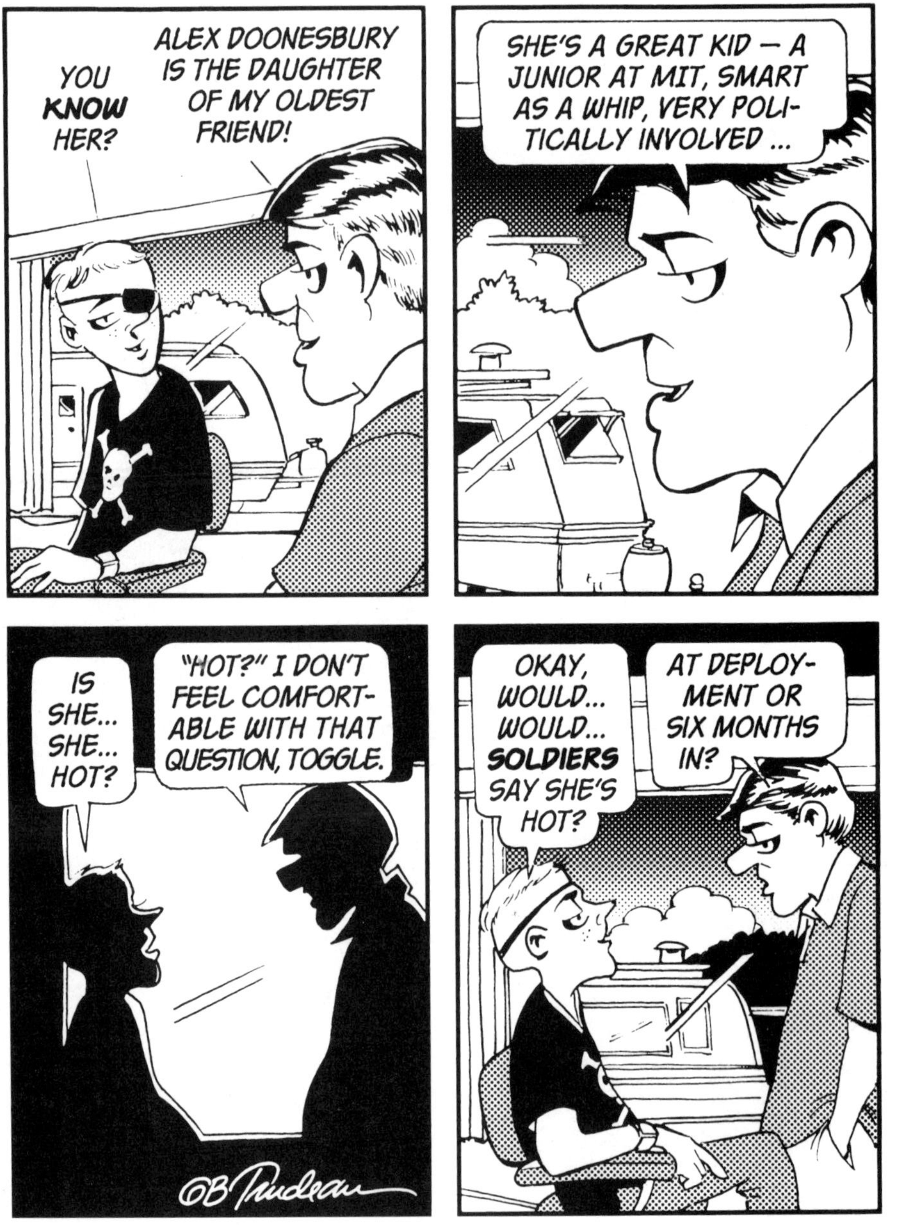
YOU KNOW HER?
ALEX DOONESBURY IS THE DAUGHTER OF MY OLDEST FRIEND!
SHE'S A GREAT KID — A JUNIOR AT MIT, SMART AS A WHIP, VERY POLITICALLY INVOLVED ...
IS SHE... SHE... HOT?
"HOT?" I DON'T FEEL COMFORTABLE WITH THAT QUESTION, TOGGLE.
OKAY, WOULD... WOULD... SOLDIERS SAY SHE'S HOT?
AT DEPLOYMENT OR SIX MONTHS IN?
©B Trudeau

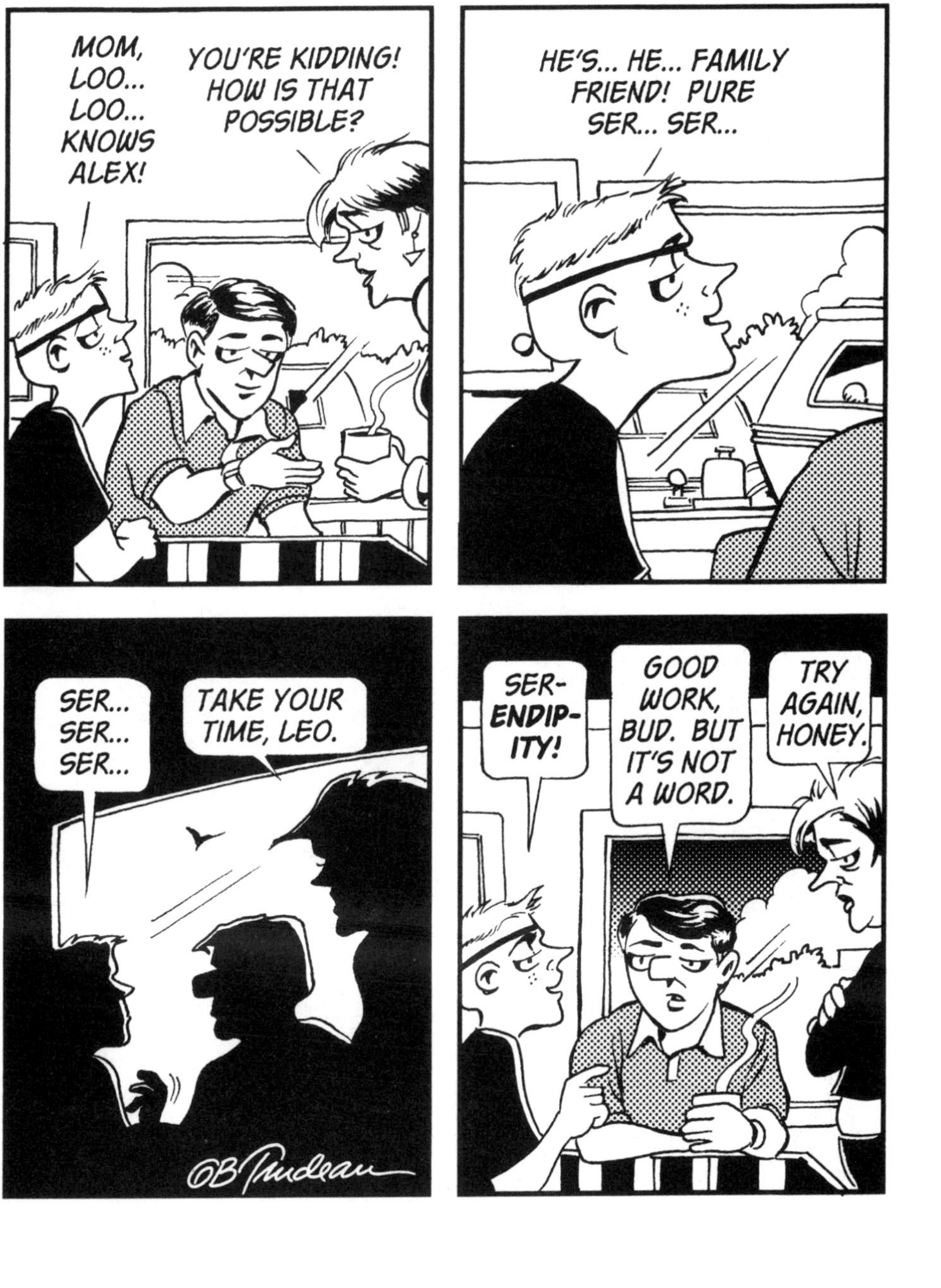
MOM, LOO... LOO... KNOWS ALEX!
YOU'RE KIDDING! HOW IS THAT POSSIBLE?
HE'S... HE... FAMILY FRIEND! PURE SER... SER...
SER... SER... SER...
TAKE YOUR TIME, LEO.
SER- ENDIP- ITY!
GOOD WORK, BUD. BUT IT'S NOT A WORD.
TRY AGAIN, HONEY.
©B Trudeau

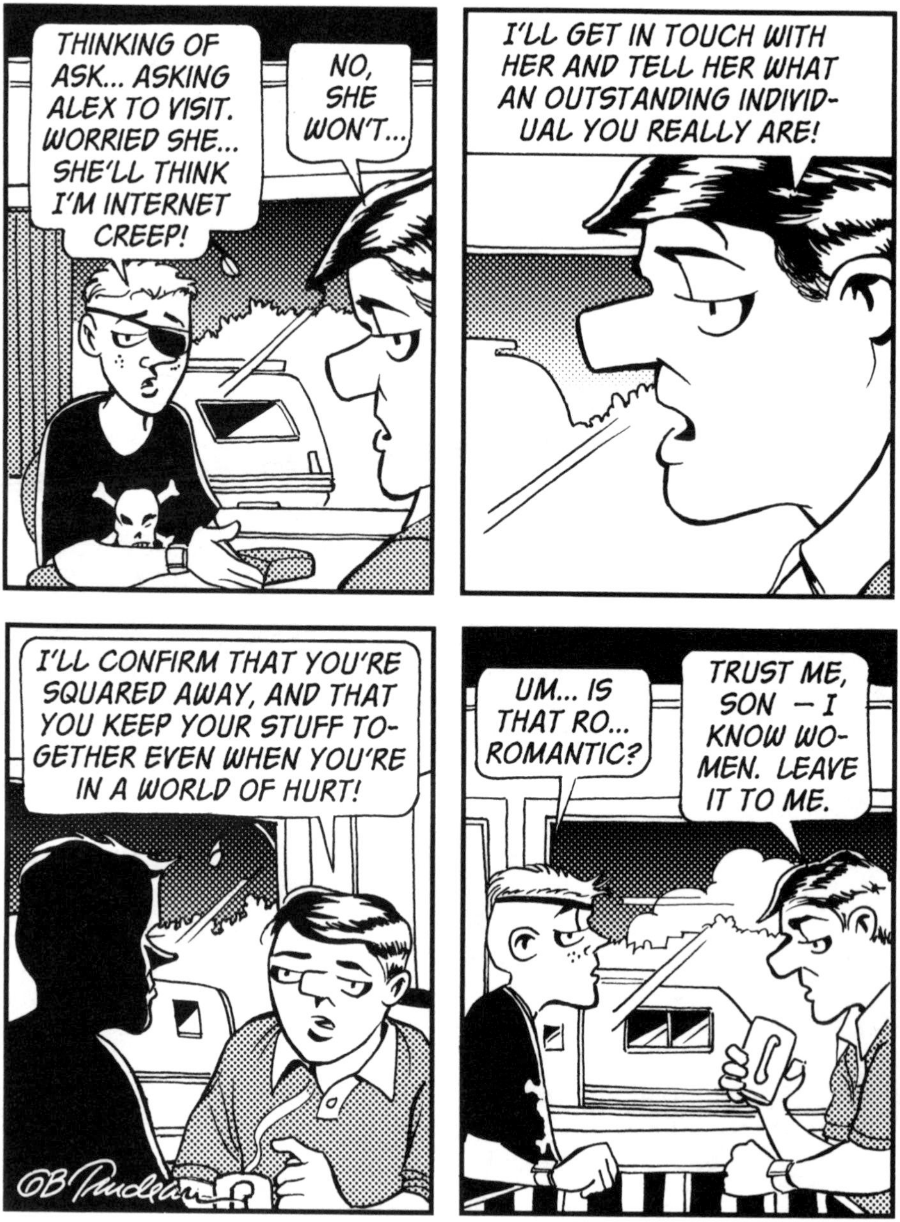
THINKING OF ASK... ASKING ALEX TO VISIT. WORRIED SHE... SHE'LL THINK I'M INTERNET CREEP!
NO, SHE WON'T...
I'LL GET IN TOUCH WITH HER AND TELL HER WHAT AN OUTSTANDING INDIVID-UAL YOU REALLY ARE!
I'LL CONFIRM THAT YOU'RE SQUARED AWAY, AND THAT YOU KEEP YOUR STUFF TO-GETHER EVEN WHEN YOU'RE IN A WORLD OF HURT!
UM... IS THAT RO... ROMANTIC?
TRUST ME, SON — I KNOW WO-MEN. LEAVE IT TO ME.
©B Trudeau

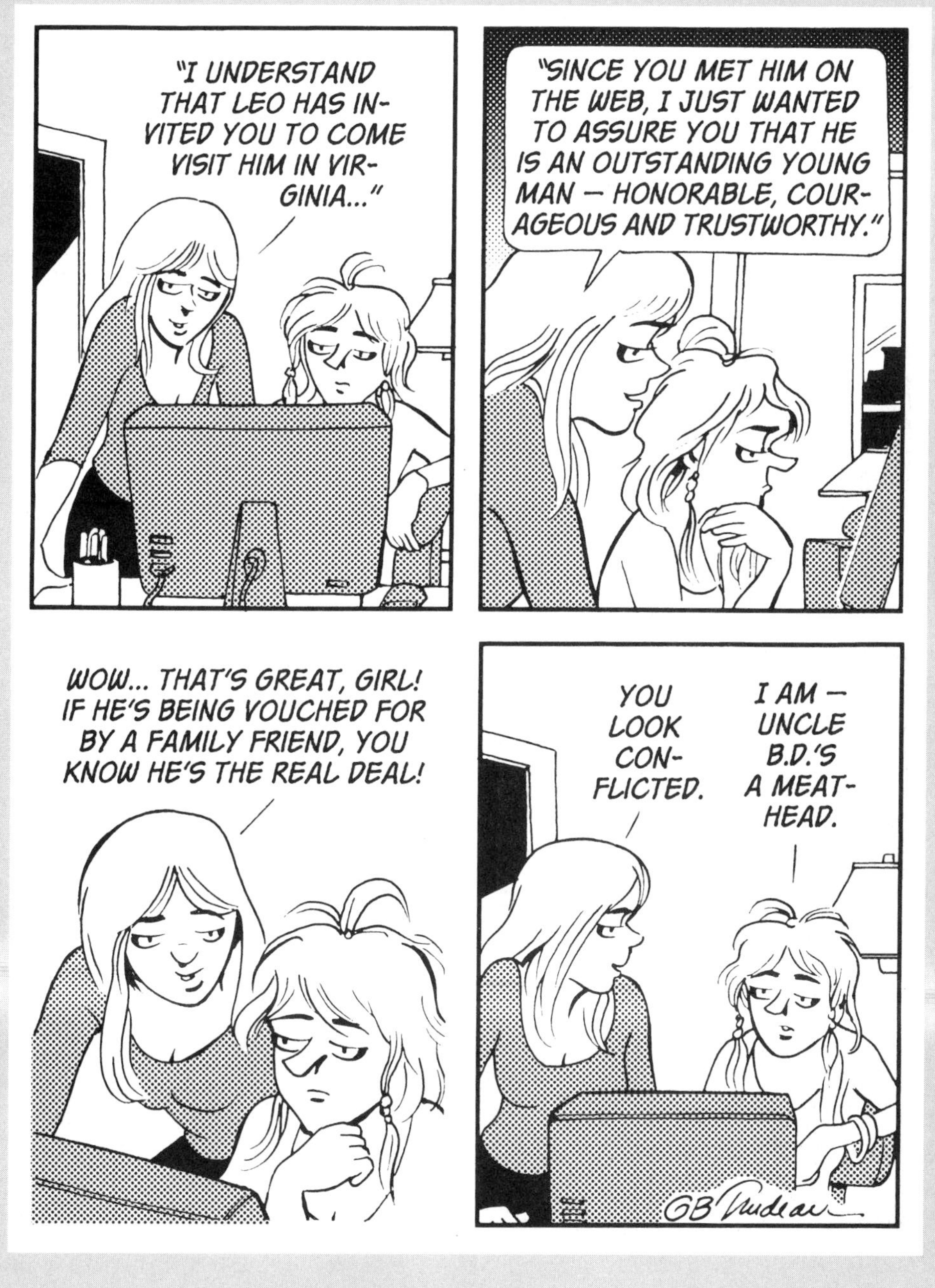
"I UNDERSTAND THAT LEO HAS INVITED YOU TO COME VISIT HIM IN VIRGINIA..."
"SINCE YOU MET HIM ON THE WEB, I JUST WANTED TO ASSURE YOU THAT HE IS AN OUTSTANDING YOUNG MAN — HONORABLE, COURAGEOUS AND TRUSTWORTHY."
WOW... THAT'S GREAT, GIRL! IF HE'S BEING VOUCHED FOR BY A FAMILY FRIEND, YOU KNOW HE'S THE REAL DEAL!
YOU LOOK CONFLICTED.
I AM — UNCLE B.D.'S A MEATHEAD.
GB Trudeau

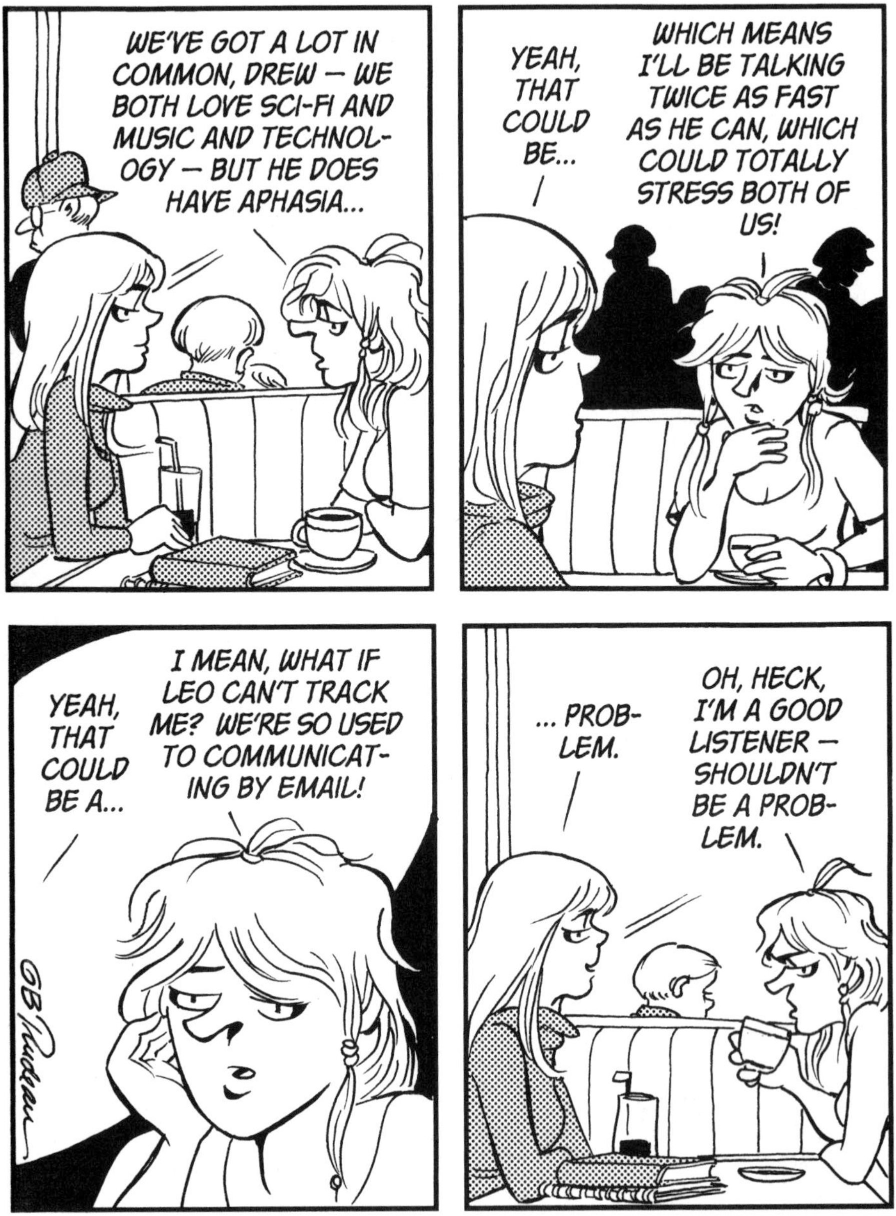
WE'VE GOT A LOT IN COMMON, DREW — WE BOTH LOVE SCI-FI AND MUSIC AND TECHNOLOGY — BUT HE DOES HAVE APHASIA...
YEAH, THAT COULD BE...
WHICH MEANS I'LL BE TALKING TWICE AS FAST AS HE CAN, WHICH COULD TOTALLY STRESS BOTH OF US!
YEAH, THAT COULD BE A...
I MEAN, WHAT IF LEO CAN'T TRACK ME? WE'RE SO USED TO COMMUNICATING BY EMAIL!
GB Rudkin
... PROBLEM.
OH, HECK, I'M A GOOD LISTENER — SHOULDN'T BE A PROBLEM.

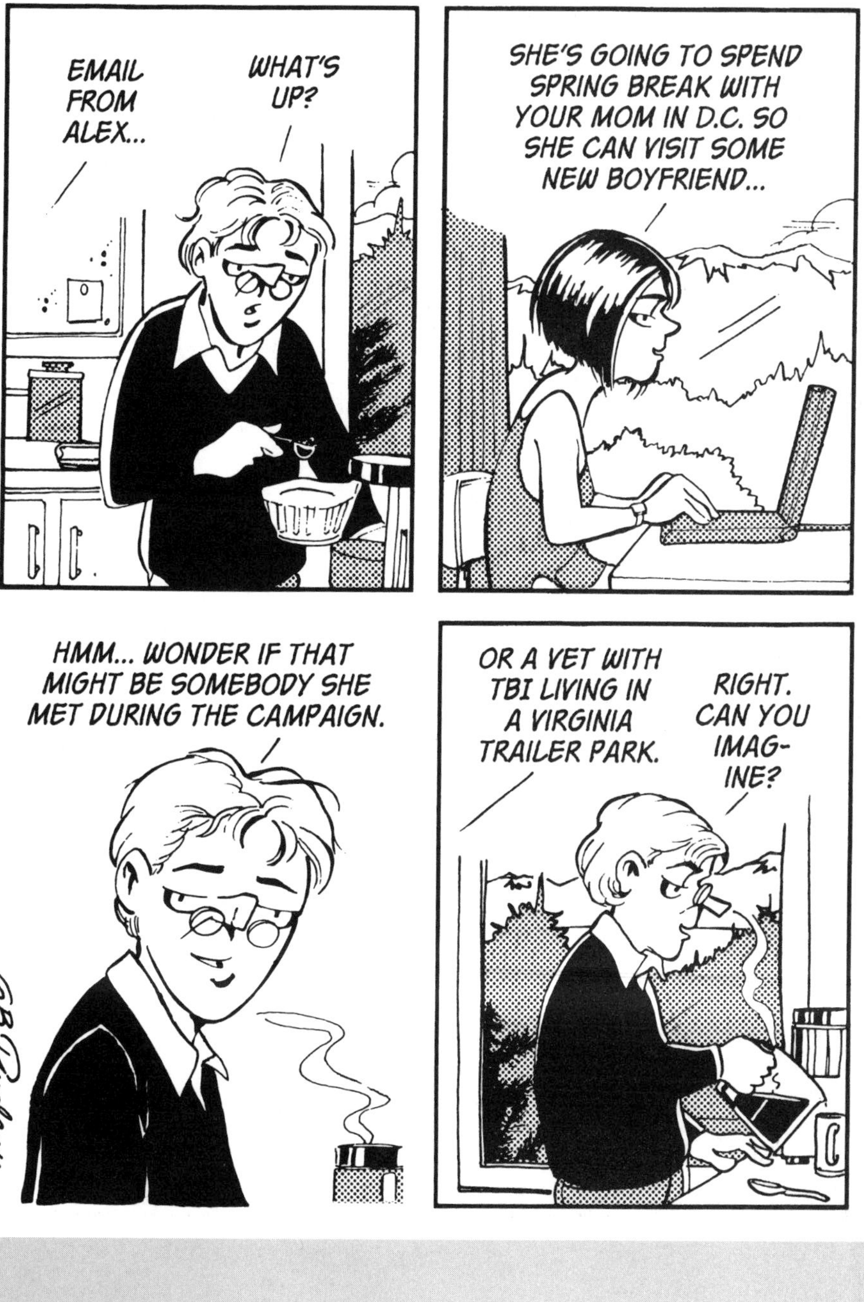
EMAIL FROM ALEX...
WHAT'S UP?
SHE'S GOING TO SPEND SPRING BREAK WITH YOUR MOM IN D.C. SO SHE CAN VISIT SOME NEW BOYFRIEND...
HMM... WONDER IF THAT MIGHT BE SOMEBODY SHE MET DURING THE CAMPAIGN.
OR A VET WITH TBI LIVING IN A VIRGINIA TRAILER PARK.
RIGHT. CAN YOU IMAG-INE?
©B Trudeau

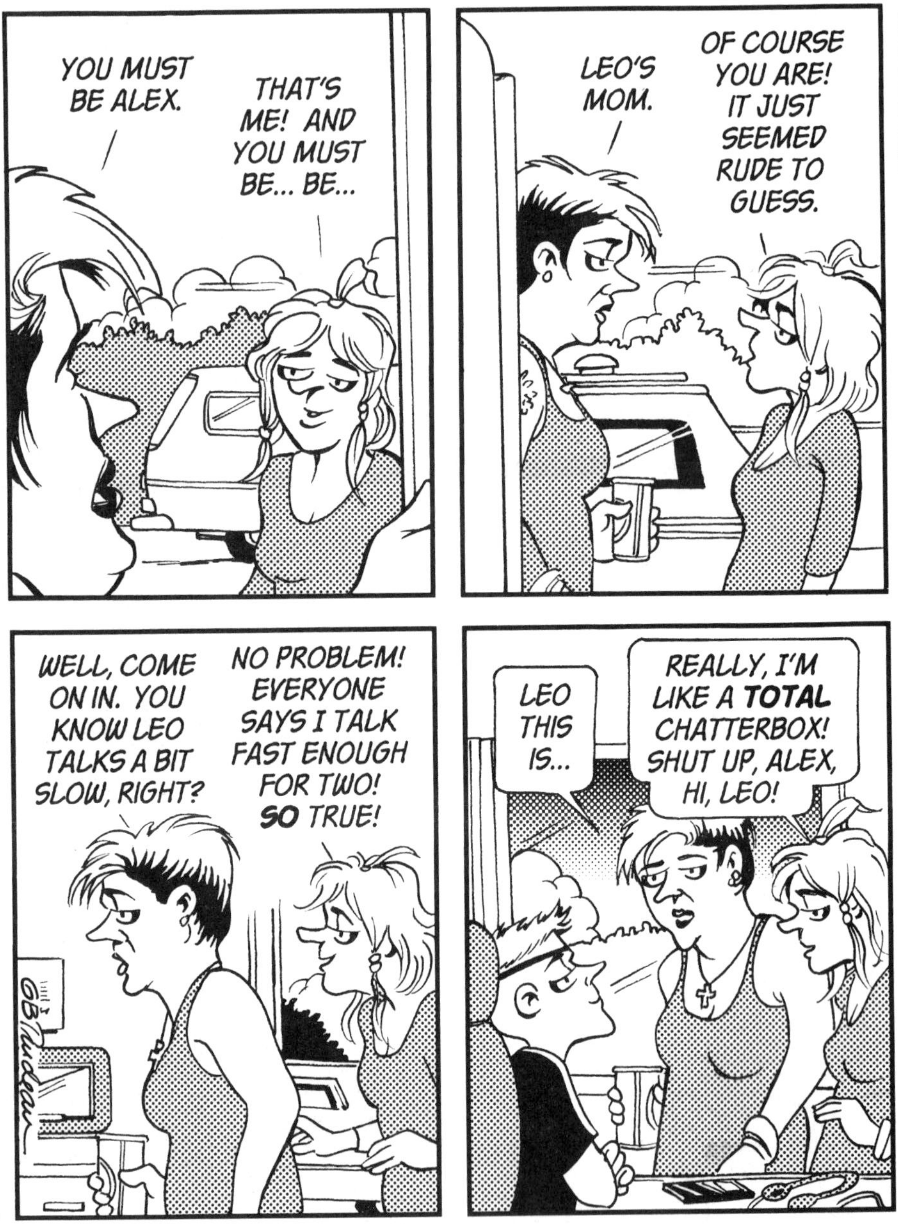
YOU MUST BE ALEX.
THAT'S ME! AND YOU MUST BE... BE...
LEO'S MOM.
OF COURSE YOU ARE! IT JUST SEEMED RUDE TO GUESS.
WELL, COME ON IN. YOU KNOW LEO TALKS A BIT SLOW, RIGHT?
NO PROBLEM! EVERYONE SAYS I TALK FAST ENOUGH FOR TWO! **SO** TRUE!
LEO THIS IS...
REALLY, I'M LIKE A **TOTAL** CHATTERBOX! SHUT UP, ALEX, HI, LEO!

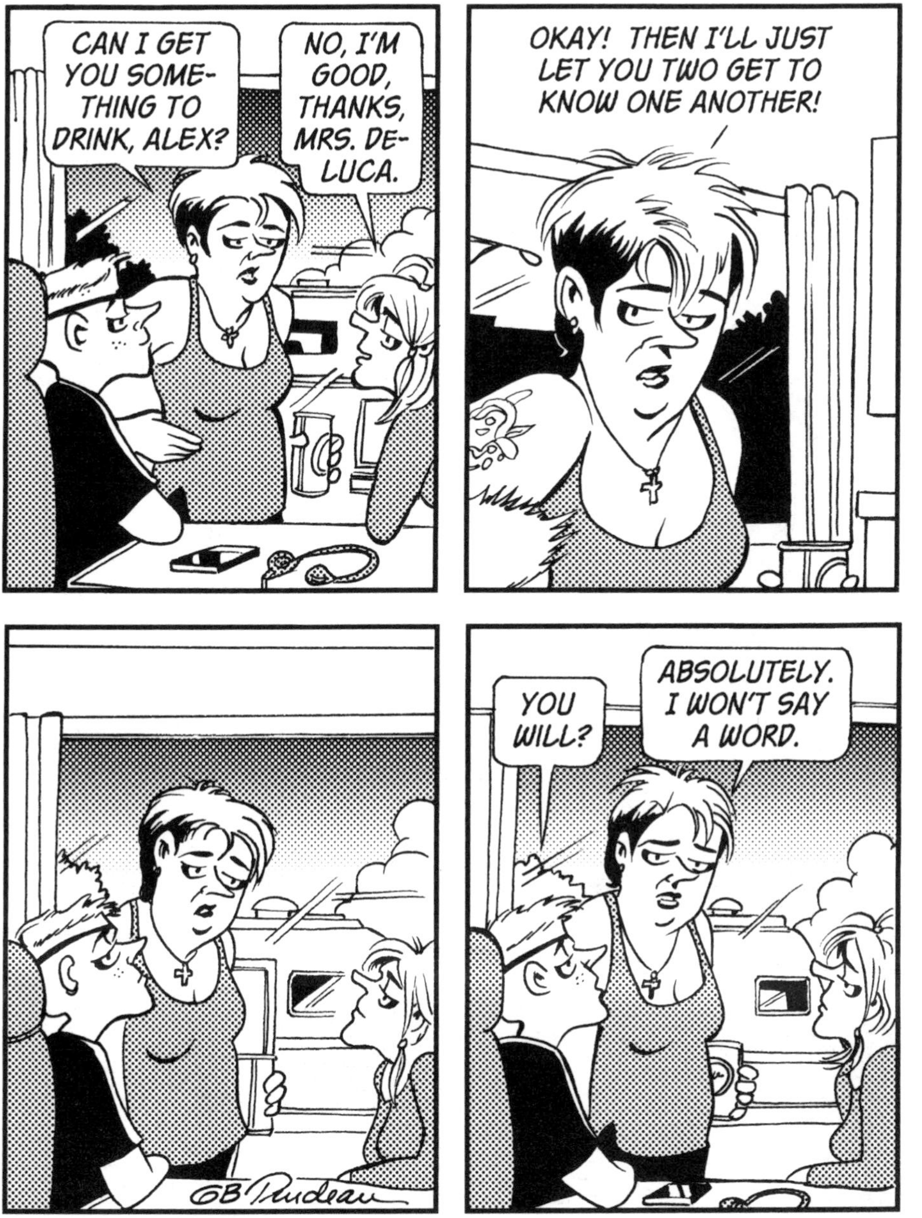
CAN I GET YOU SOME-THING TO DRINK, ALEX?
NO, I'M GOOD, THANKS, MRS. DE-LUCA.
OKAY! THEN I'LL JUST LET YOU TWO GET TO KNOW ONE ANOTHER!
GB Trudeau
YOU WILL?
ABSOLUTELY. I WON'T SAY A WORD.

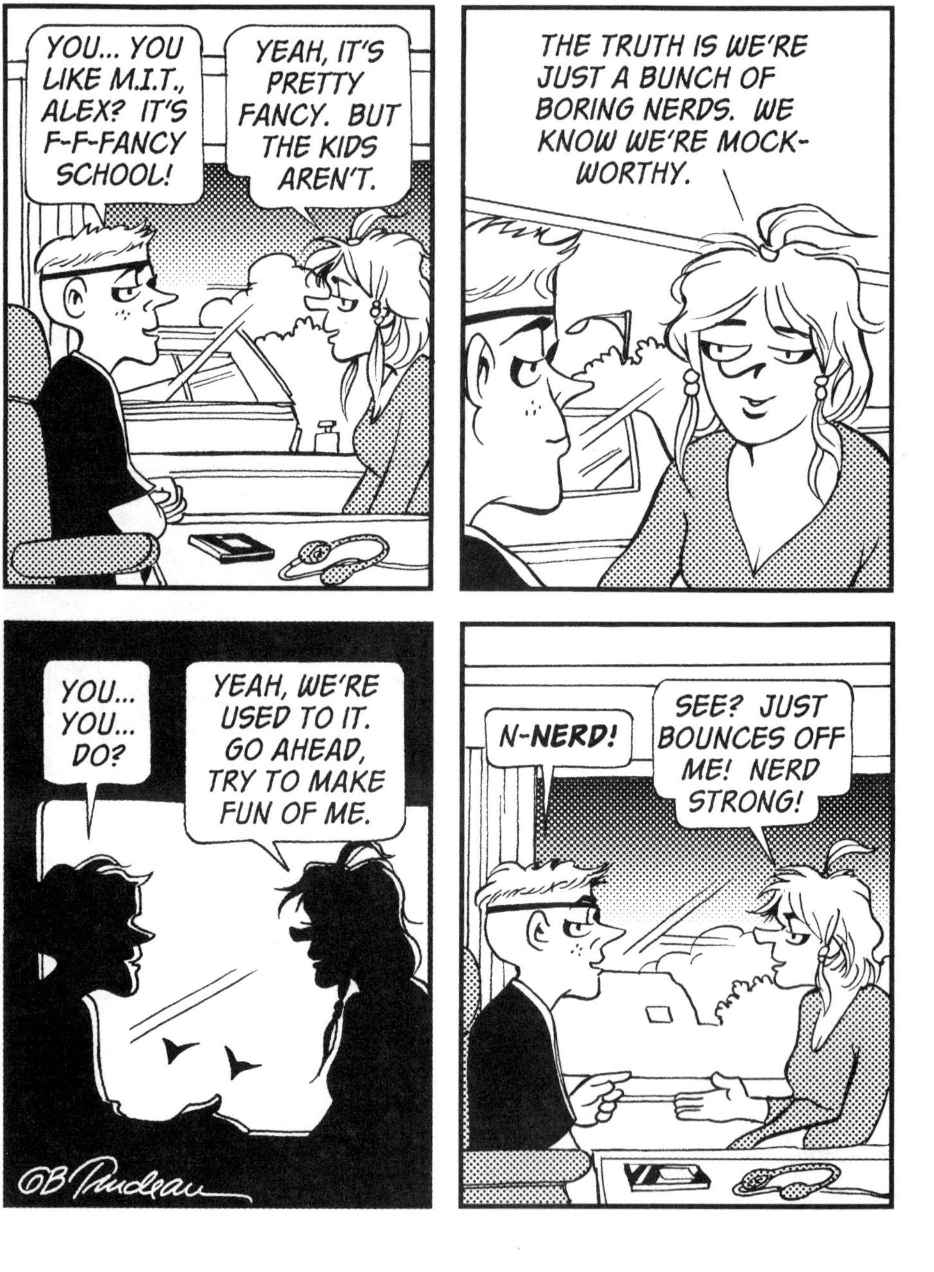
YOU... YOU LIKE M.I.T., ALEX? IT'S F-F-FANCY SCHOOL!
YEAH, IT'S PRETTY FANCY. BUT THE KIDS AREN'T.
THE TRUTH IS WE'RE JUST A BUNCH OF BORING NERDS. WE KNOW WE'RE MOCK-WORTHY.
YOU... YOU... DO?
YEAH, WE'RE USED TO IT. GO AHEAD, TRY TO MAKE FUN OF ME.
©B. Trudeau
N-NERD!
SEE? JUST BOUNCES OFF ME! NERD STRONG!

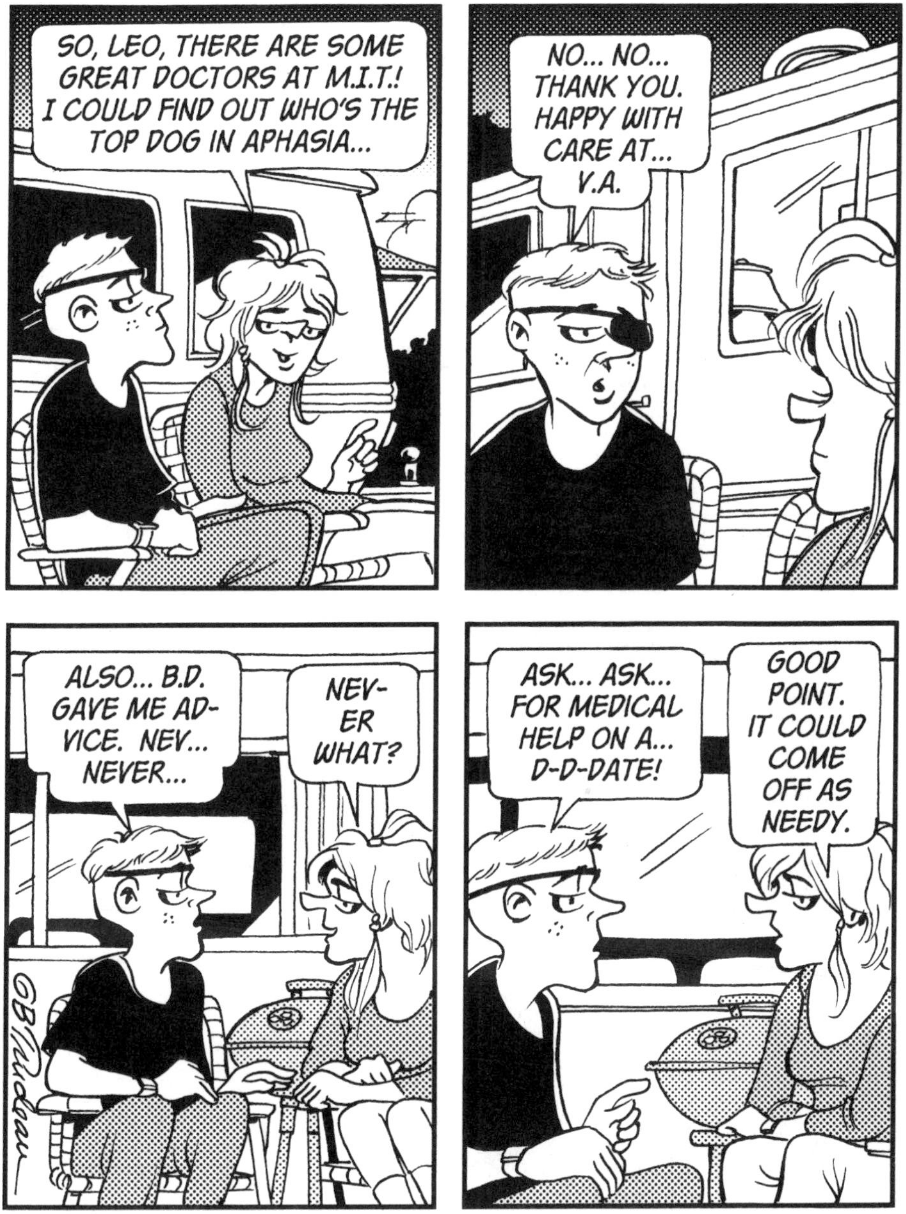
SO, LEO, THERE ARE SOME GREAT DOCTORS AT M.I.T.! I COULD FIND OUT WHO'S THE TOP DOG IN APHASIA...
NO... NO... THANK YOU. HAPPY WITH CARE AT... V.A.
ALSO... B.D. GAVE ME ADVICE. NEV... NEVER...
NEVER WHAT?
ASK... ASK... FOR MEDICAL HELP ON A... D-D-DATE!
GOOD POINT. IT COULD COME OFF AS NEEDY.
GBTrudeau

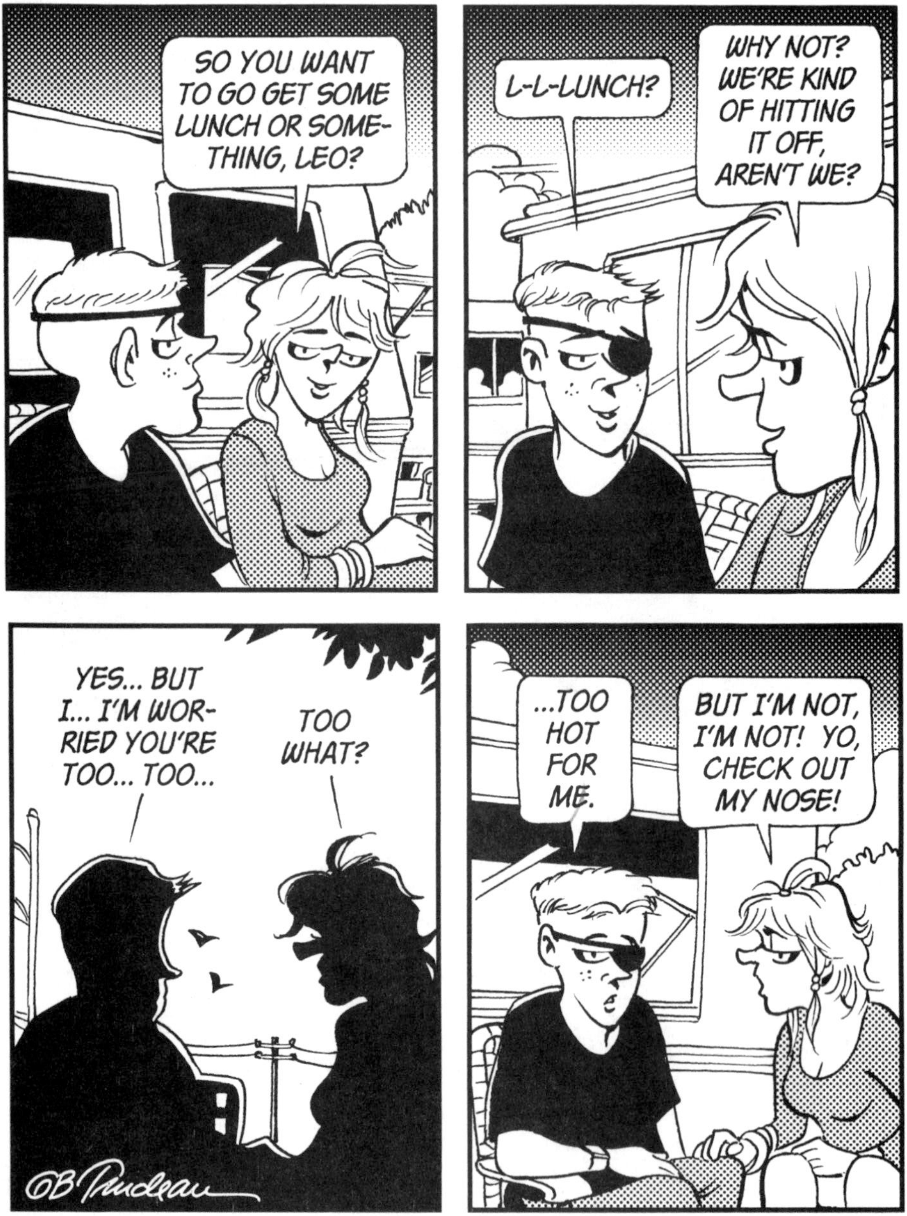
SO YOU WANT TO GO GET SOME LUNCH OR SOME-THING, LEO?
L-L-LUNCH?
WHY NOT? WE'RE KIND OF HITTING IT OFF, AREN'T WE?
YES... BUT I... I'M WOR-RIED YOU'RE TOO... TOO...
TOO WHAT?
...TOO HOT FOR ME.
BUT I'M NOT, I'M NOT! YO, CHECK OUT MY NOSE!
©B Trudeau

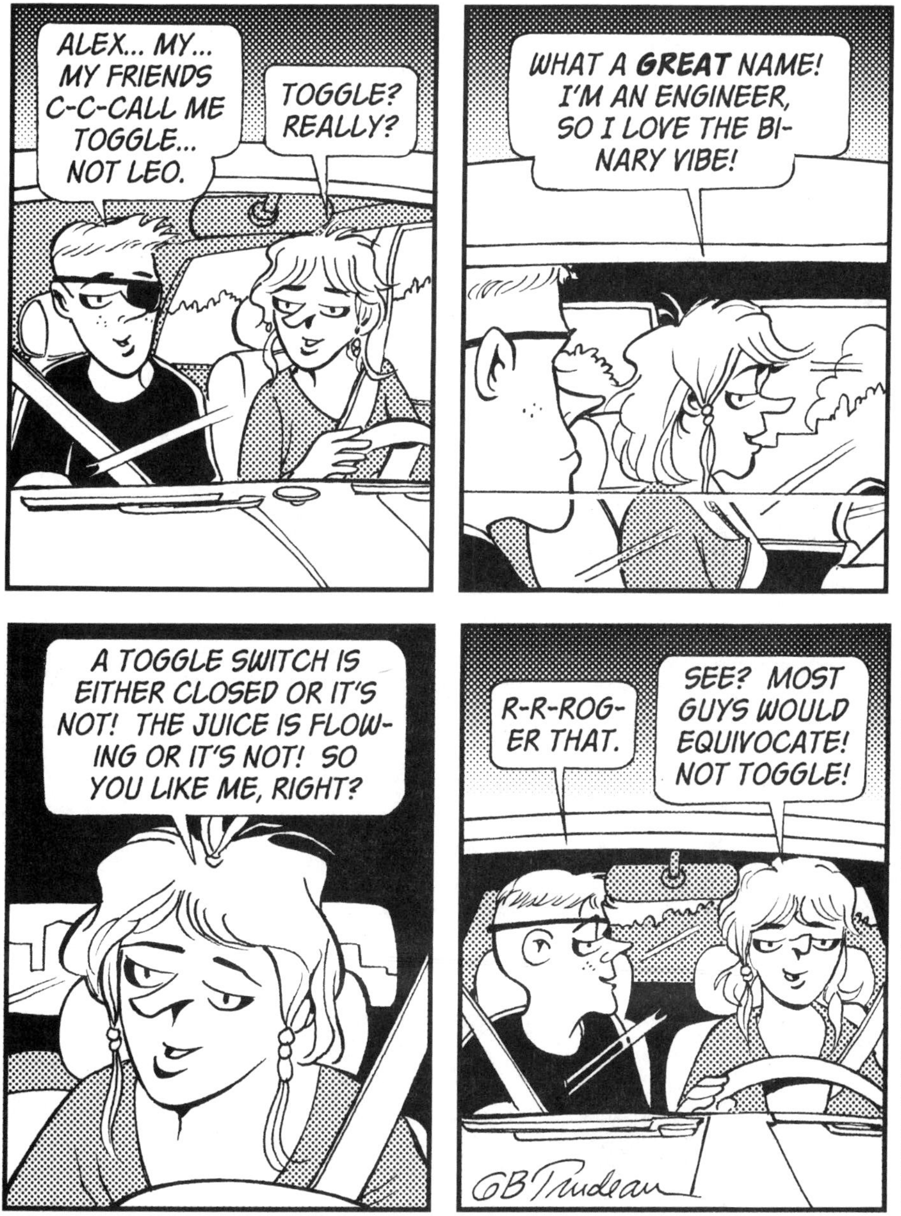
ALEX... MY... MY FRIENDS C-C-CALL ME TOGGLE... NOT LEO.
TOGGLE? REALLY?
WHAT A **GREAT** NAME! I'M AN ENGINEER, SO I LOVE THE BI-NARY VIBE!
A TOGGLE SWITCH IS EITHER CLOSED OR IT'S NOT! THE JUICE IS FLOW-ING OR IT'S NOT! SO YOU LIKE ME, RIGHT?
R-R-ROG-ER THAT.
SEE? MOST GUYS WOULD EQUIVOCATE! NOT TOGGLE!
GB Trudeau

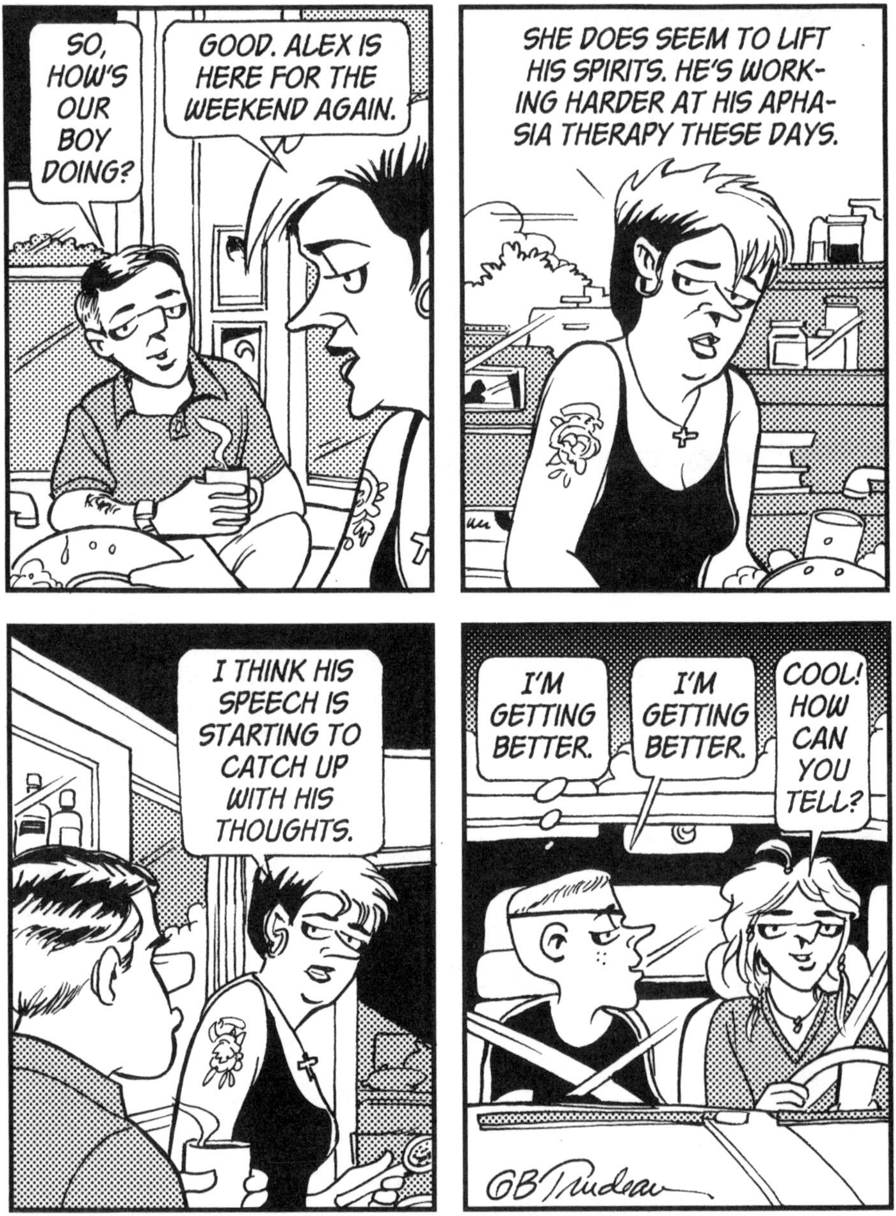

SO, HOW'S OUR BOY DOING?
GOOD. ALEX IS HERE FOR THE WEEKEND AGAIN.
SHE DOES SEEM TO LIFT HIS SPIRITS. HE'S WORKING HARDER AT HIS APHASIA THERAPY THESE DAYS.
I THINK HIS SPEECH IS STARTING TO CATCH UP WITH HIS THOUGHTS.
I'M GETTING BETTER.
I'M GETTING BETTER.
COOL! HOW CAN YOU TELL?
GB Trudeau

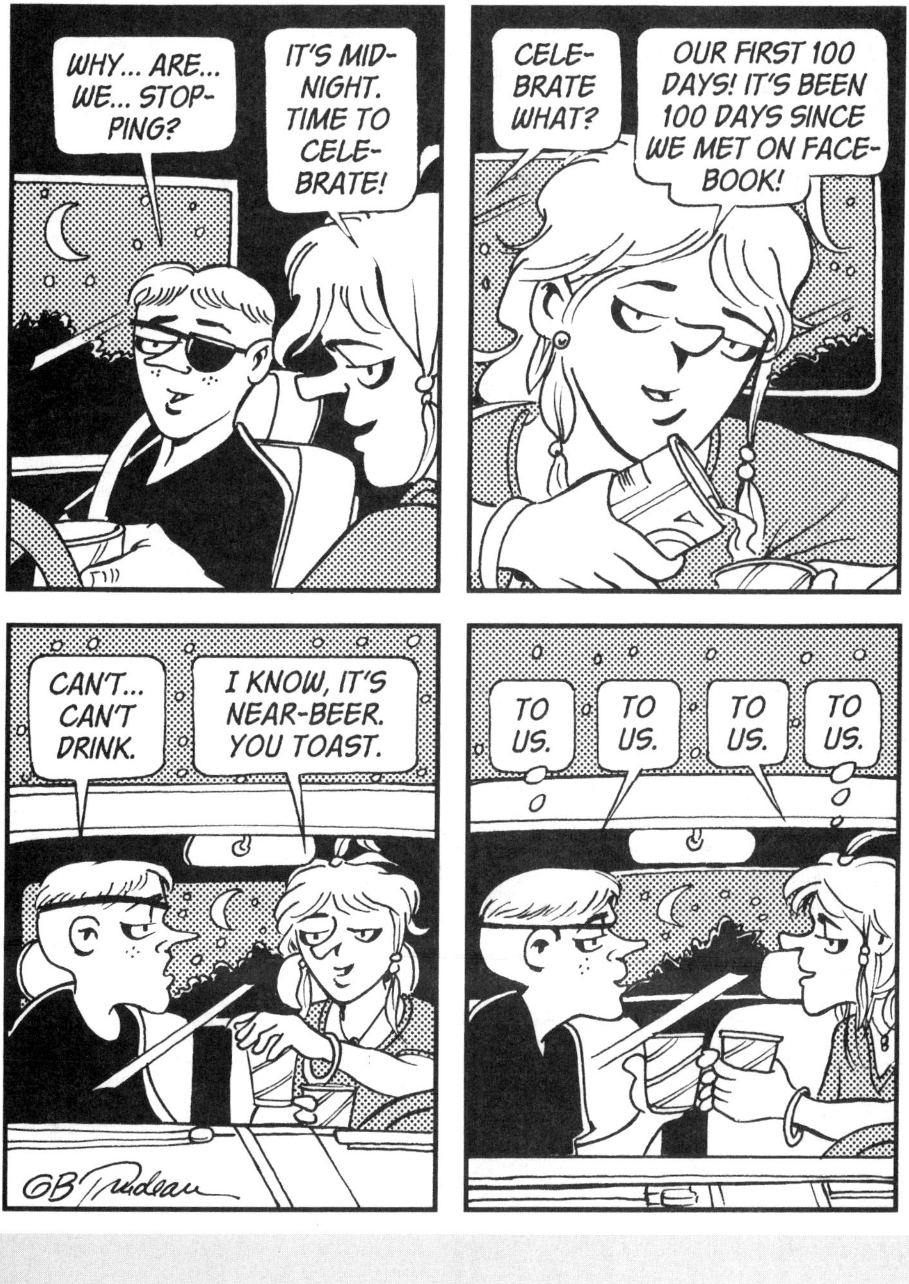
WHY... ARE... WE... STOP-PING?
IT'S MID-NIGHT. TIME TO CELE-BRATE!
CELE-BRATE WHAT?
OUR FIRST 100 DAYS! IT'S BEEN 100 DAYS SINCE WE MET ON FACE-BOOK!
CAN'T... CAN'T DRINK.
I KNOW, IT'S NEAR-BEER. YOU TOAST.
TO US.
TO US.
TO US.
TO US.
GB Trudeau

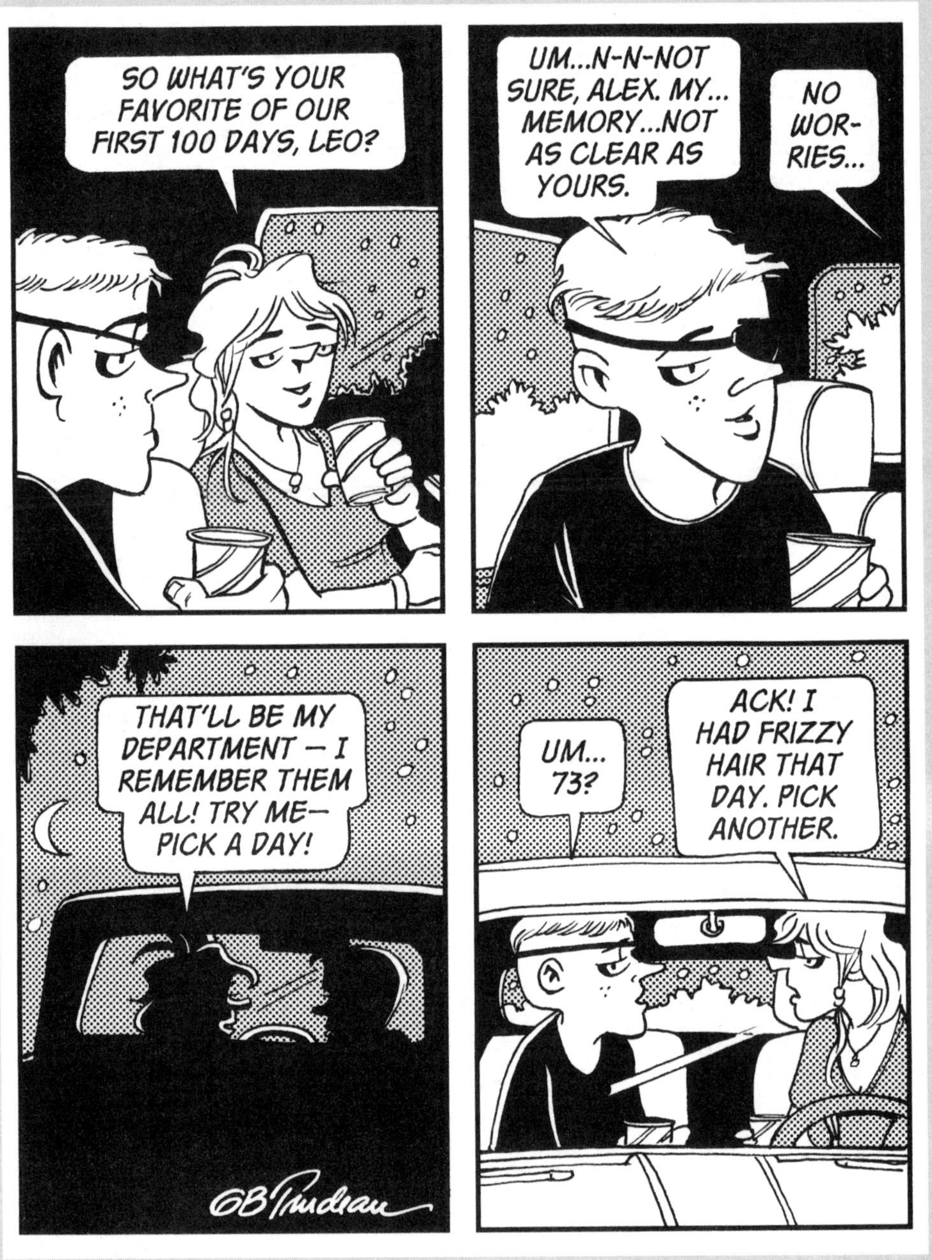
SO WHAT'S YOUR FAVORITE OF OUR FIRST 100 DAYS, LEO?
UM...N-N-NOT SURE, ALEX. MY... MEMORY...NOT AS CLEAR AS YOURS.
NO WOR-RIES...
THAT'LL BE MY DEPARTMENT — I REMEMBER THEM ALL! TRY ME— PICK A DAY!
UM... 73?
ACK! I HAD FRIZZY HAIR THAT DAY. PICK ANOTHER.
GB Trudeau

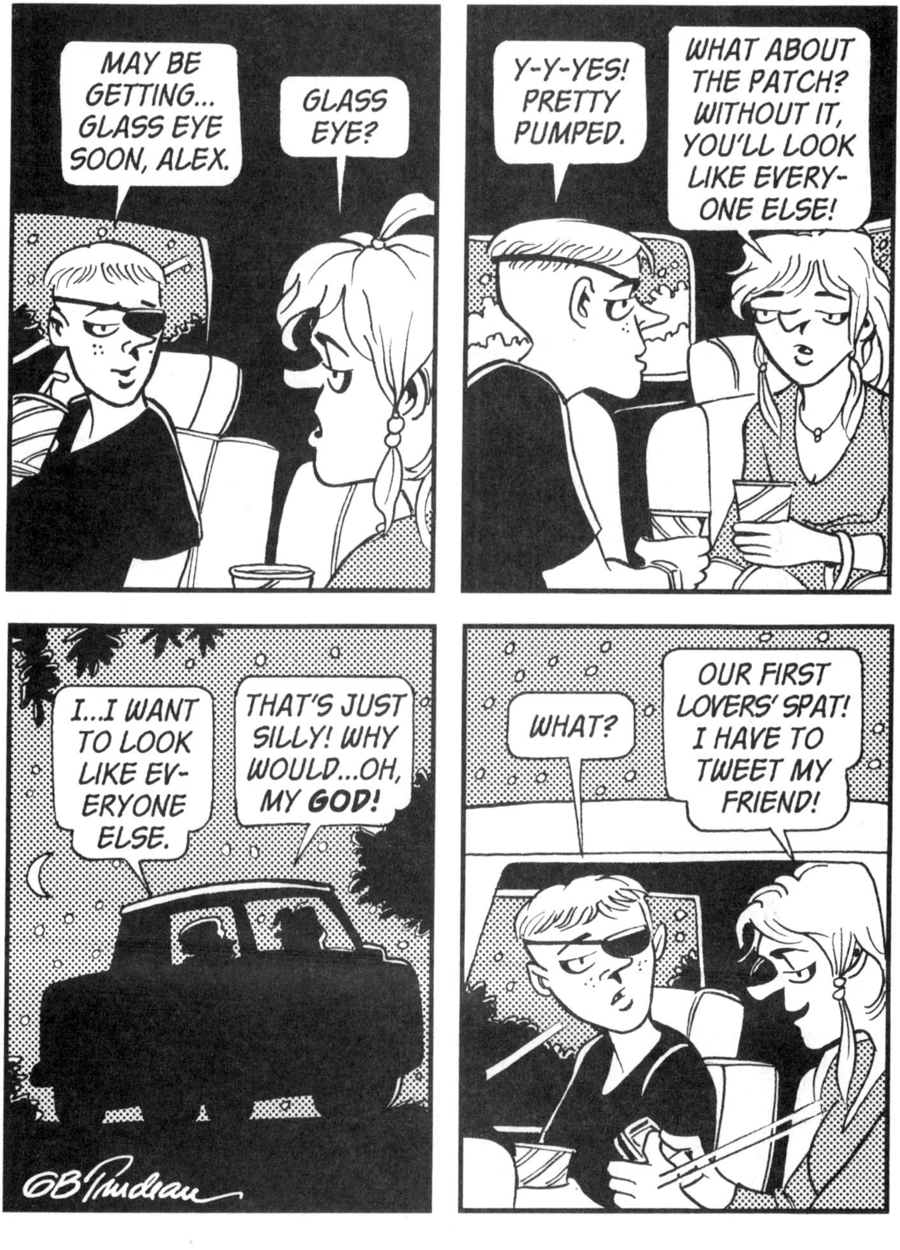
MAY BE GETTING... GLASS EYE SOON, ALEX.
GLASS EYE?
Y-Y-YES! PRETTY PUMPED.
WHAT ABOUT THE PATCH? WITHOUT IT, YOU'LL LOOK LIKE EVERY-ONE ELSE!
I...I WANT TO LOOK LIKE EV-ERYONE ELSE.
THAT'S JUST SILLY! WHY WOULD...OH, MY **GOD**!
WHAT?
OUR FIRST LOVERS' SPAT! I HAVE TO TWEET MY FRIEND!
GB Trudeau

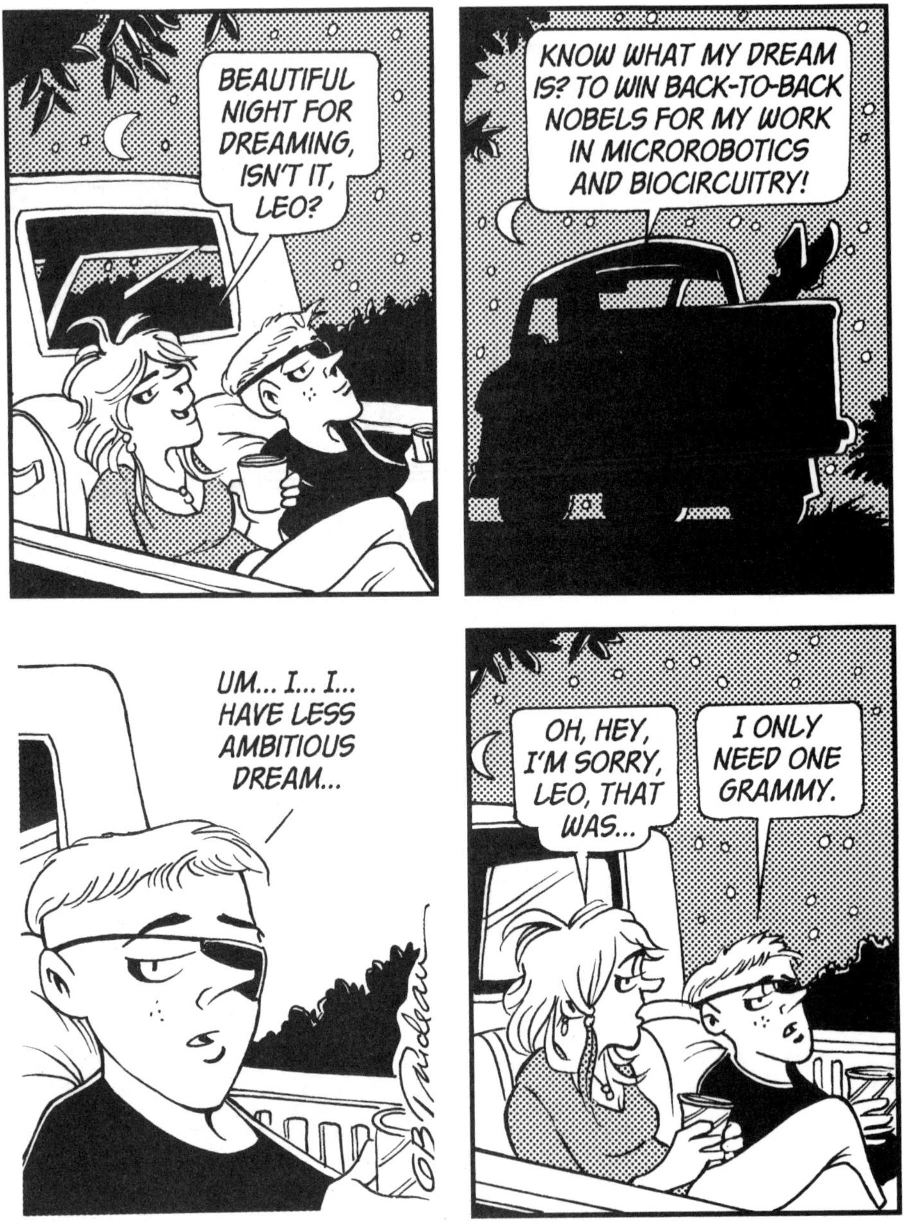
BEAUTIFUL NIGHT FOR DREAMING, ISN'T IT, LEO?
KNOW WHAT MY DREAM IS? TO WIN BACK-TO-BACK NOBELS FOR MY WORK IN MICROROBOTICS AND BIOCIRCUITRY!
UM... I... I... HAVE LESS AMBITIOUS DREAM...
OH, HEY, I'M SORRY, LEO, THAT WAS...
I ONLY NEED ONE GRAMMY.

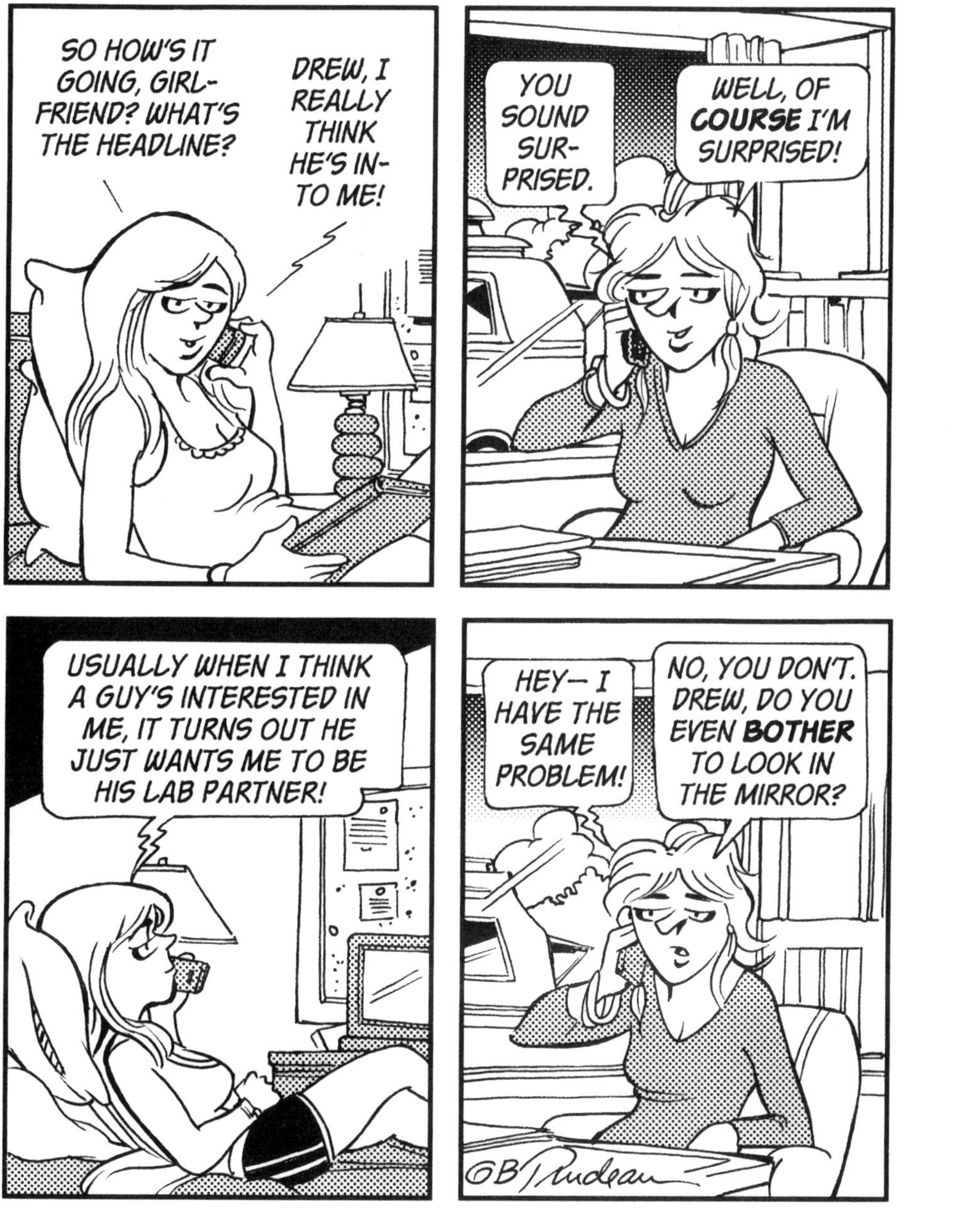
SO HOW'S IT GOING, GIRL-FRIEND? WHAT'S THE HEADLINE?
DREW, I REALLY THINK HE'S IN-TO ME!
YOU SOUND SUR-PRISED.
WELL, OF **COURSE** I'M SURPRISED!
USUALLY WHEN I THINK A GUY'S INTERESTED IN ME, IT TURNS OUT HE JUST WANTS ME TO BE HIS LAB PARTNER!
HEY— I HAVE THE SAME PROBLEM!
NO, YOU DON'T. DREW, DO YOU EVEN **BOTHER** TO LOOK IN THE MIRROR?
©B Trudeau

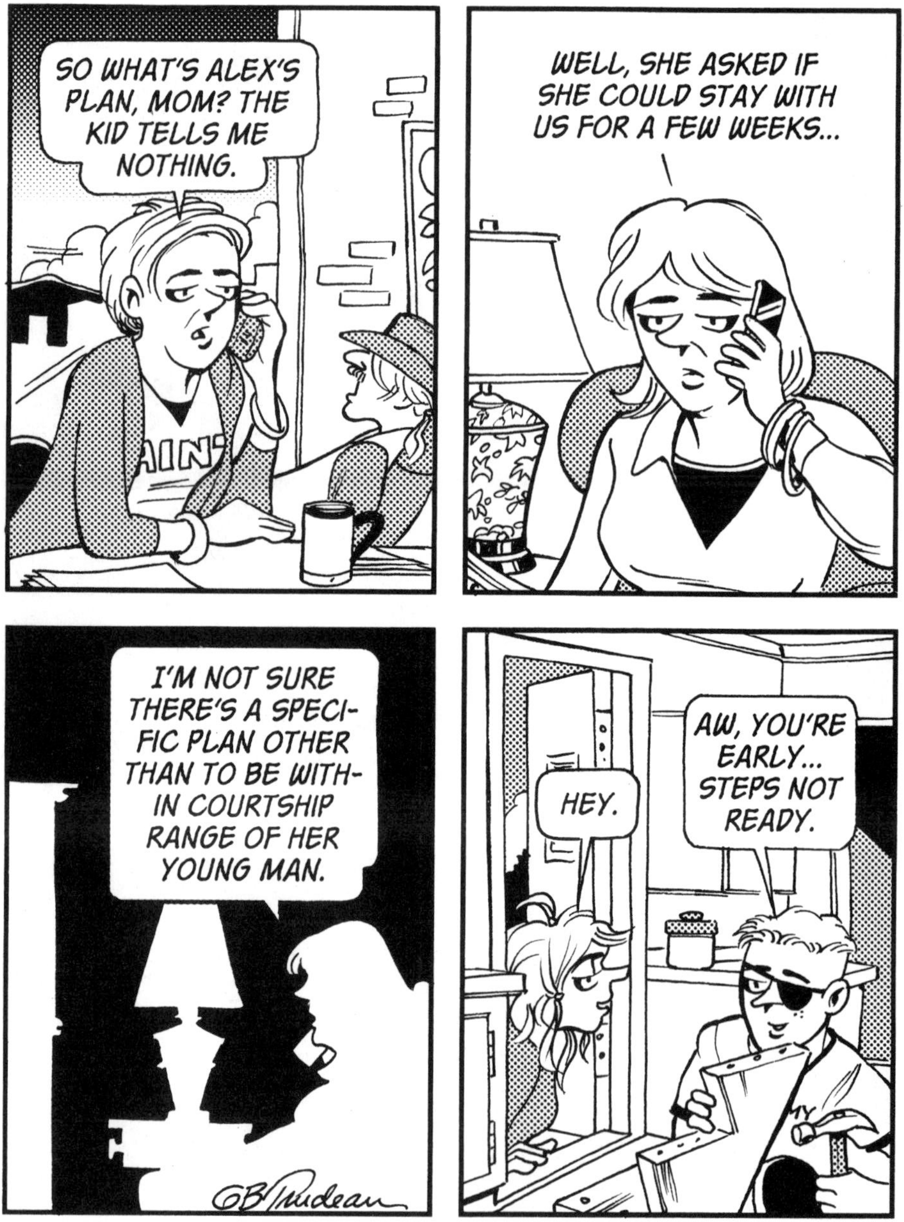
SO WHAT'S ALEX'S PLAN, MOM? THE KID TELLS ME NOTHING.
WELL, SHE ASKED IF SHE COULD STAY WITH US FOR A FEW WEEKS...
I'M NOT SURE THERE'S A SPECIFIC PLAN OTHER THAN TO BE WITHIN COURTSHIP RANGE OF HER YOUNG MAN.
GB Trudeau
HEY.
AW, YOU'RE EARLY... STEPS NOT READY.

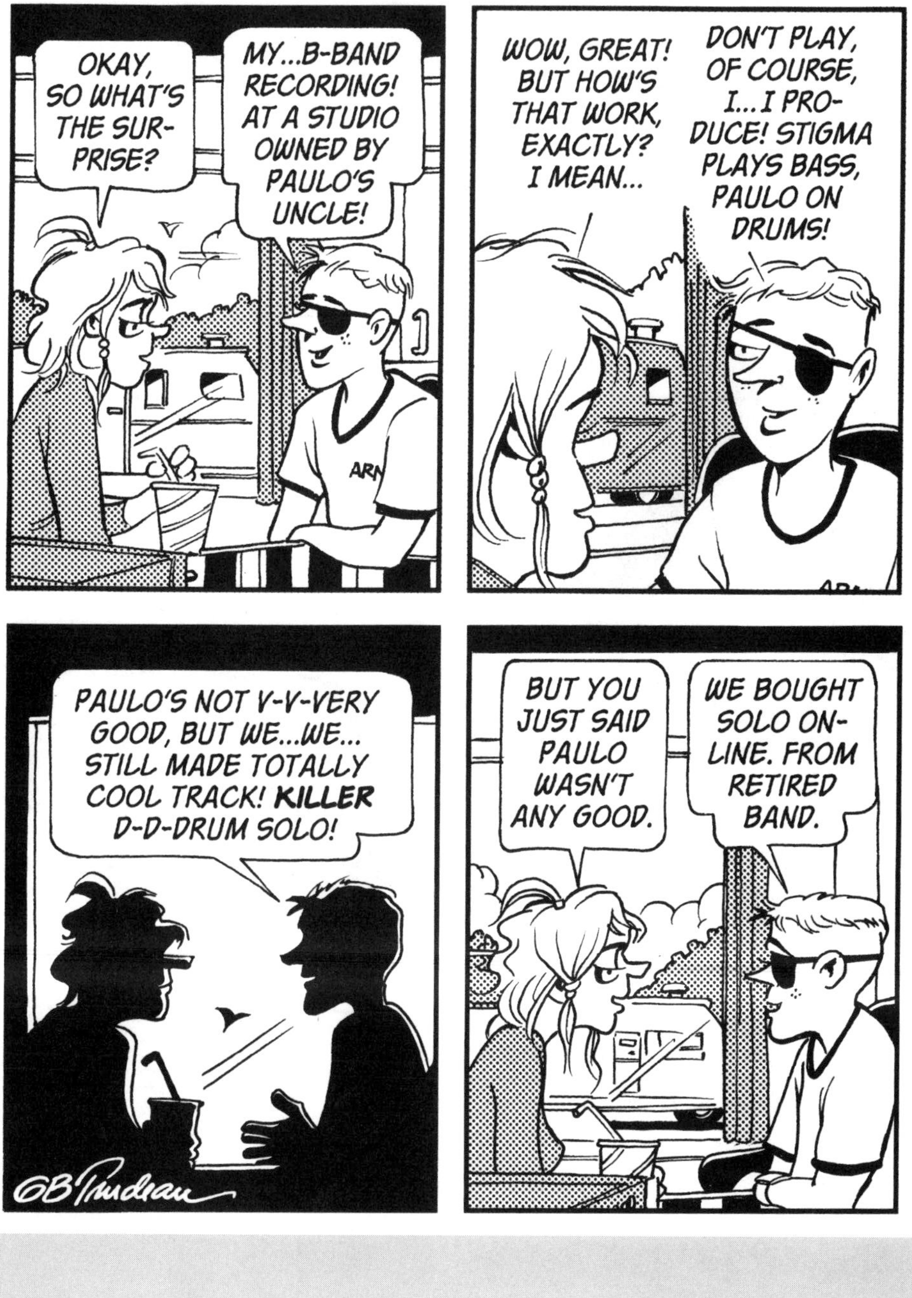
OKAY, SO WHAT'S THE SURPRISE?
MY...B-BAND RECORDING! AT A STUDIO OWNED BY PAULO'S UNCLE!
WOW, GREAT! BUT HOW'S THAT WORK, EXACTLY? I MEAN...
DON'T PLAY, OF COURSE, I...I PRODUCE! STIGMA PLAYS BASS, PAULO ON DRUMS!
PAULO'S NOT V-V-VERY GOOD, BUT WE...WE... STILL MADE TOTALLY COOL TRACK! **KILLER** D-D-DRUM SOLO!
BUT YOU JUST SAID PAULO WASN'T ANY GOOD.
WE BOUGHT SOLO ONLINE. FROM RETIRED BAND.
GB Trudeau

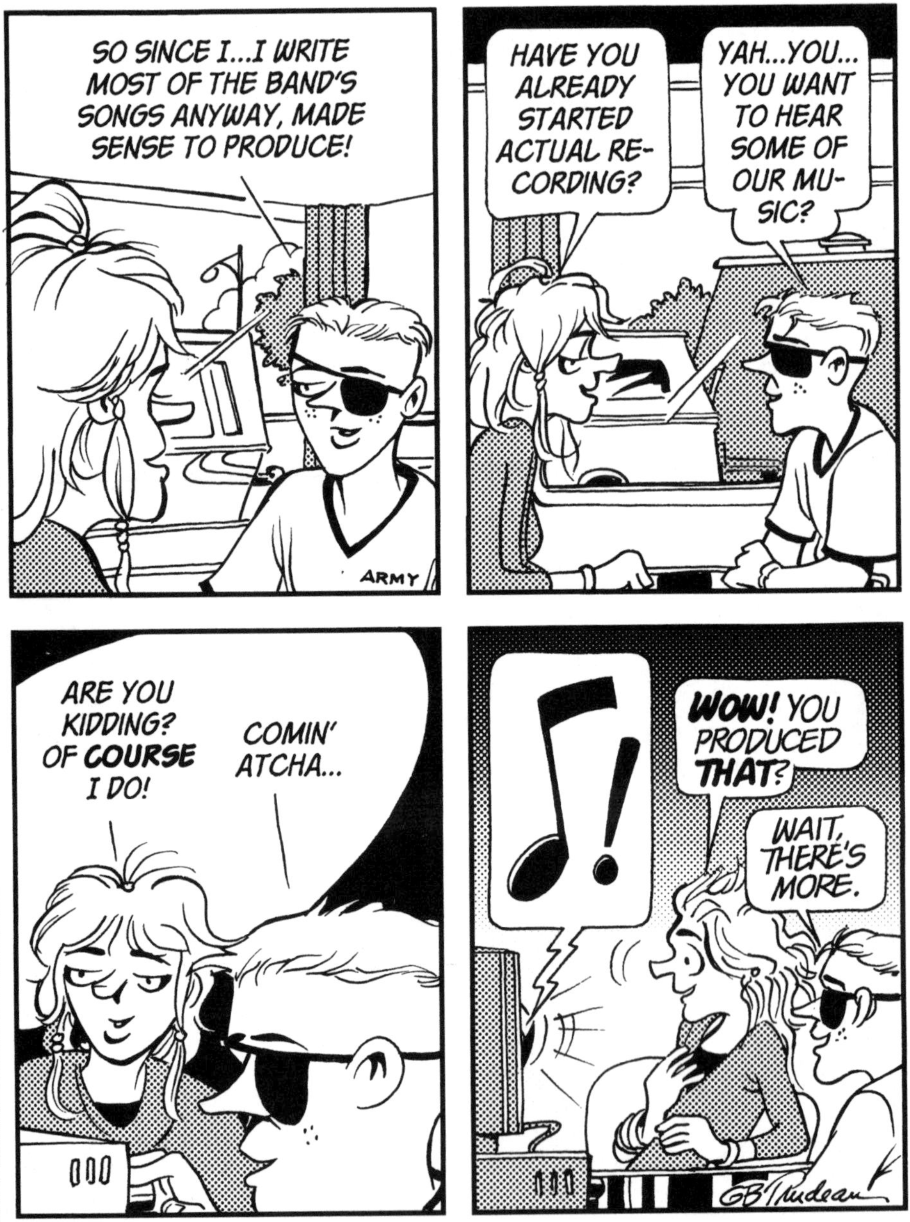
SO SINCE I...I WRITE MOST OF THE BAND'S SONGS ANYWAY, MADE SENSE TO PRODUCE!
ARMY
HAVE YOU ALREADY STARTED ACTUAL RE-CORDING?
YAH...YOU... YOU WANT TO HEAR SOME OF OUR MU-SIC?
ARE YOU KIDDING? OF **COURSE** I DO!
COMIN' ATCHA...
WOW! YOU PRODUCED **THAT**?
WAIT, THERE'S MORE.
GB Trudeau

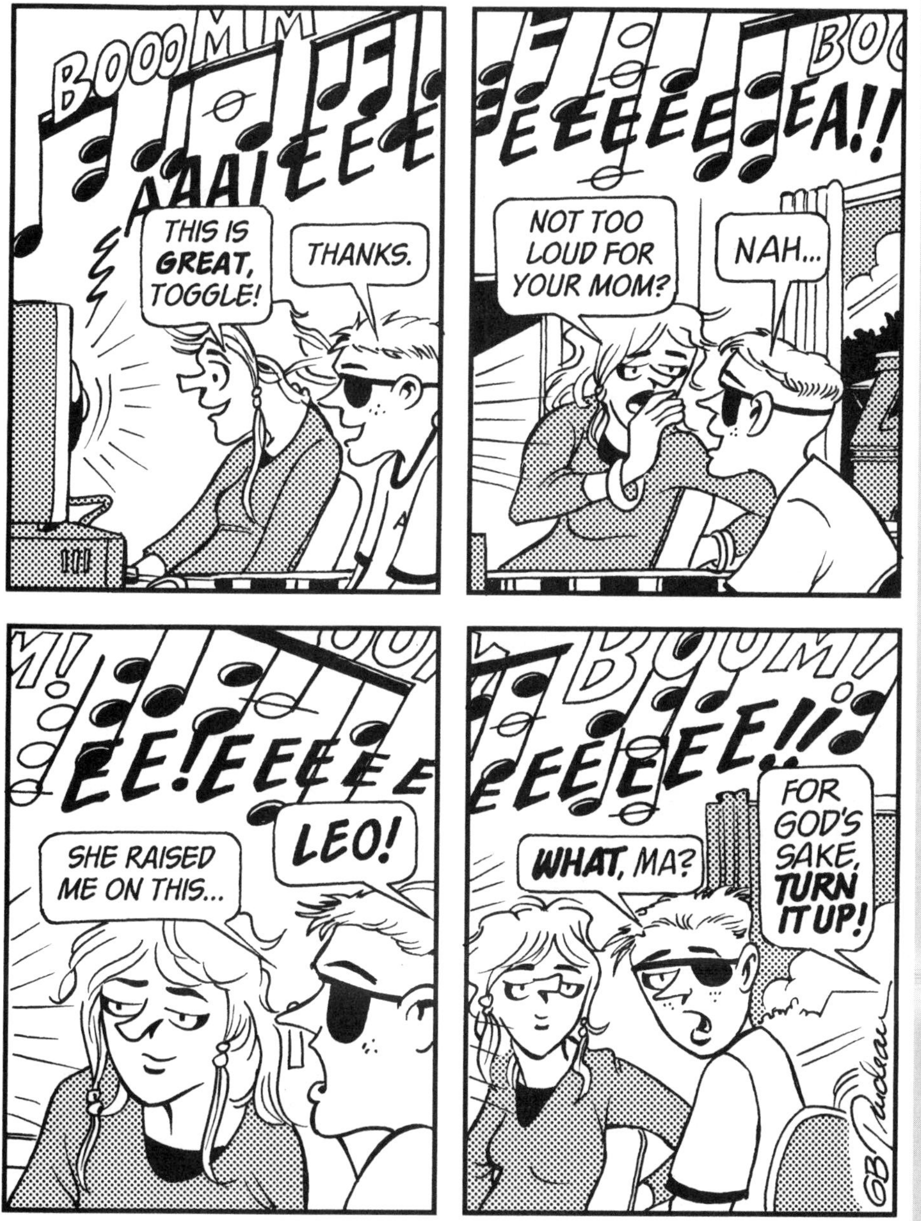

BOOOMM
AAAIEEEE
THIS IS GREAT, TOGGLE!
THANKS.
EEEEEEEA!!
BOO
NOT TOO LOUD FOR YOUR MOM?
NAH...
EE!EEEEE
SHE RAISED ME ON THIS...
LEO!
BOOM
EEEEEE!!
WHAT, MA?
FOR GOD'S SAKE, TURN IT UP!

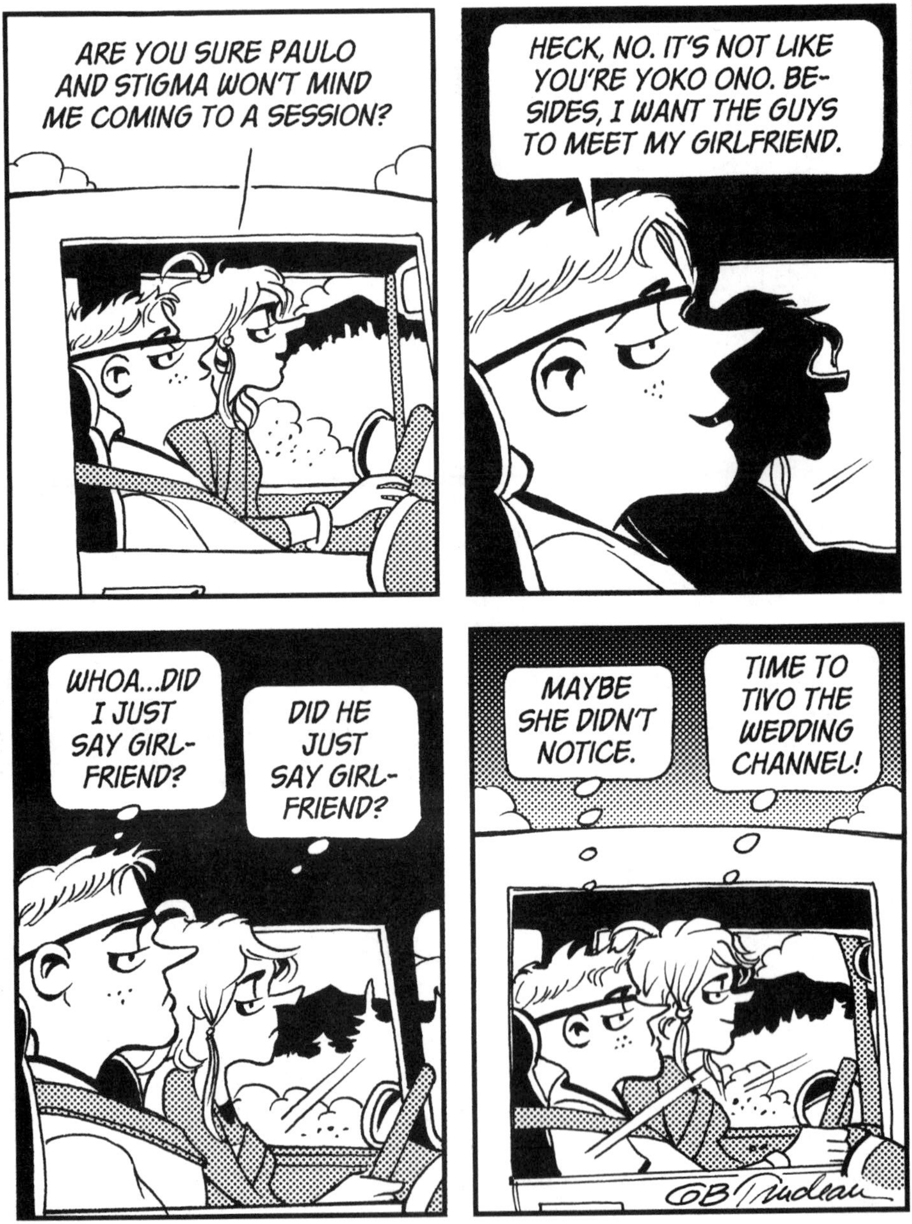
ARE YOU SURE PAULO AND STIGMA WON'T MIND ME COMING TO A SESSION?
HECK, NO. IT'S NOT LIKE YOU'RE YOKO ONO. BESIDES, I WANT THE GUYS TO MEET MY GIRLFRIEND.
WHOA...DID I JUST SAY GIRLFRIEND?
DID HE JUST SAY GIRLFRIEND?
MAYBE SHE DIDN'T NOTICE.
TIME TO TIVO THE WEDDING CHANNEL!
GB Trudeau

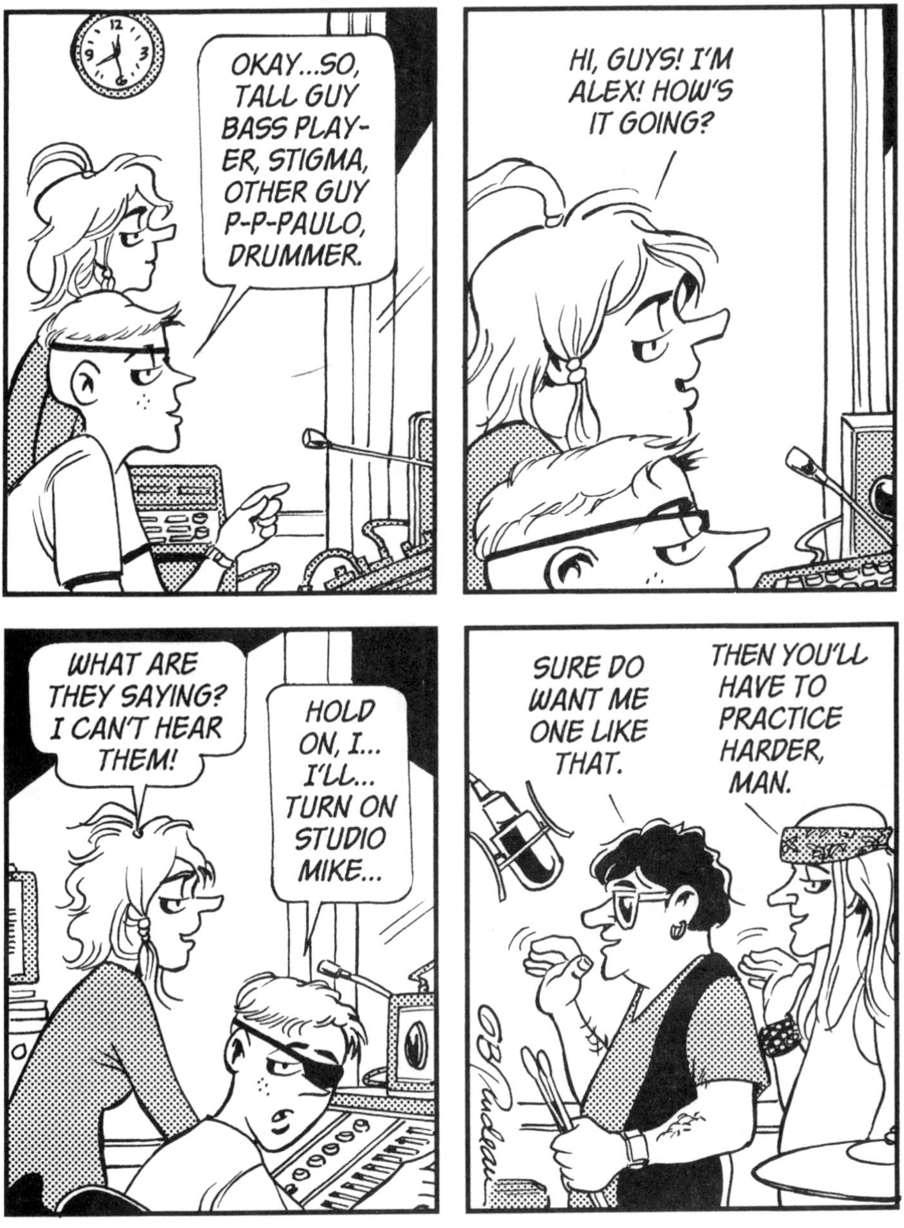
OKAY...SO, TALL GUY BASS PLAYER, STIGMA, OTHER GUY P-P-PAULO, DRUMMER.
HI, GUYS! I'M ALEX! HOW'S IT GOING?
WHAT ARE THEY SAYING? I CAN'T HEAR THEM!
HOLD ON, I... I'LL... TURN ON STUDIO MIKE...
SURE DO WANT ME ONE LIKE THAT.
THEN YOU'LL HAVE TO PRACTICE HARDER, MAN.

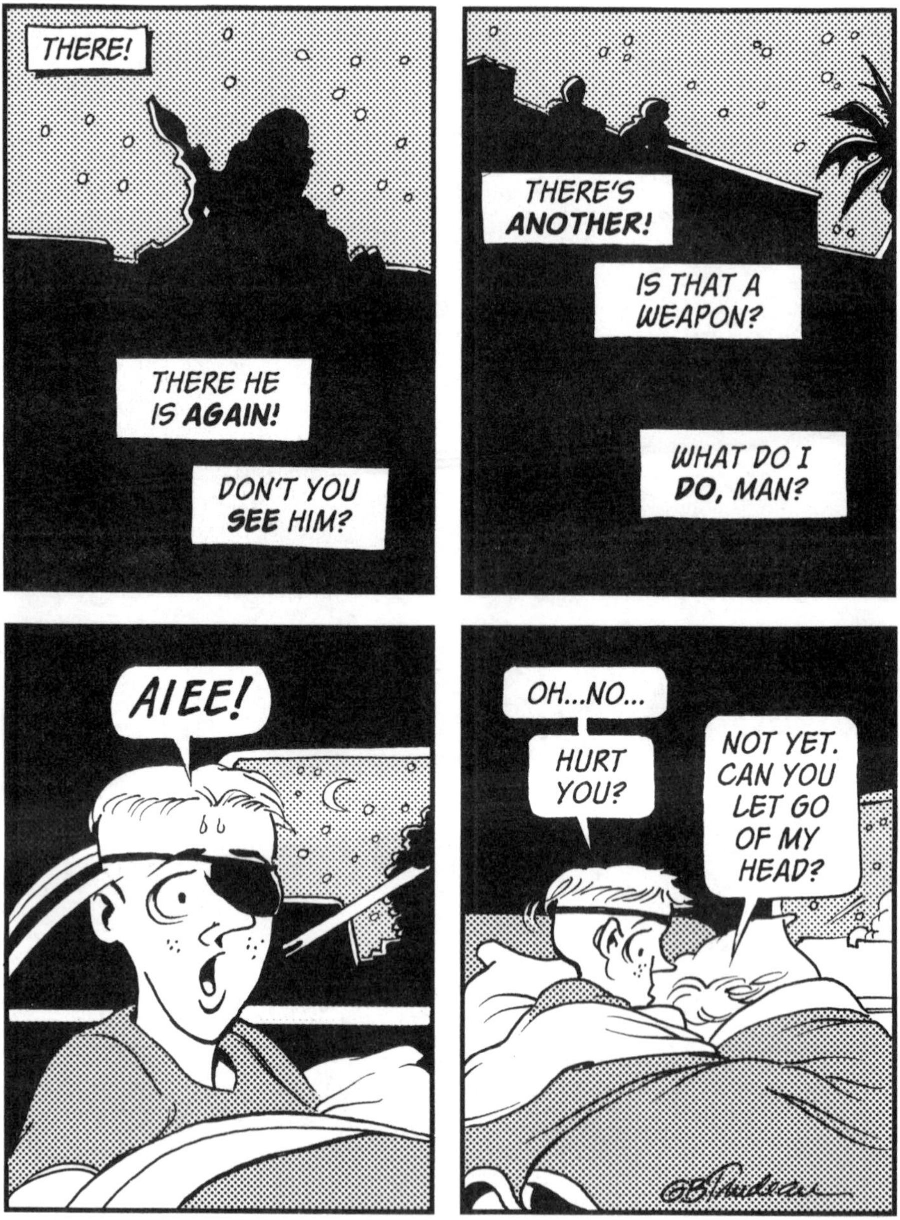
THERE!
THERE HE IS AGAIN!
DON'T YOU SEE HIM?
THERE'S ANOTHER!
IS THAT A WEAPON?
WHAT DO I DO, MAN?
AIEE!
OH...NO...
HURT YOU?
NOT YET. CAN YOU LET GO OF MY HEAD?

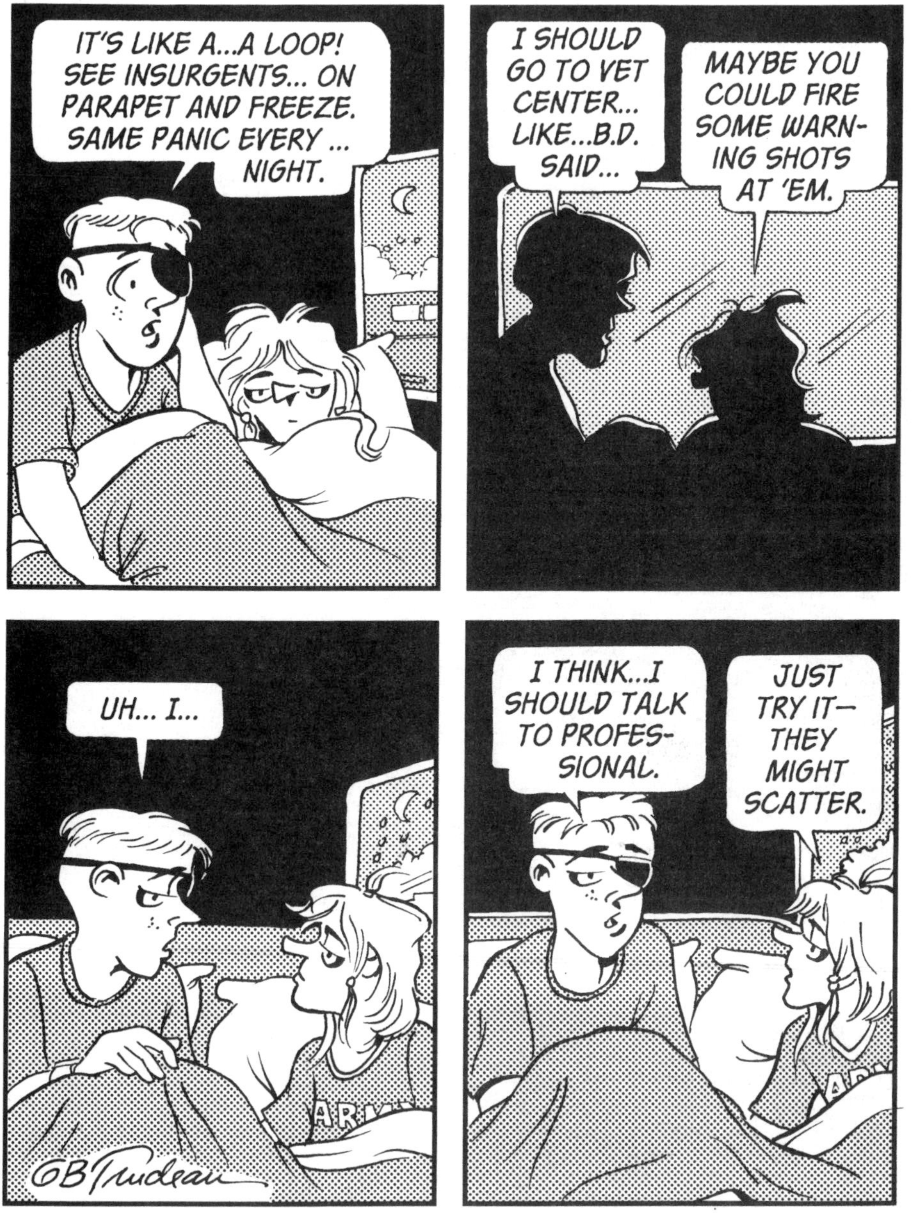
IT'S LIKE A...A LOOP! SEE INSURGENTS... ON PARAPET AND FREEZE. SAME PANIC EVERY ... NIGHT.
I SHOULD GO TO VET CENTER... LIKE...B.D. SAID...
MAYBE YOU COULD FIRE SOME WARNING SHOTS AT 'EM.
UH... I...
GB Trudeau
I THINK...I SHOULD TALK TO PROFESSIONAL.
JUST TRY IT— THEY MIGHT SCATTER.

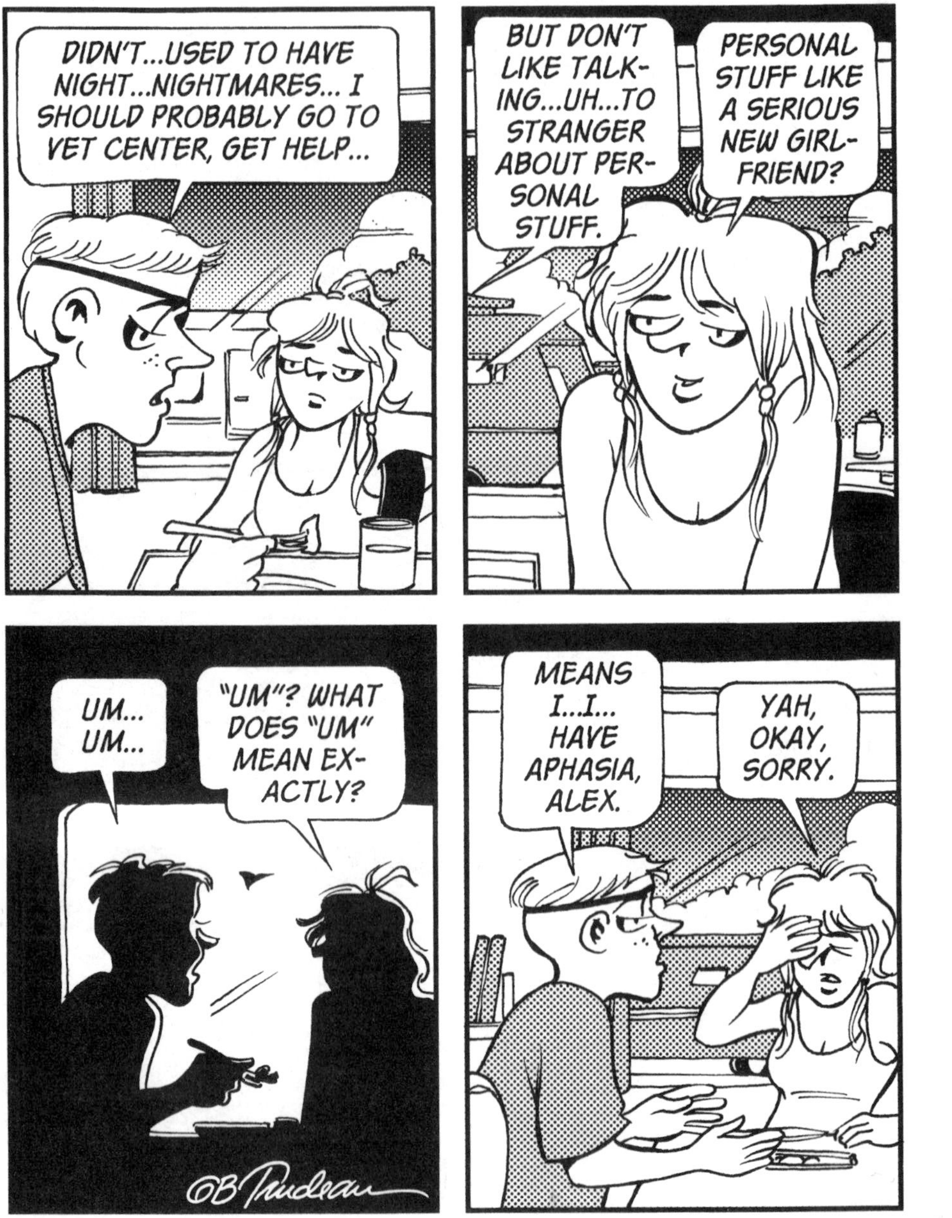
DIDN'T...USED TO HAVE NIGHT...NIGHTMARES... I SHOULD PROBABLY GO TO VET CENTER, GET HELP...
BUT DON'T LIKE TALK-ING...UH...TO STRANGER ABOUT PER-SONAL STUFF.
PERSONAL STUFF LIKE A SERIOUS NEW GIRL-FRIEND?
UM... UM...
"UM"? WHAT DOES "UM" MEAN EX-ACTLY?
©B Trudeau
MEANS I...I... HAVE APHASIA, ALEX.
YAH, OKAY, SORRY.

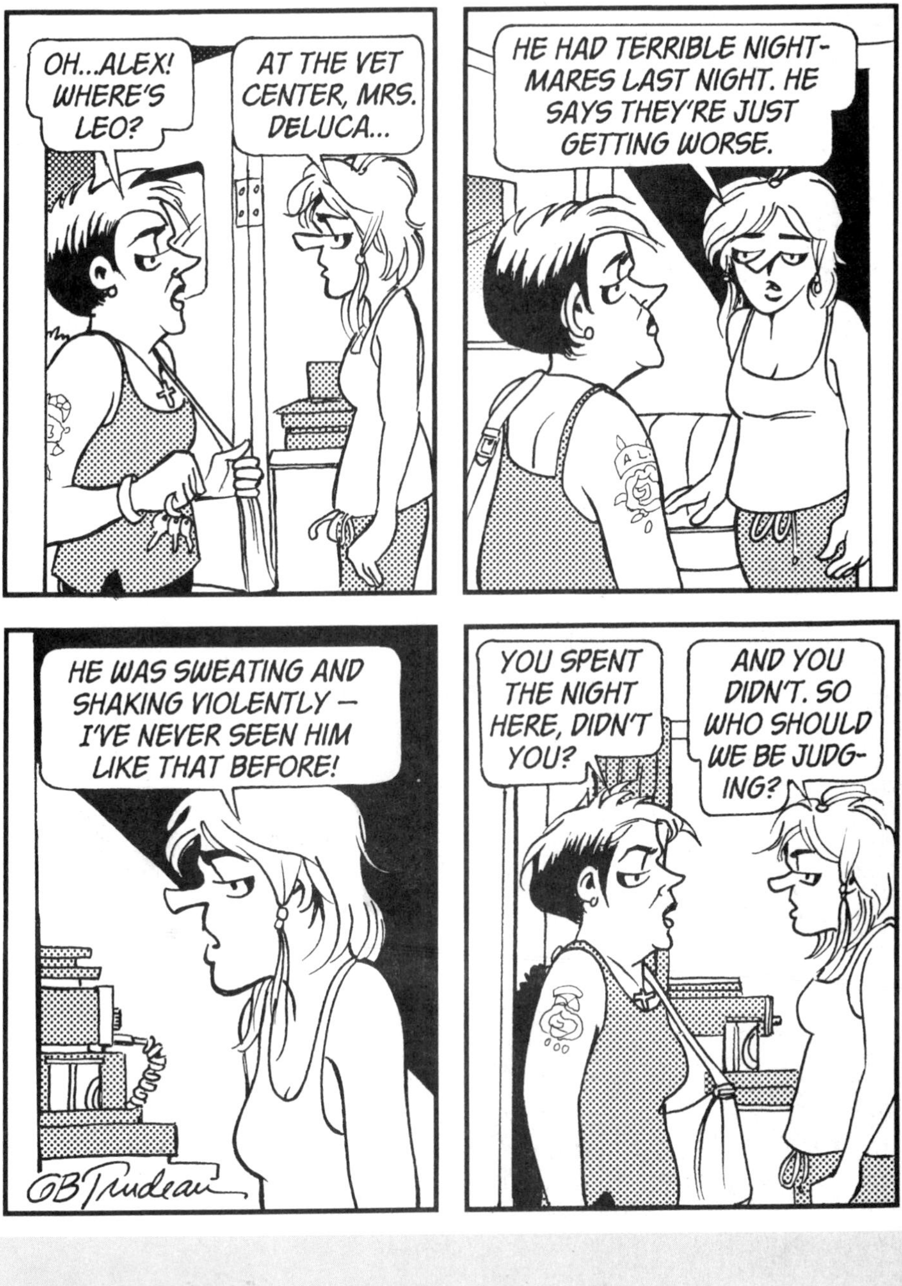
OH...ALEX! WHERE'S LEO?
AT THE VET CENTER, MRS. DELUCA...
HE HAD TERRIBLE NIGHT-MARES LAST NIGHT. HE SAYS THEY'RE JUST GETTING WORSE.
HE WAS SWEATING AND SHAKING VIOLENTLY — I'VE NEVER SEEN HIM LIKE THAT BEFORE!
GB Trudeau
YOU SPENT THE NIGHT HERE, DIDN'T YOU?
AND YOU DIDN'T. SO WHO SHOULD WE BE JUDG-ING?

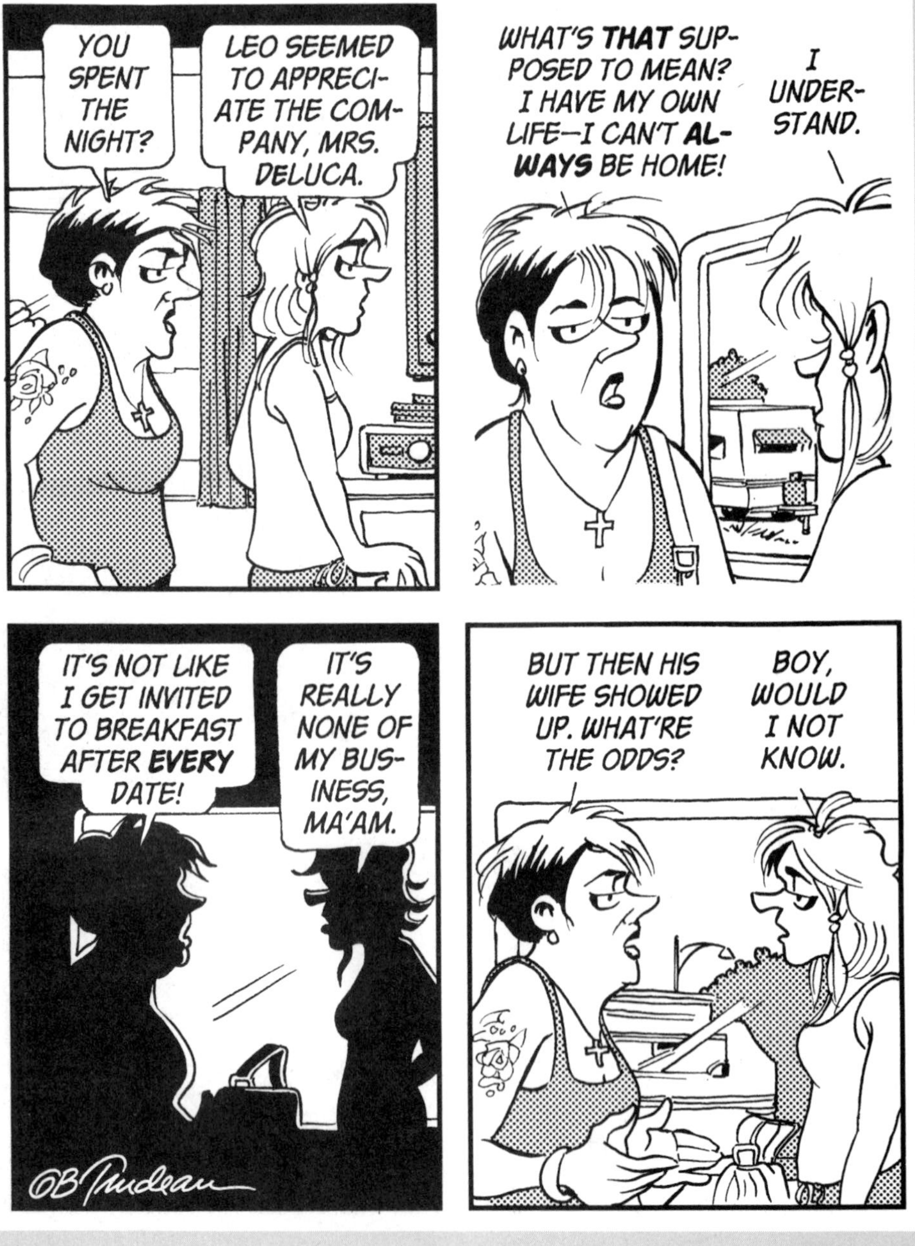
YOU SPENT THE NIGHT?
LEO SEEMED TO APPRECIATE THE COMPANY, MRS. DELUCA.
WHAT'S **THAT** SUPPOSED TO MEAN? I HAVE MY OWN LIFE—I CAN'T **ALWAYS** BE HOME!
I UNDERSTAND.
IT'S NOT LIKE I GET INVITED TO BREAKFAST AFTER **EVERY** DATE!
IT'S REALLY NONE OF MY BUSINESS, MA'AM.
©B Trudeau
BUT THEN HIS WIFE SHOWED UP. WHAT'RE THE ODDS?
BOY, WOULD I NOT KNOW.

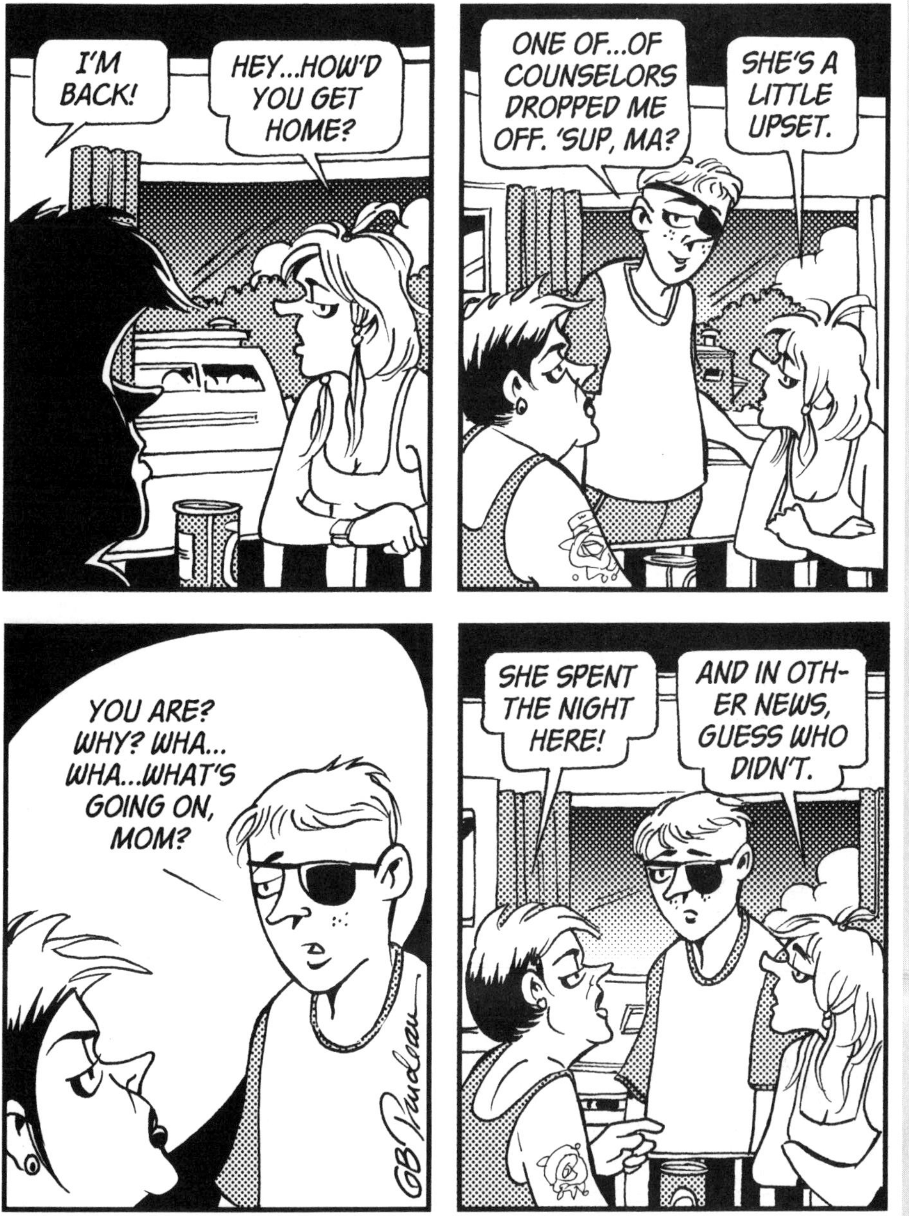
I'M BACK!
HEY...HOW'D YOU GET HOME?
ONE OF...OF COUNSELORS DROPPED ME OFF. 'SUP, MA?
SHE'S A LITTLE UPSET.
YOU ARE? WHY? WHA... WHA...WHAT'S GOING ON, MOM?
SHE SPENT THE NIGHT HERE!
AND IN OTH-ER NEWS, GUESS WHO DIDN'T.

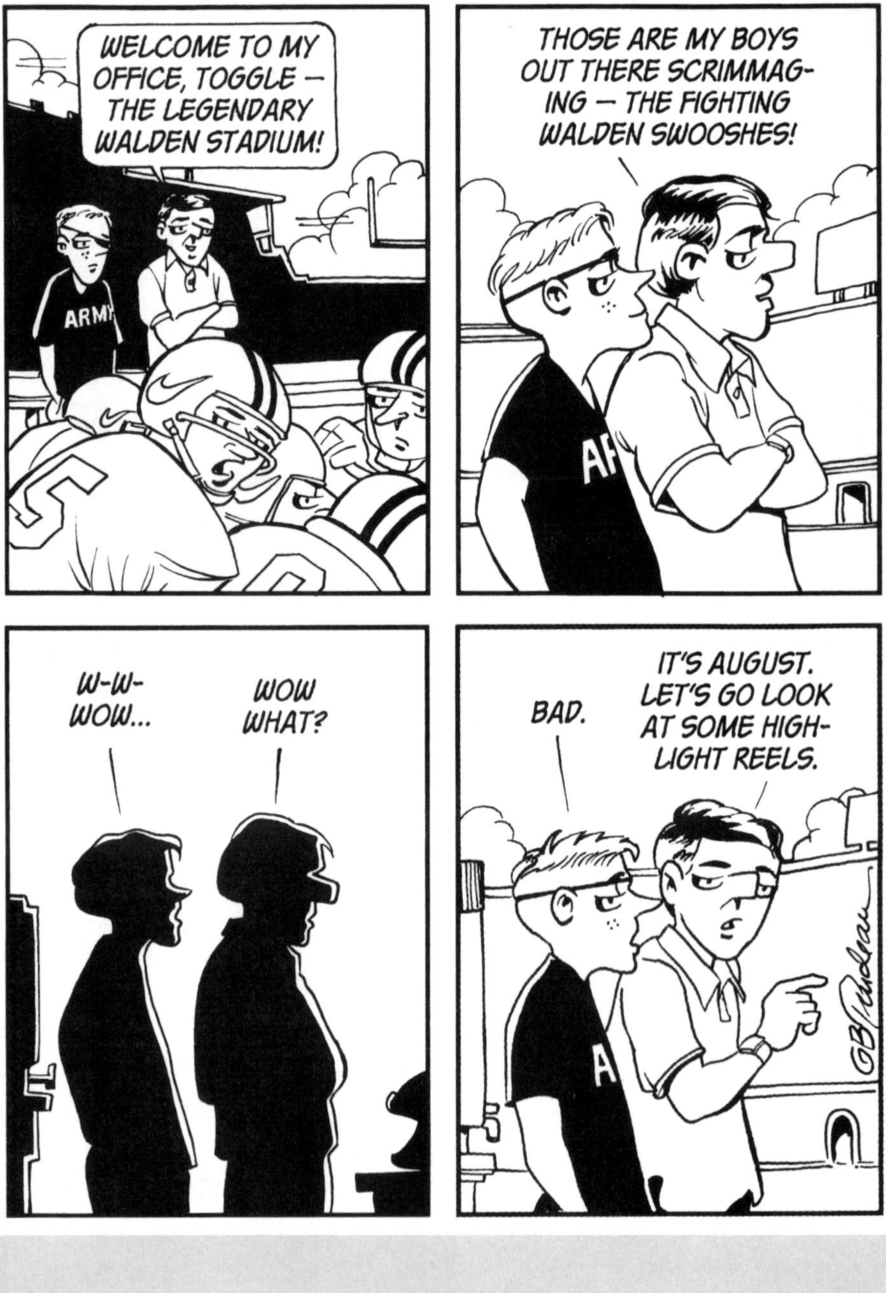
WELCOME TO MY OFFICE, TOGGLE — THE LEGENDARY WALDEN STADIUM!
ARMY
THOSE ARE MY BOYS OUT THERE SCRIMMAGING — THE FIGHTING WALDEN SWOOSHES!
W-W-WOW...
WOW WHAT?
BAD.
IT'S AUGUST. LET'S GO LOOK AT SOME HIGHLIGHT REELS.

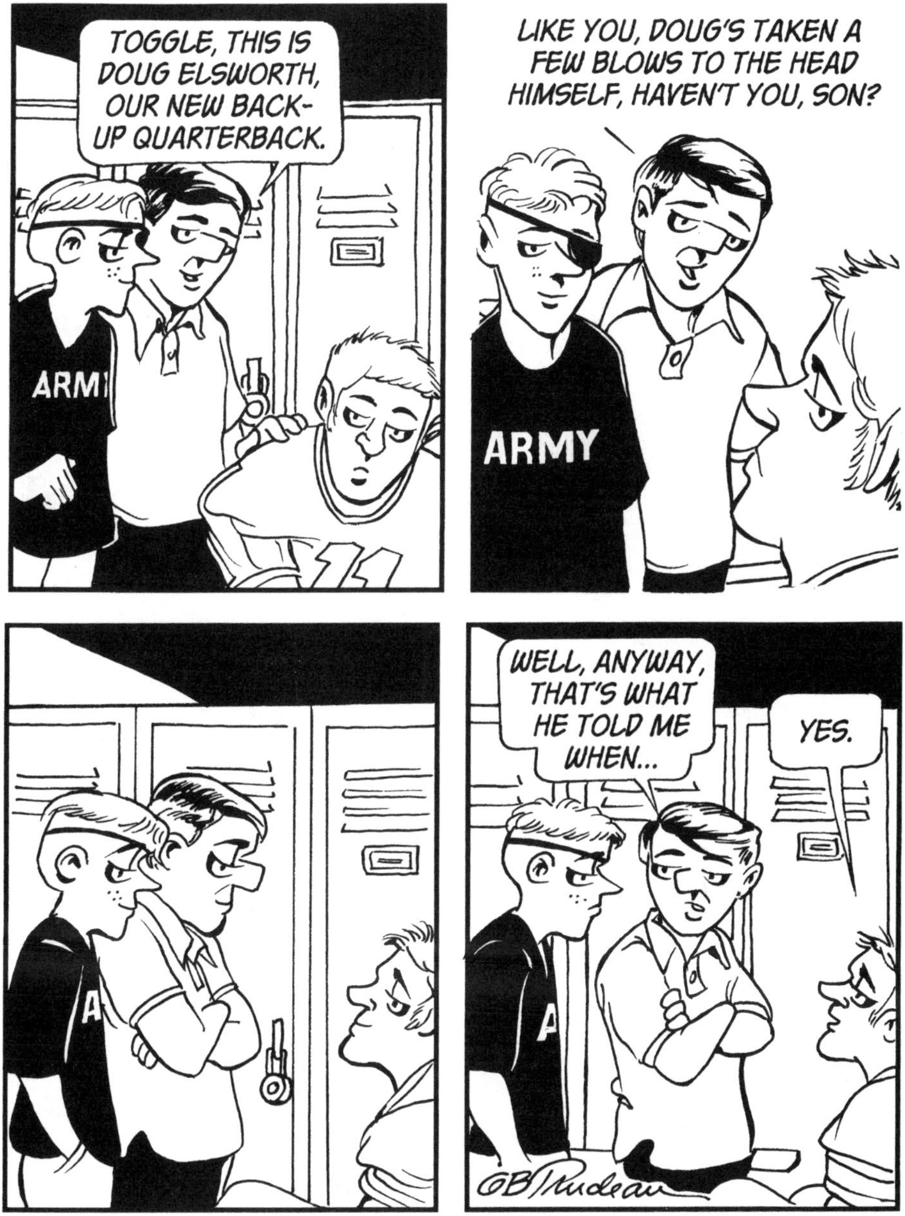
TOGGLE, THIS IS DOUG ELSWORTH, OUR NEW BACK-UP QUARTERBACK.
ARMY
11
LIKE YOU, DOUG'S TAKEN A FEW BLOWS TO THE HEAD HIMSELF, HAVEN'T YOU, SON?
ARMY
WELL, ANYWAY, THAT'S WHAT HE TOLD ME WHEN...
YES.
GB Trudeau

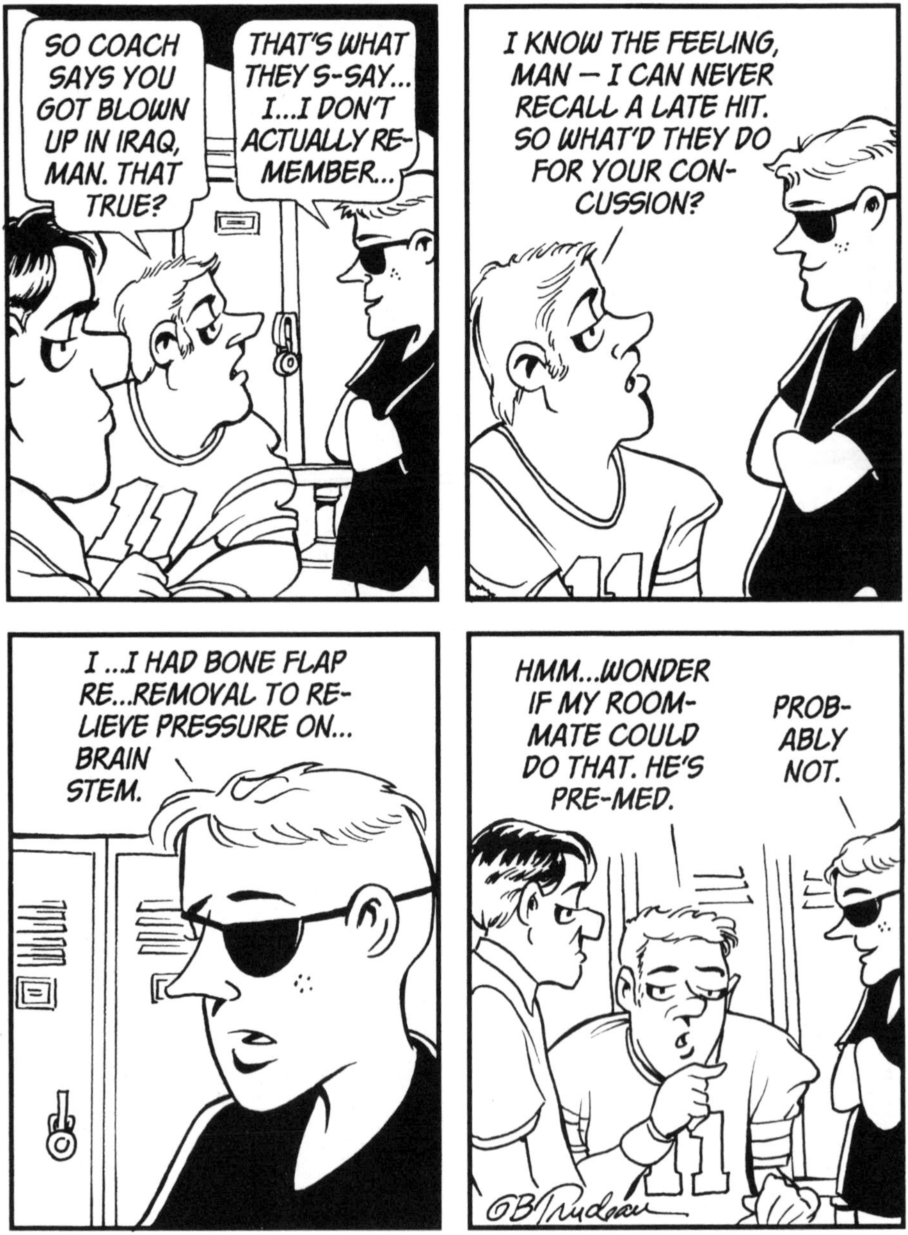
SO COACH SAYS YOU GOT BLOWN UP IN IRAQ, MAN. THAT TRUE?
THAT'S WHAT THEY S-SAY... I...I DON'T ACTUALLY RE-MEMBER...
I KNOW THE FEELING, MAN — I CAN NEVER RECALL A LATE HIT. SO WHAT'D THEY DO FOR YOUR CON-CUSSION?
I ...I HAD BONE FLAP RE...REMOVAL TO RE-LIEVE PRESSURE ON... BRAIN STEM.
HMM...WONDER IF MY ROOM-MATE COULD DO THAT. HE'S PRE-MED.
PROB-ABLY NOT.
©B Trudeau

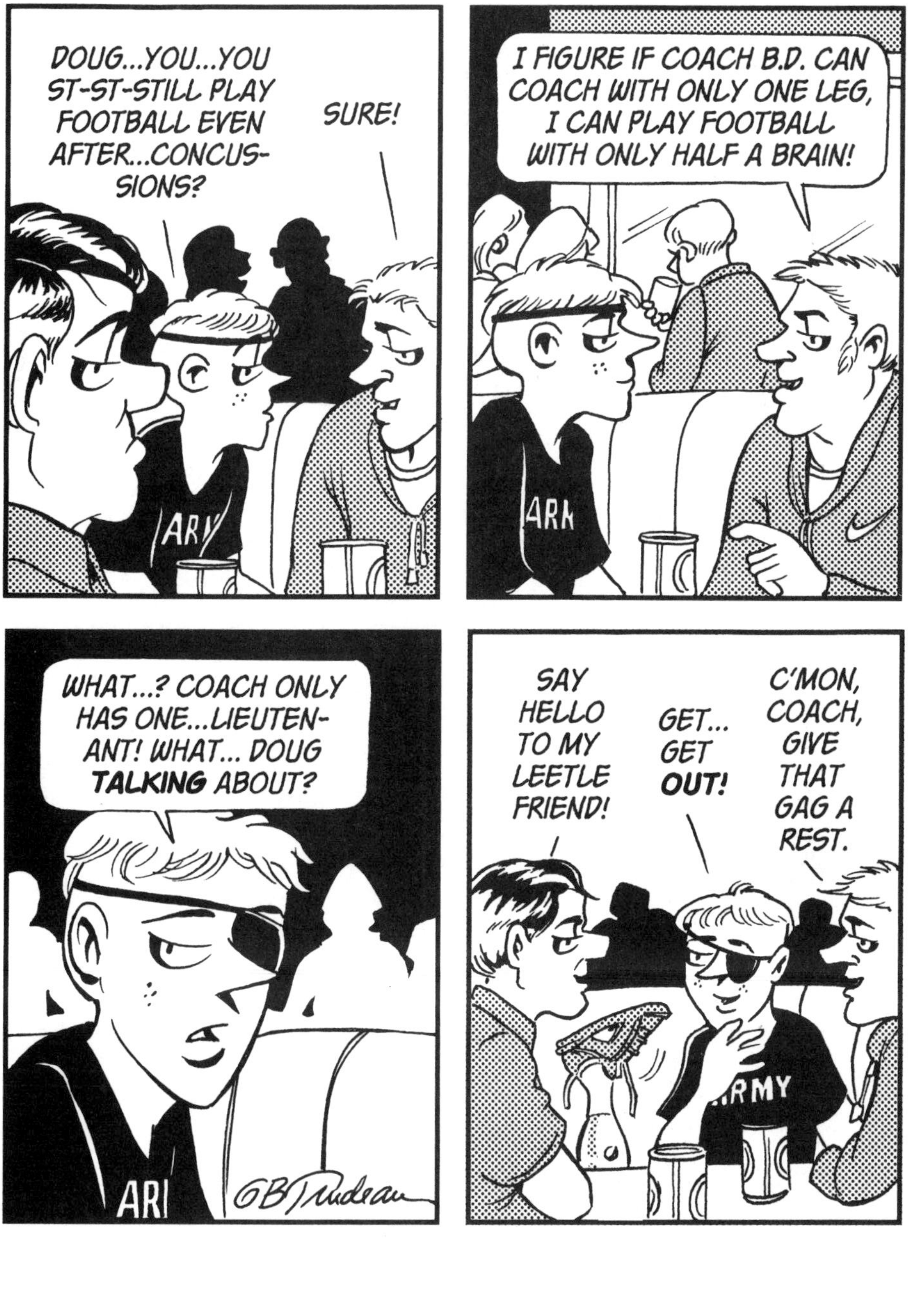
DOUG...YOU...YOU ST-ST-STILL PLAY FOOTBALL EVEN AFTER...CONCUS-SIONS?
SURE!
I FIGURE IF COACH B.D. CAN COACH WITH ONLY ONE LEG, I CAN PLAY FOOTBALL WITH ONLY HALF A BRAIN!
WHAT...? COACH ONLY HAS ONE...LIEUTEN-ANT! WHAT... DOUG TALKING ABOUT?
SAY HELLO TO MY LEETLE FRIEND!
GET... GET OUT!
C'MON, COACH, GIVE THAT GAG A REST.
ARMY
©B Trudeau

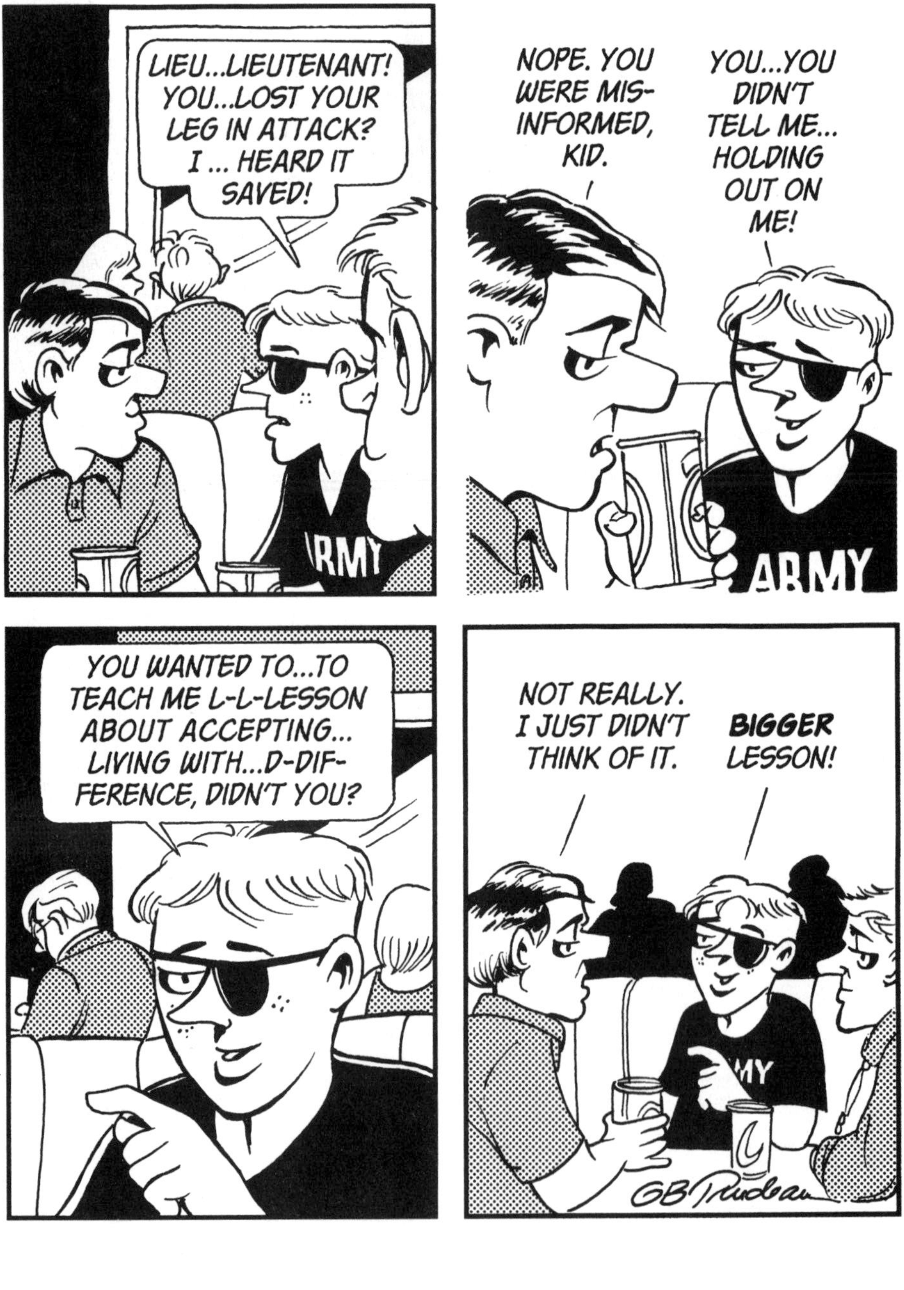
LIEU...LIEUTENANT! YOU...LOST YOUR LEG IN ATTACK? I ... HEARD IT SAVED!
ARMY
NOPE. YOU WERE MIS-INFORMED, KID.
YOU...YOU DIDN'T TELL ME... HOLDING OUT ON ME!
ARMY
YOU WANTED TO...TO TEACH ME L-L-LESSON ABOUT ACCEPTING... LIVING WITH...D-DIF-FERENCE, DIDN'T YOU?
NOT REALLY. I JUST DIDN'T THINK OF IT.
BIGGER LESSON!
GB Trudeau

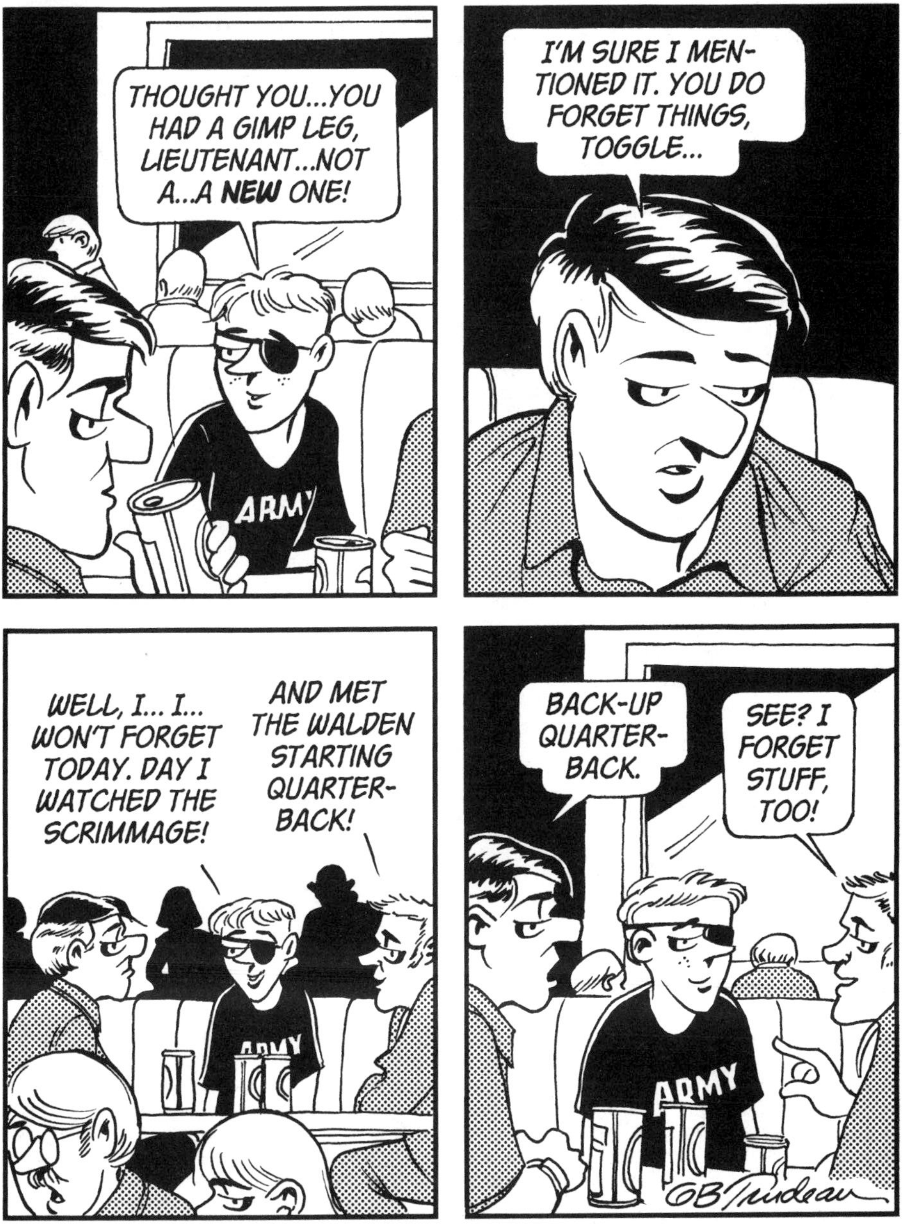
THOUGHT YOU...YOU HAD A GIMP LEG, LIEUTENANT...NOT A...A NEW ONE!
ARMY
I'M SURE I MEN-TIONED IT. YOU DO FORGET THINGS, TOGGLE...
WELL, I... I... WON'T FORGET TODAY. DAY I WATCHED THE SCRIMMAGE!
AND MET THE WALDEN STARTING QUARTER-BACK!
BACK-UP QUARTER-BACK.
SEE? I FORGET STUFF, TOO!
ARMY
GB Trudeau

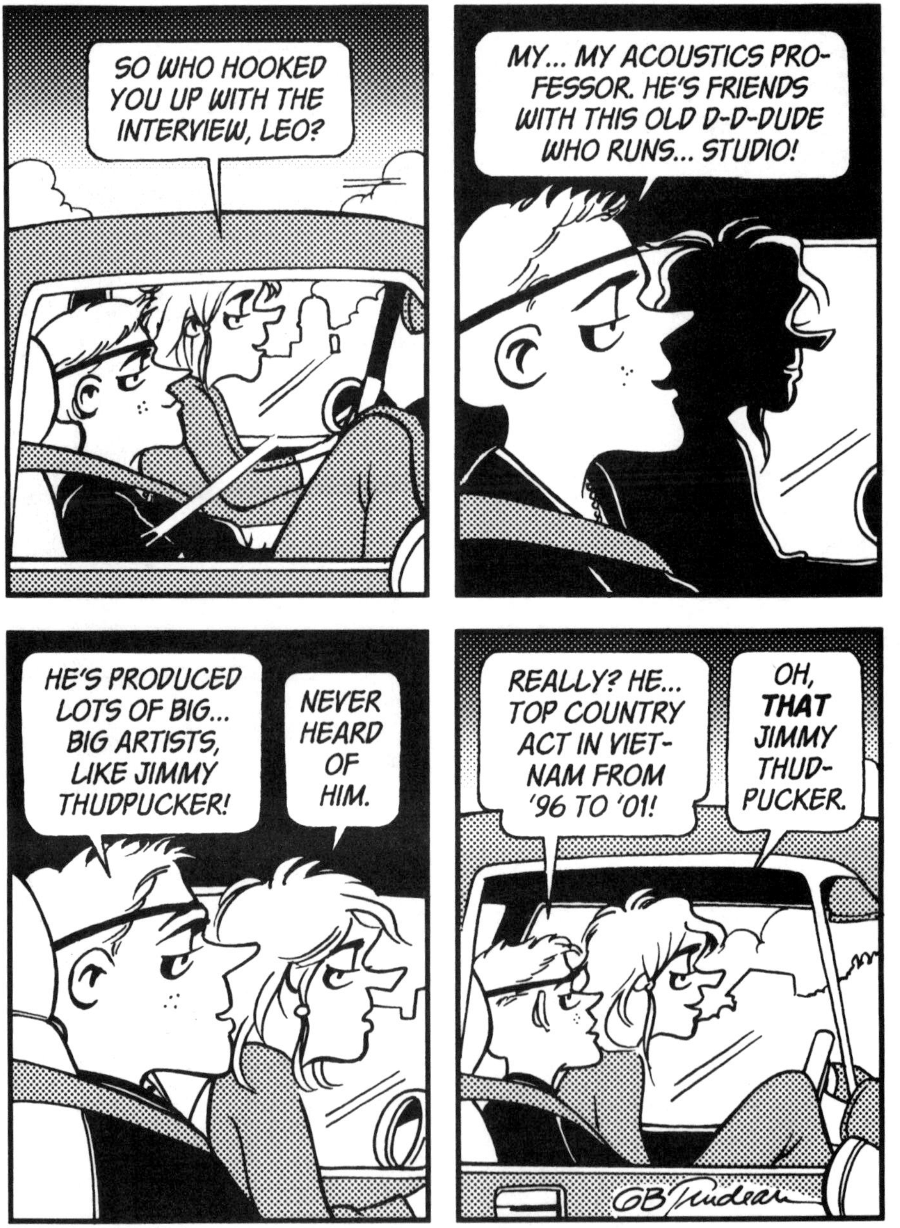
SO WHO HOOKED YOU UP WITH THE INTERVIEW, LEO?
MY... MY ACOUSTICS PROFESSOR. HE'S FRIENDS WITH THIS OLD D-D-DUDE WHO RUNS... STUDIO!
HE'S PRODUCED LOTS OF BIG... BIG ARTISTS, LIKE JIMMY THUDPUCKER!
NEVER HEARD OF HIM.
REALLY? HE... TOP COUNTRY ACT IN VIETNAM FROM '96 TO '01!
OH, **THAT** JIMMY THUDPUCKER.
GB Trudeau

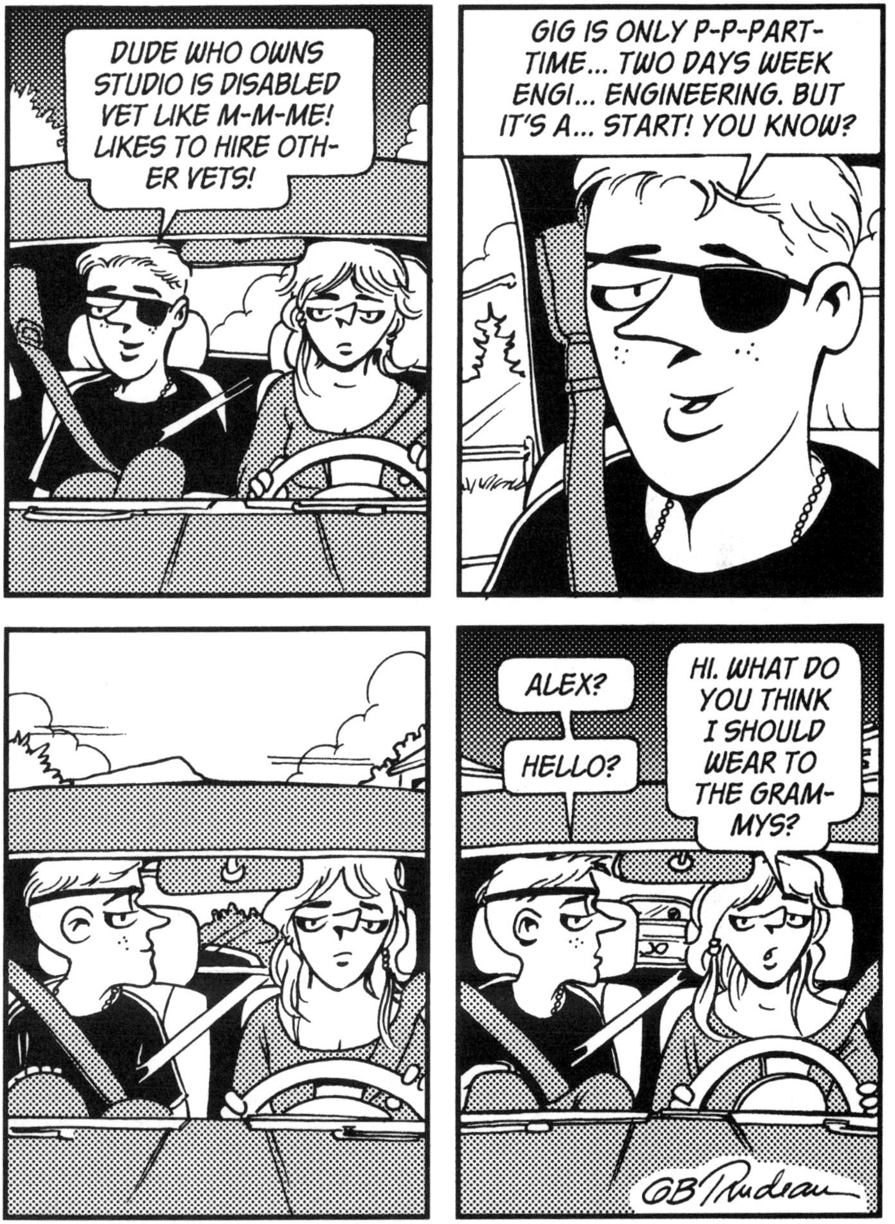

DUDE WHO OWNS STUDIO IS DISABLED VET LIKE M-M-ME! LIKES TO HIRE OTH-ER VETS!
GIG IS ONLY P-P-PART-TIME... TWO DAYS WEEK ENGI... ENGINEERING. BUT IT'S A... START! YOU KNOW?
ALEX?
HELLO?
HI. WHAT DO YOU THINK I SHOULD WEAR TO THE GRAM-MYS?
GB Trudeau

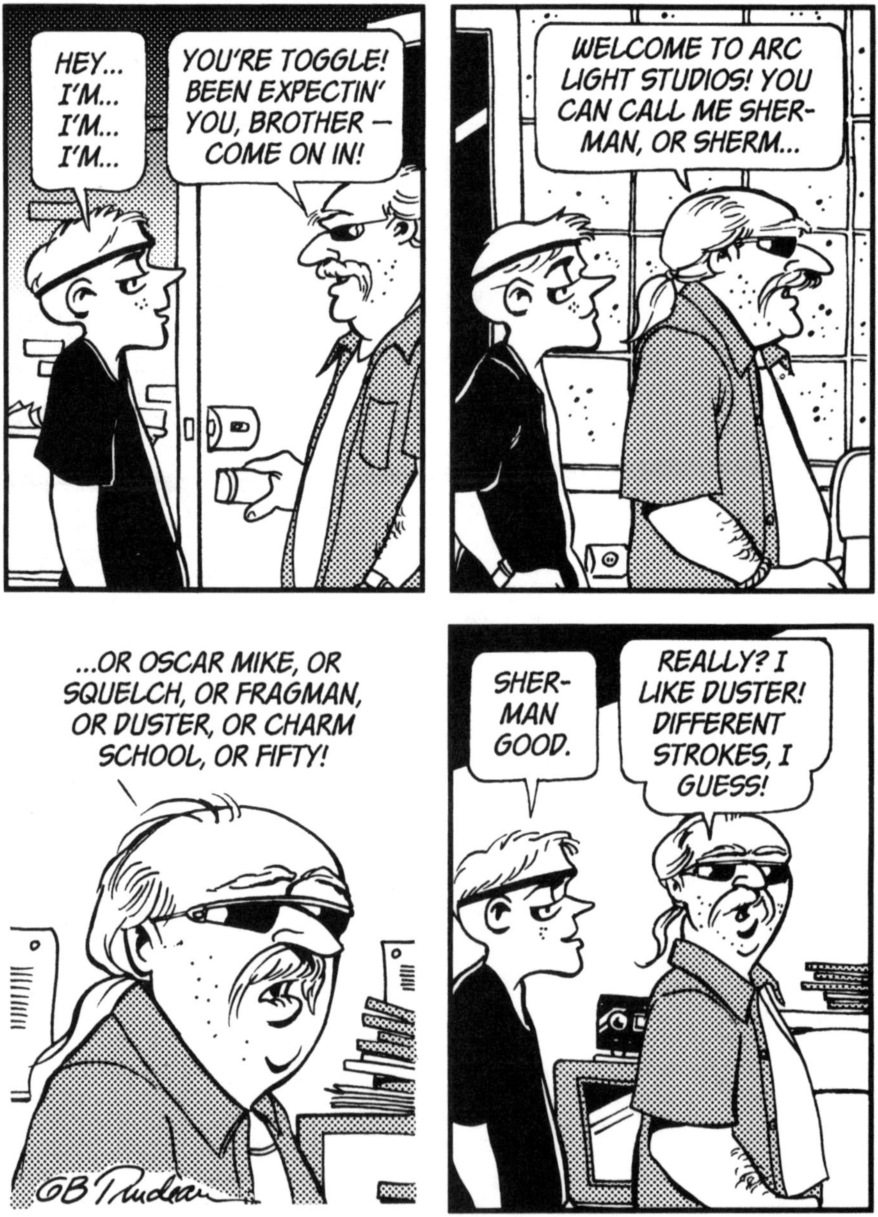
HEY... I'M... I'M... I'M...
YOU'RE TOGGLE! BEEN EXPECTIN' YOU, BROTHER — COME ON IN!
WELCOME TO ARC LIGHT STUDIOS! YOU CAN CALL ME SHER-MAN, OR SHERM...
...OR OSCAR MIKE, OR SQUELCH, OR FRAGMAN, OR DUSTER, OR CHARM SCHOOL, OR FIFTY!
SHER-MAN GOOD.
REALLY? I LIKE DUSTER! DIFFERENT STROKES, I GUESS!
GB Trudeau

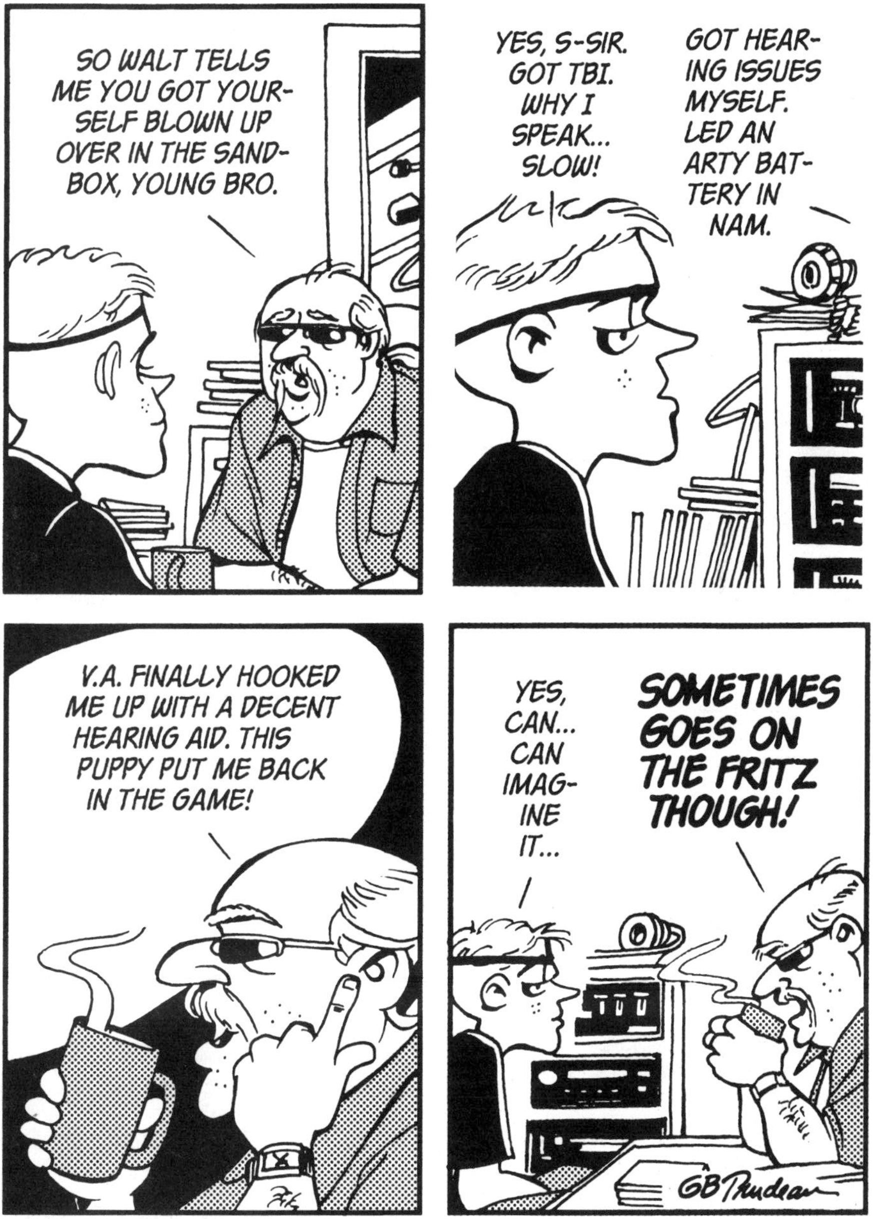
SO WALT TELLS ME YOU GOT YOURSELF BLOWN UP OVER IN THE SANDBOX, YOUNG BRO.
YES, S-SIR. GOT TBI. WHY I SPEAK... SLOW!
GOT HEARING ISSUES MYSELF. LED AN ARTY BATTERY IN NAM.
V.A. FINALLY HOOKED ME UP WITH A DECENT HEARING AID. THIS PUPPY PUT ME BACK IN THE GAME!
YES, CAN... CAN IMAGINE IT...
SOMETIMES GOES ON THE FRITZ THOUGH!
GB Trudeau

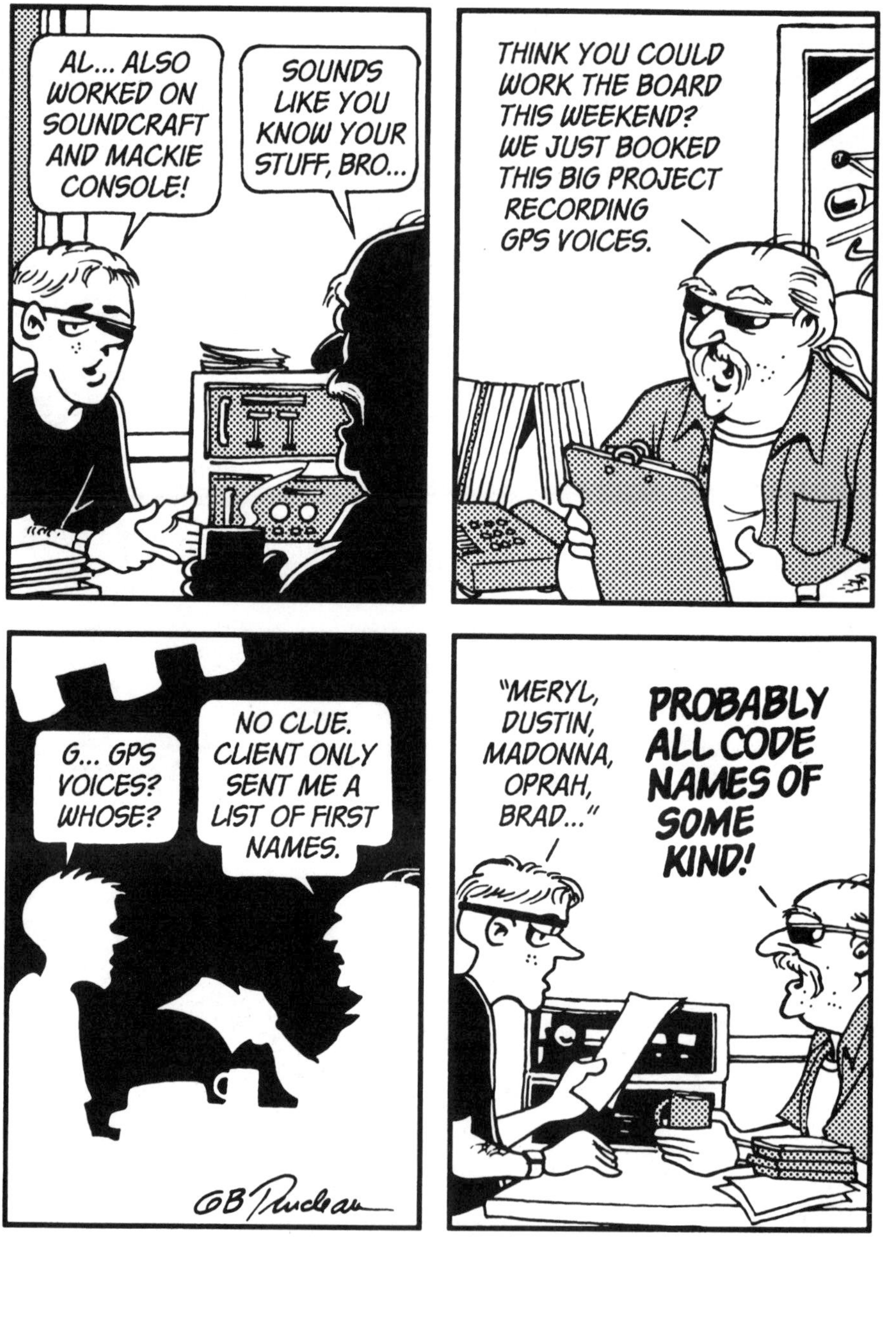
AL... ALSO WORKED ON SOUNDCRAFT AND MACKIE CONSOLE!
SOUNDS LIKE YOU KNOW YOUR STUFF, BRO...
THINK YOU COULD WORK THE BOARD THIS WEEKEND? WE JUST BOOKED THIS BIG PROJECT RECORDING GPS VOICES.
G... GPS VOICES? WHOSE?
NO CLUE. CLIENT ONLY SENT ME A LIST OF FIRST NAMES.
"MERYL, DUSTIN, MADONNA, OPRAH, BRAD..."
PROBABLY ALL CODE NAMES OF SOME KIND!

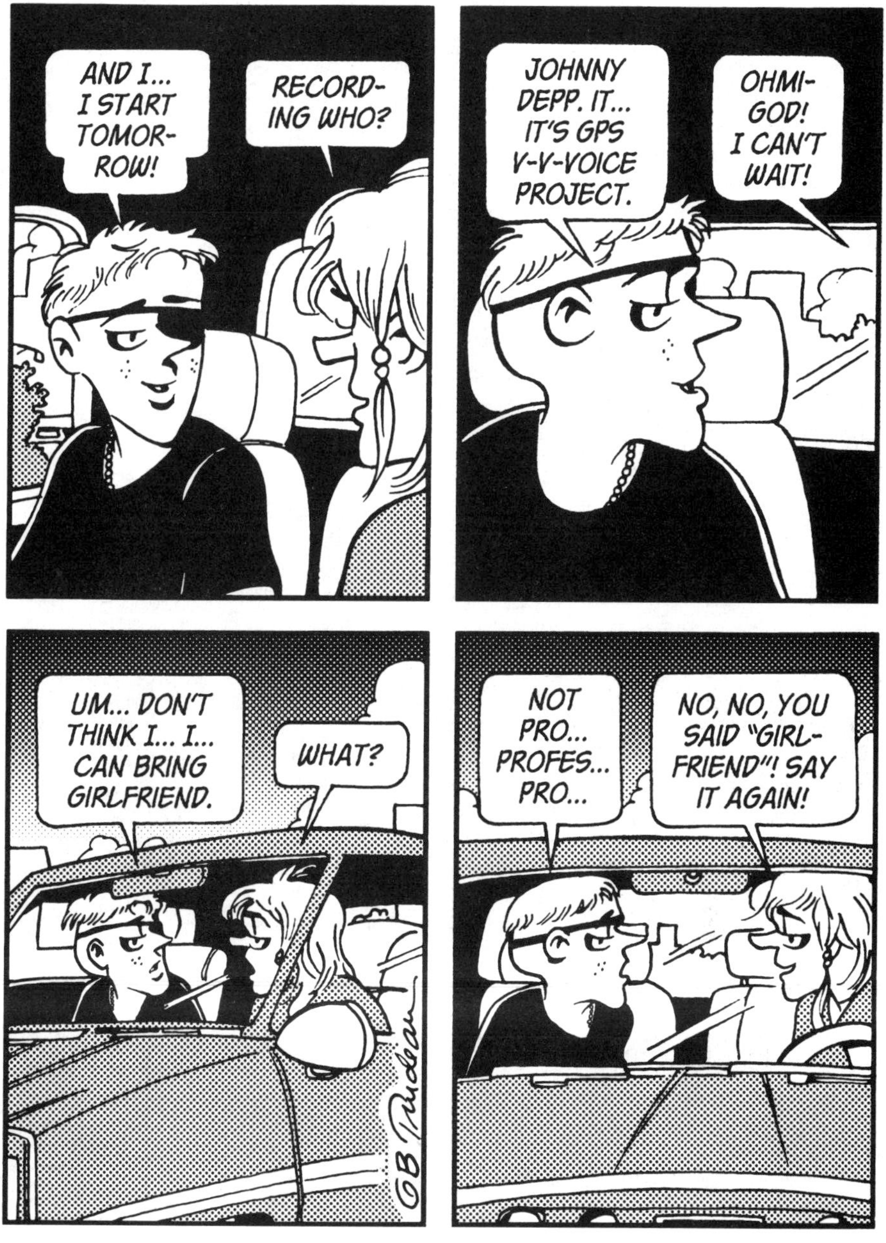
AND I... I START TOMOR-ROW!
RECORD-ING WHO?
JOHNNY DEPP. IT... IT'S GPS V-V-VOICE PROJECT.
OHMI-GOD! I CAN'T WAIT!
UM... DON'T THINK I... I... CAN BRING GIRLFRIEND.
WHAT?
NOT PRO... PROFES... PRO...
NO, NO, YOU SAID "GIRL-FRIEND"! SAY IT AGAIN!
GB Trudeau

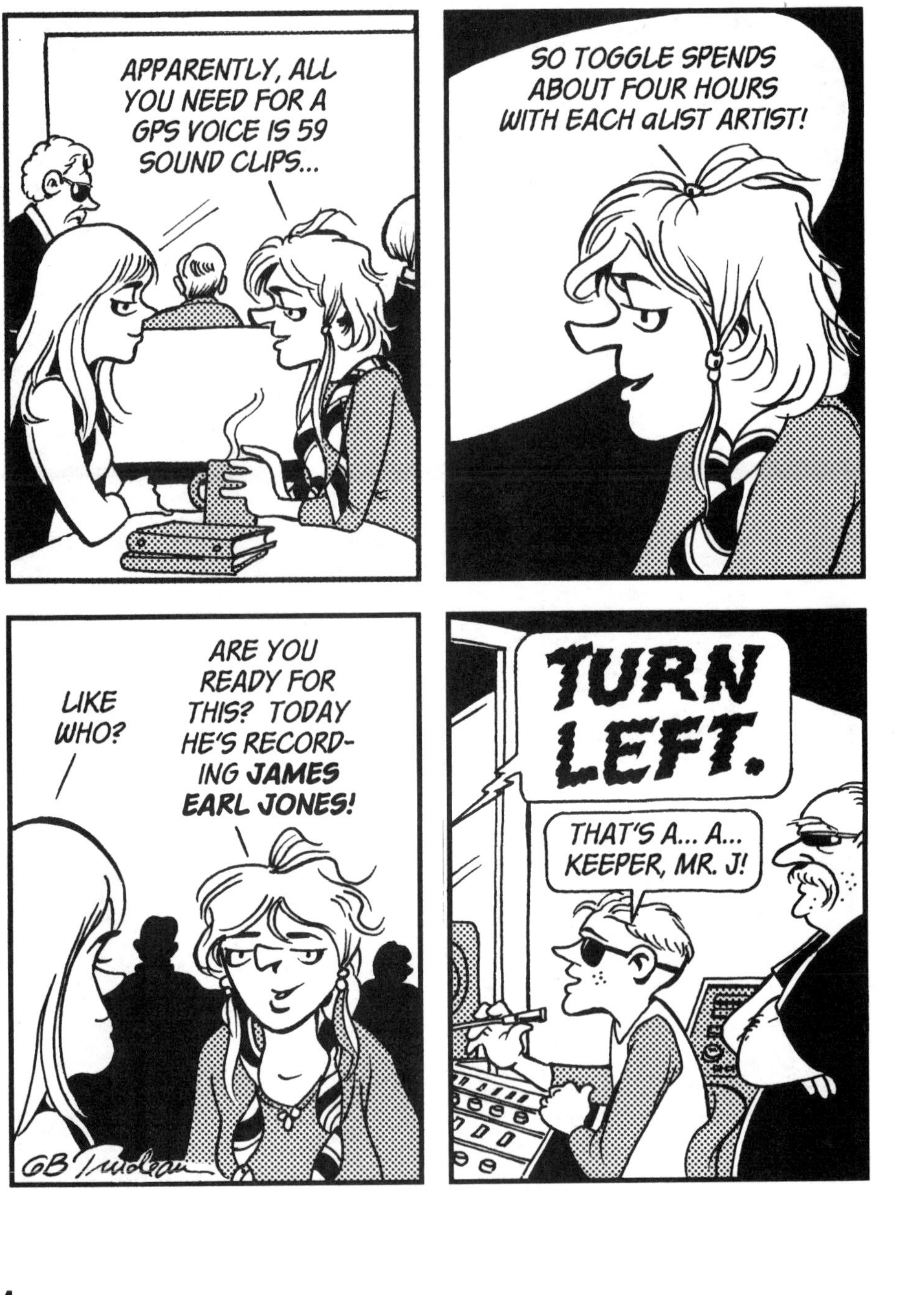
APPARENTLY, ALL YOU NEED FOR A GPS VOICE IS 59 SOUND CLIPS...
SO TOGGLE SPENDS ABOUT FOUR HOURS WITH EACH aLIST ARTIST!
LIKE WHO?
ARE YOU READY FOR THIS? TODAY HE'S RECORD-ING **JAMES EARL JONES!**
TURN LEFT.
THAT'S A... A... KEEPER, MR. J!
GB Trudeau

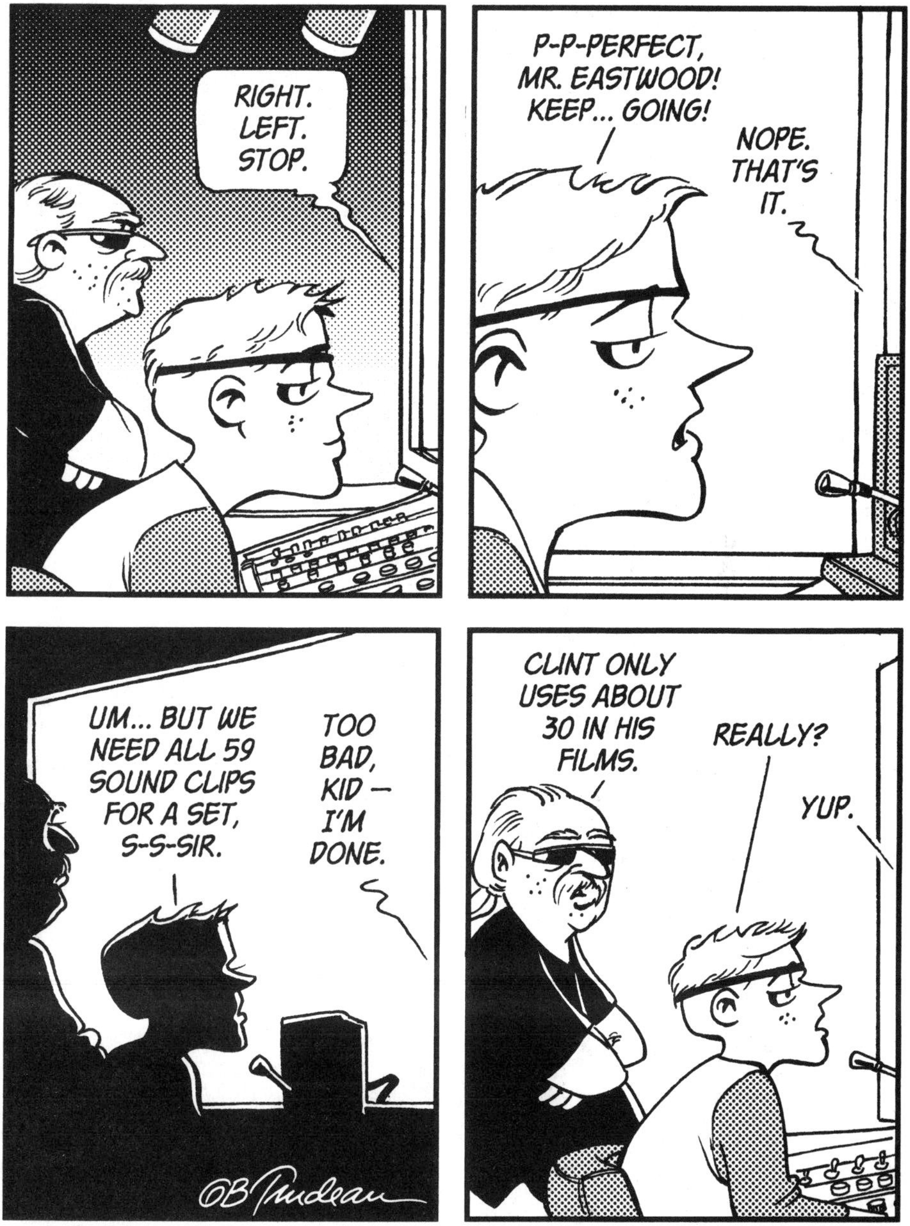
RIGHT. LEFT. STOP.
P-P-PERFECT, MR. EASTWOOD! KEEP... GOING!
NOPE. THAT'S IT.
UM... BUT WE NEED ALL 59 SOUND CLIPS FOR A SET, S-S-SIR.
TOO BAD, KID — I'M DONE.
CLINT ONLY USES ABOUT 30 IN HIS FILMS.
REALLY?
YUP.

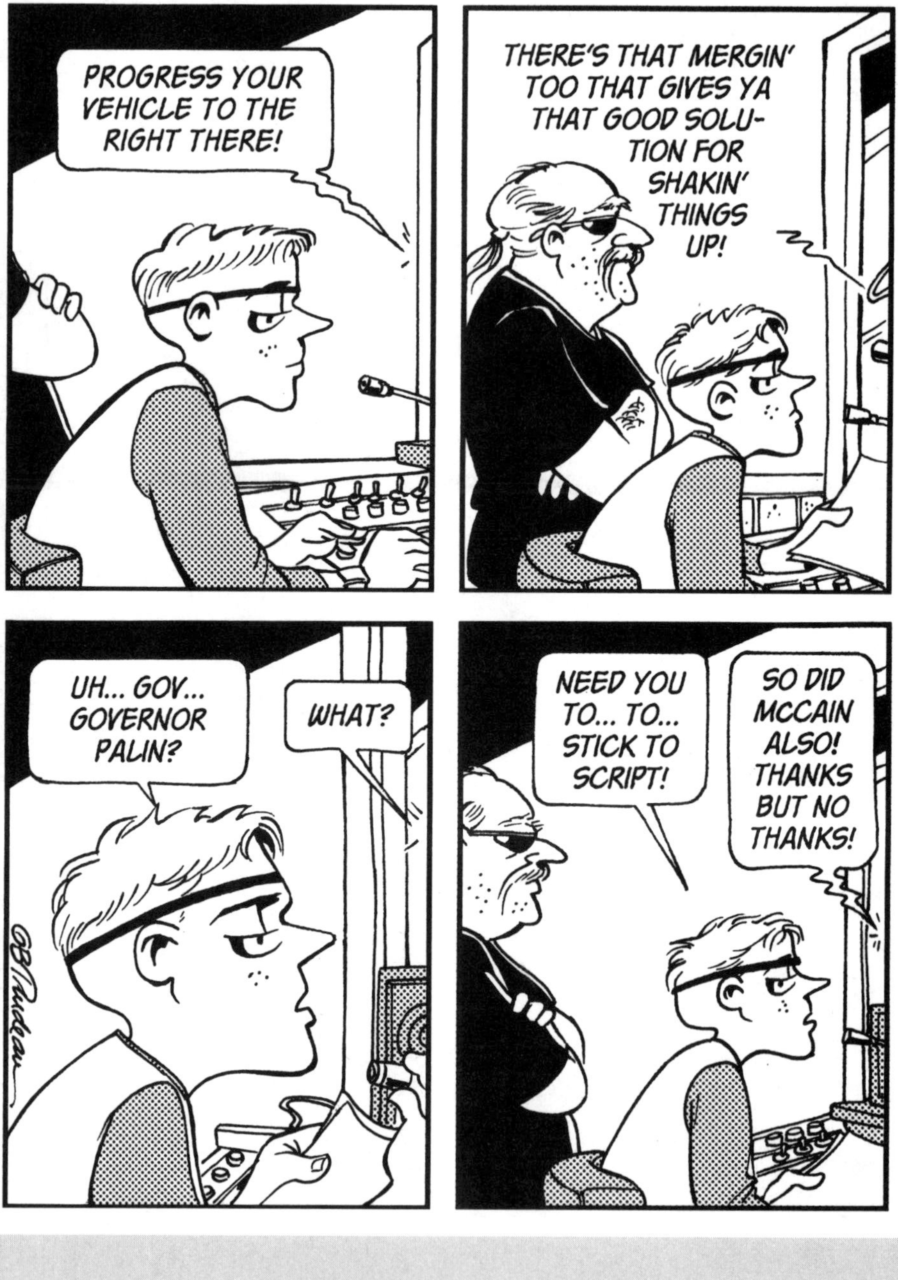
PROGRESS YOUR VEHICLE TO THE RIGHT THERE!
THERE'S THAT MERGIN' TOO THAT GIVES YA THAT GOOD SOLU-TION FOR SHAKIN' THINGS UP!
UH... GOV... GOVERNOR PALIN?
WHAT?
NEED YOU TO... TO... STICK TO SCRIPT!
SO DID MCCAIN ALSO! THANKS BUT NO THANKS!

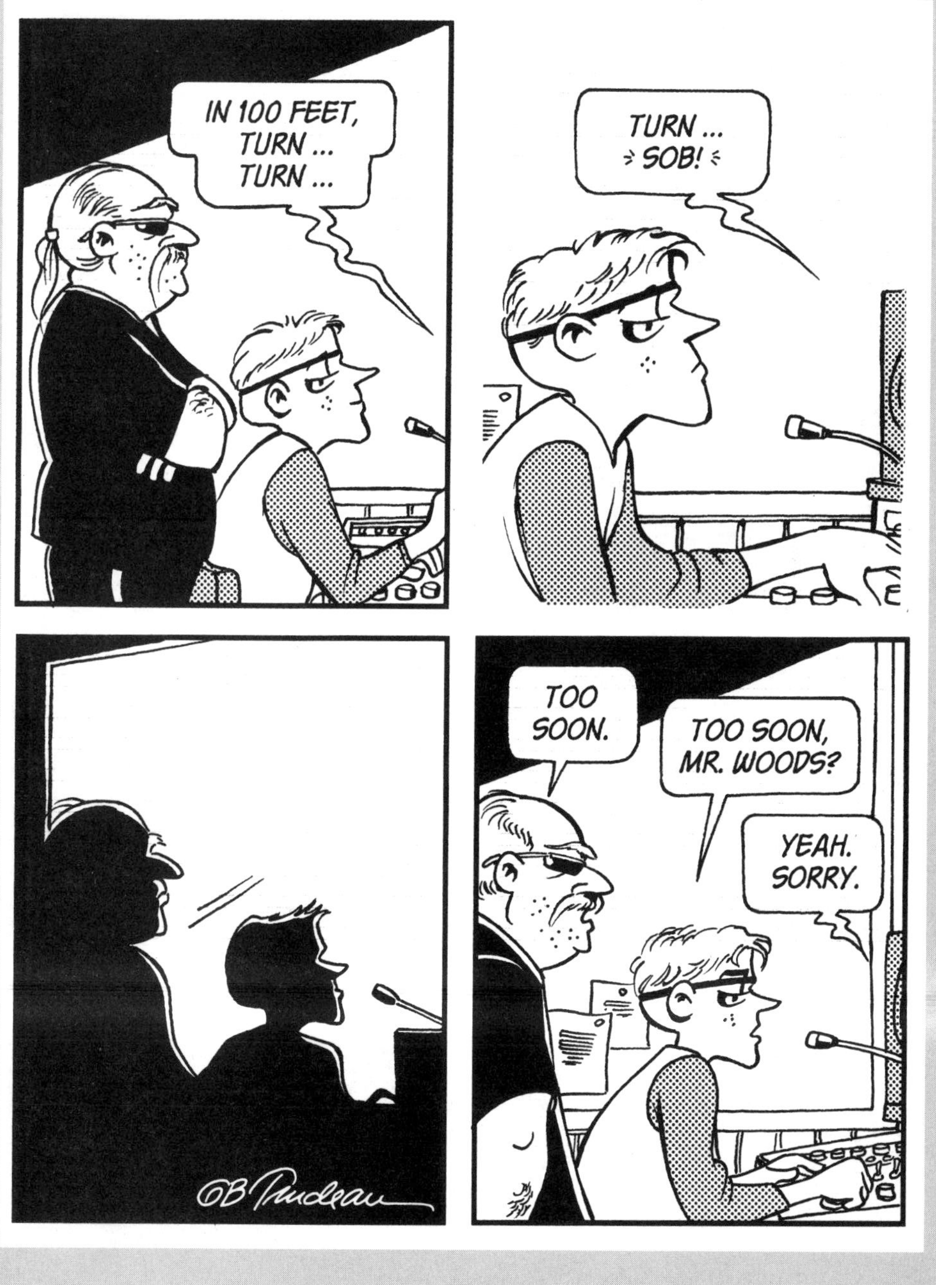
IN 100 FEET,
TURN ...
TURN ...
TURN ...
SOB!
TOO
SOON.
TOO SOON,
MR. WOODS?
YEAH.
SORRY.

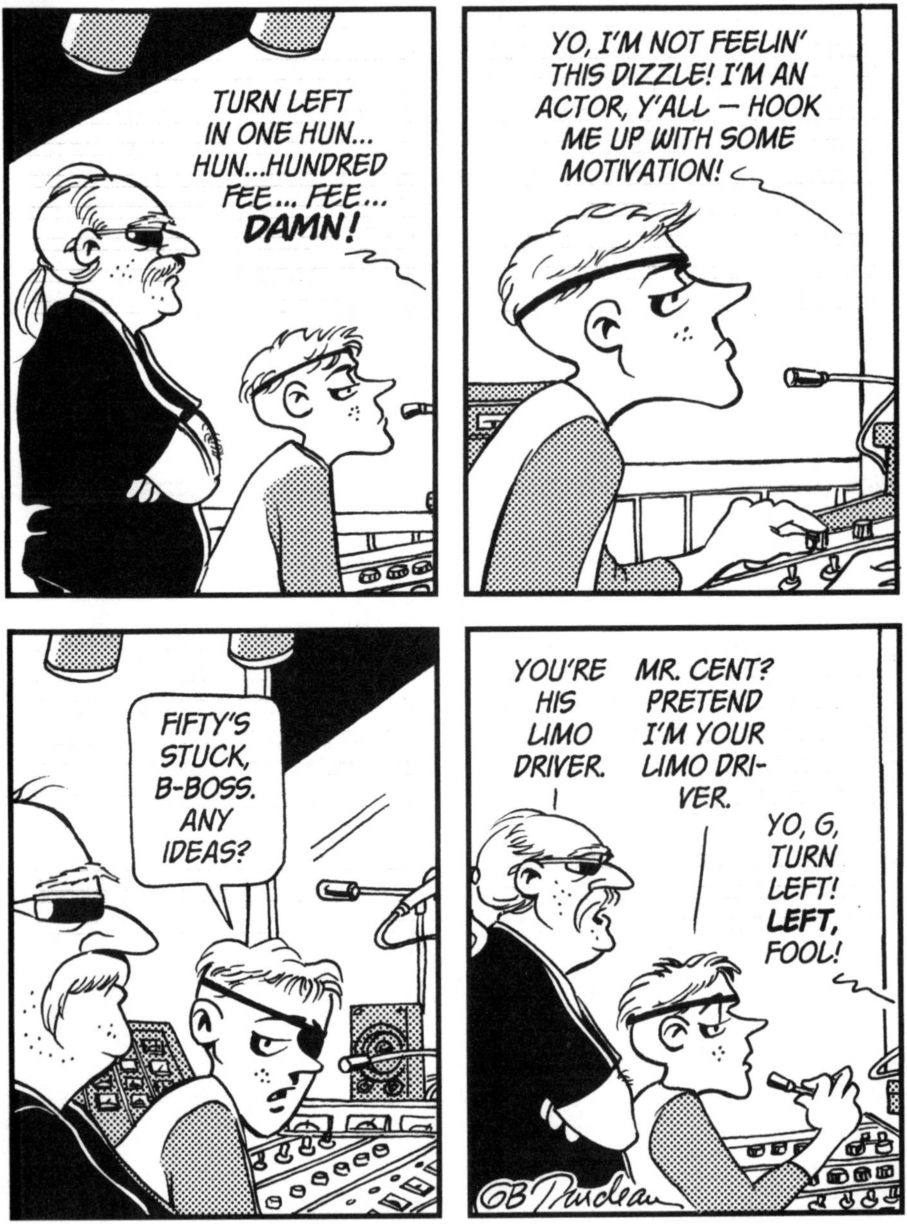
TURN LEFT IN ONE HUN... HUN...HUNDRED FEE... FEE... **DAMN!**
YO, I'M NOT FEELIN' THIS DIZZLE! I'M AN ACTOR, Y'ALL — HOOK ME UP WITH SOME MOTIVATION!
FIFTY'S STUCK, B-BOSS. ANY IDEAS?
YOU'RE HIS LIMO DRIVER.
MR. CENT? PRETEND I'M YOUR LIMO DRI-VER.
YO, G, TURN LEFT! **LEFT,** FOOL!
GB Trudeau

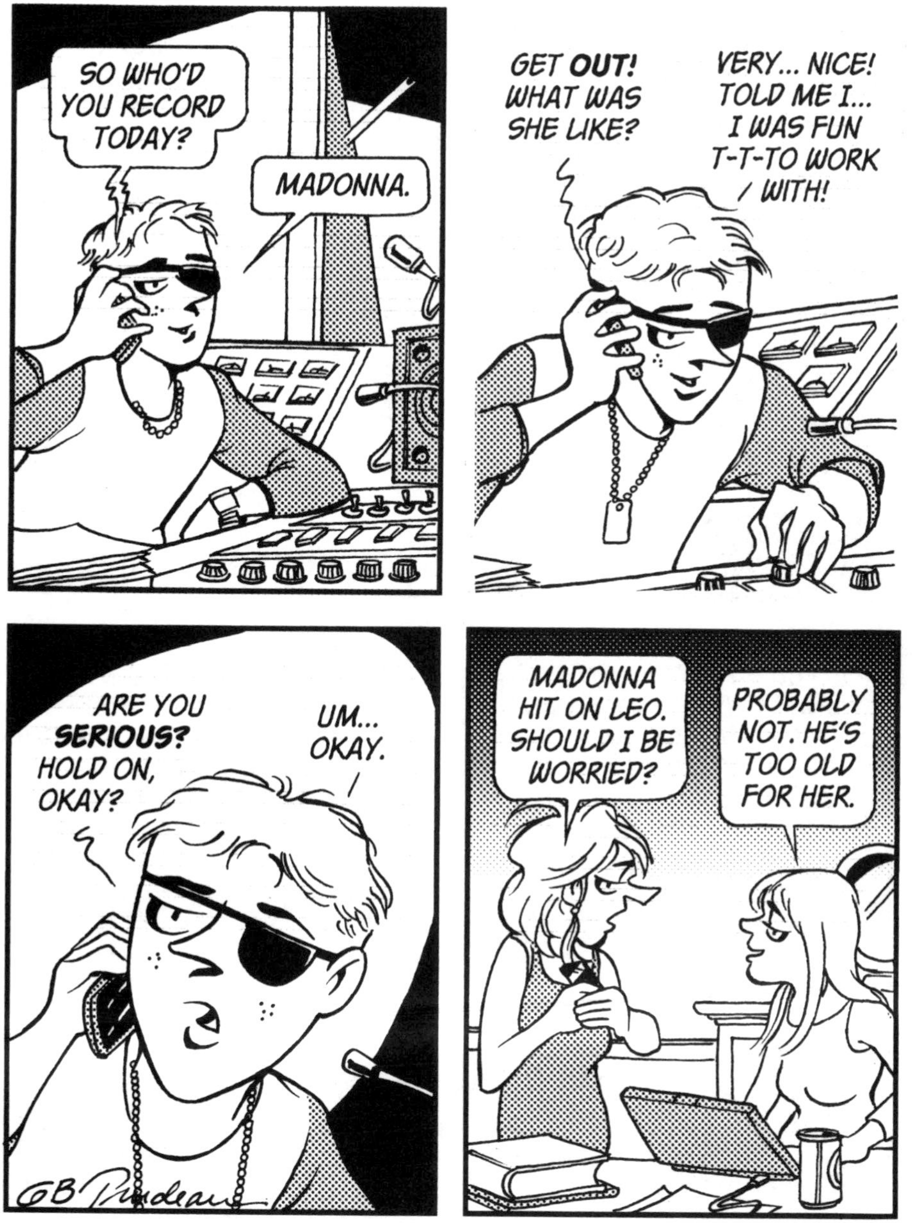

SO WHO'D YOU RECORD TODAY?
MADONNA.
GET **OUT!** WHAT WAS SHE LIKE?
VERY... NICE! TOLD ME I... I WAS FUN T-T-TO WORK WITH!
ARE YOU **SERIOUS?** HOLD ON, OKAY?
UM... OKAY.
MADONNA HIT ON LEO. SHOULD I BE WORRIED?
PROBABLY NOT. HE'S TOO OLD FOR HER.
GB Trudeau

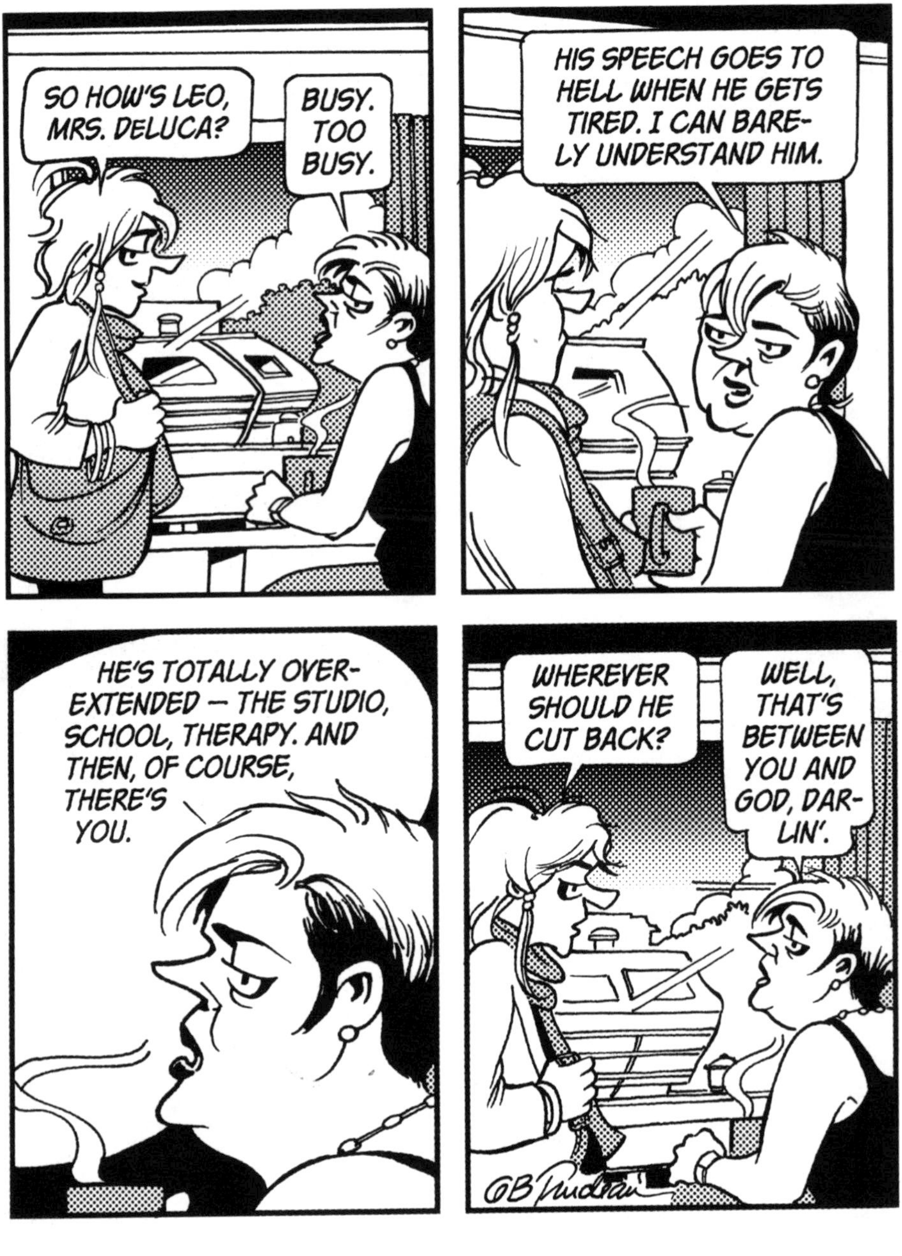
SO HOW'S LEO, MRS. DELUCA?
BUSY. TOO BUSY.
HIS SPEECH GOES TO HELL WHEN HE GETS TIRED. I CAN BARE-LY UNDERSTAND HIM.
HE'S TOTALLY OVER-EXTENDED — THE STUDIO, SCHOOL, THERAPY. AND THEN, OF COURSE, THERE'S YOU.
WHEREVER SHOULD HE CUT BACK?
WELL, THAT'S BETWEEN YOU AND GOD, DAR-LIN'.
©B Trudeau

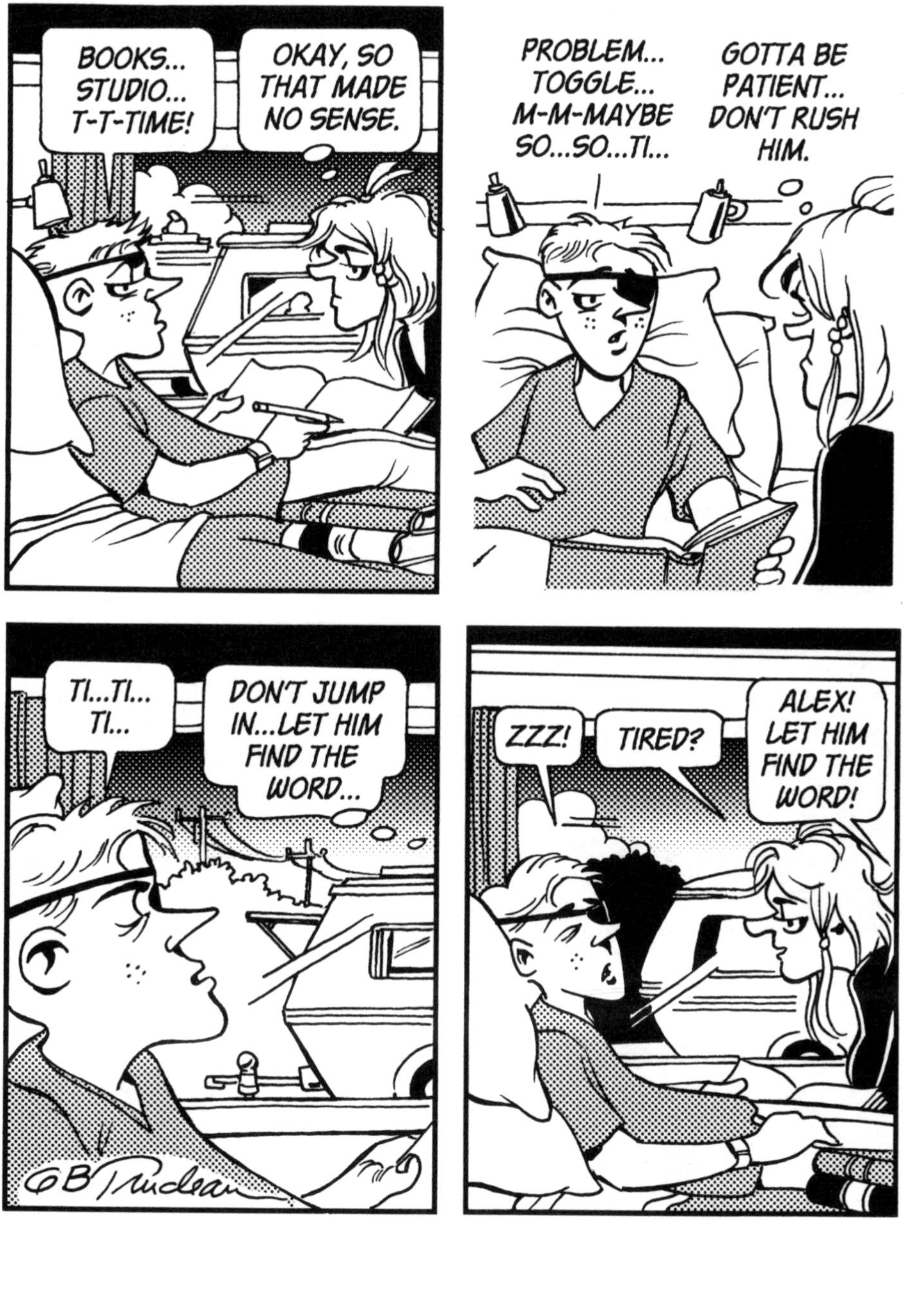
BOOKS... STUDIO... T-T-TIME!
OKAY, SO THAT MADE NO SENSE.
PROBLEM... TOGGLE... M-M-MAYBE SO...SO...TI...
GOTTA BE PATIENT... DON'T RUSH HIM.
TI...TI... TI...
DON'T JUMP IN...LET HIM FIND THE WORD...
ZZZ!
TIRED?
ALEX! LET HIM FIND THE WORD!
GB Trudeau

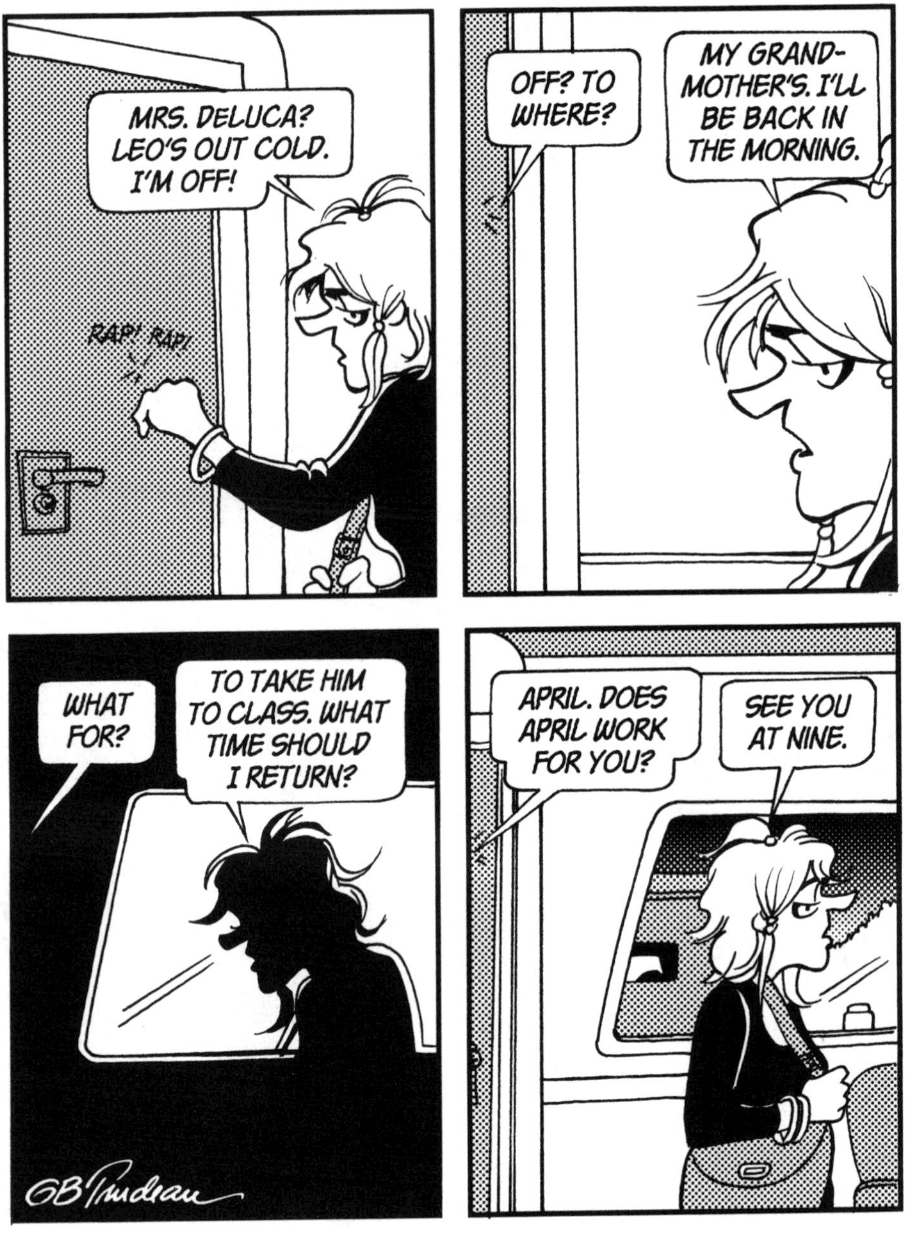
MRS. DELUCA? LEO'S OUT COLD. I'M OFF!
RAP! RAP!
OFF? TO WHERE?
MY GRAND-MOTHER'S. I'LL BE BACK IN THE MORNING.
WHAT FOR?
TO TAKE HIM TO CLASS. WHAT TIME SHOULD I RETURN?
GB Trudeau
APRIL. DOES APRIL WORK FOR YOU?
SEE YOU AT NINE.

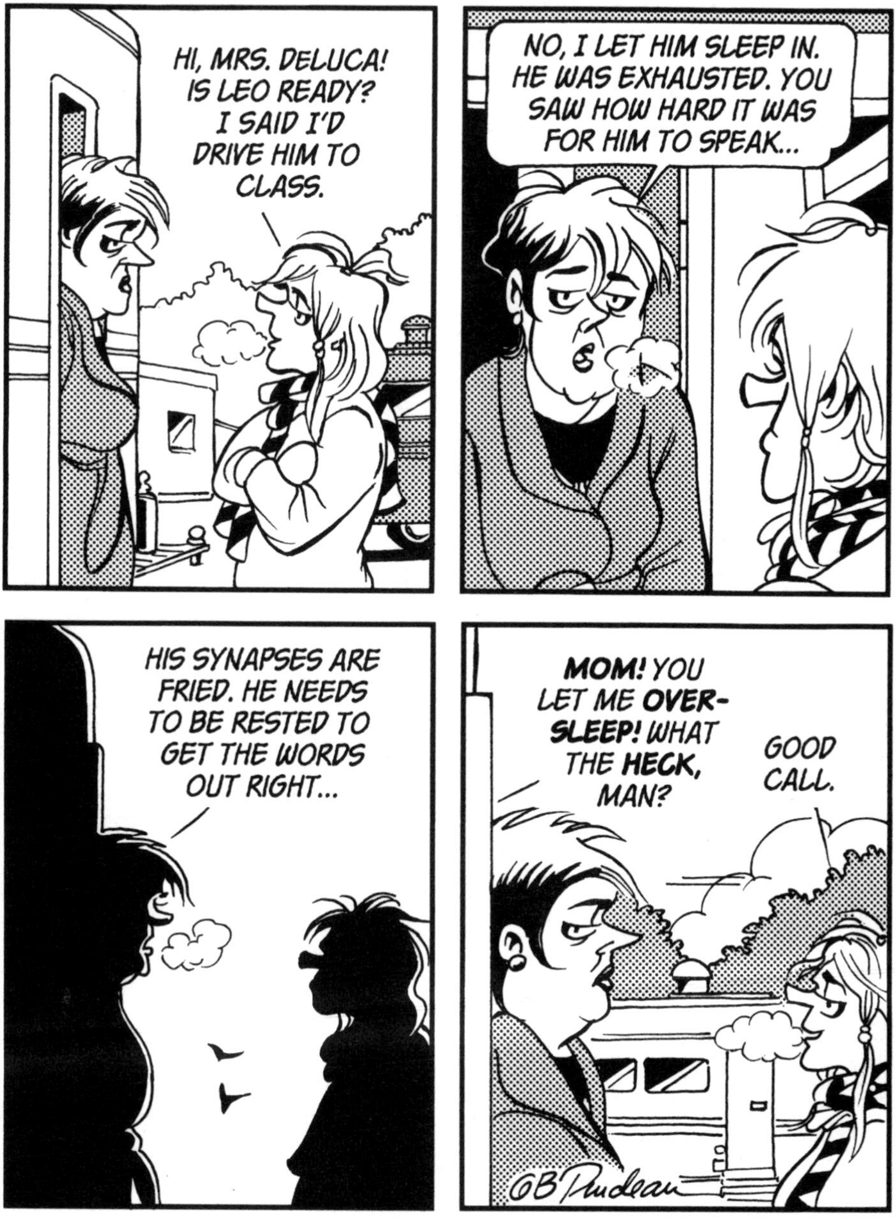
HI, MRS. DELUCA! IS LEO READY? I SAID I'D DRIVE HIM TO CLASS.
NO, I LET HIM SLEEP IN. HE WAS EXHAUSTED. YOU SAW HOW HARD IT WAS FOR HIM TO SPEAK...
HIS SYNAPSES ARE FRIED. HE NEEDS TO BE RESTED TO GET THE WORDS OUT RIGHT...
MOM! YOU LET ME OVER-SLEEP! WHAT THE HECK, MAN?
GOOD CALL.

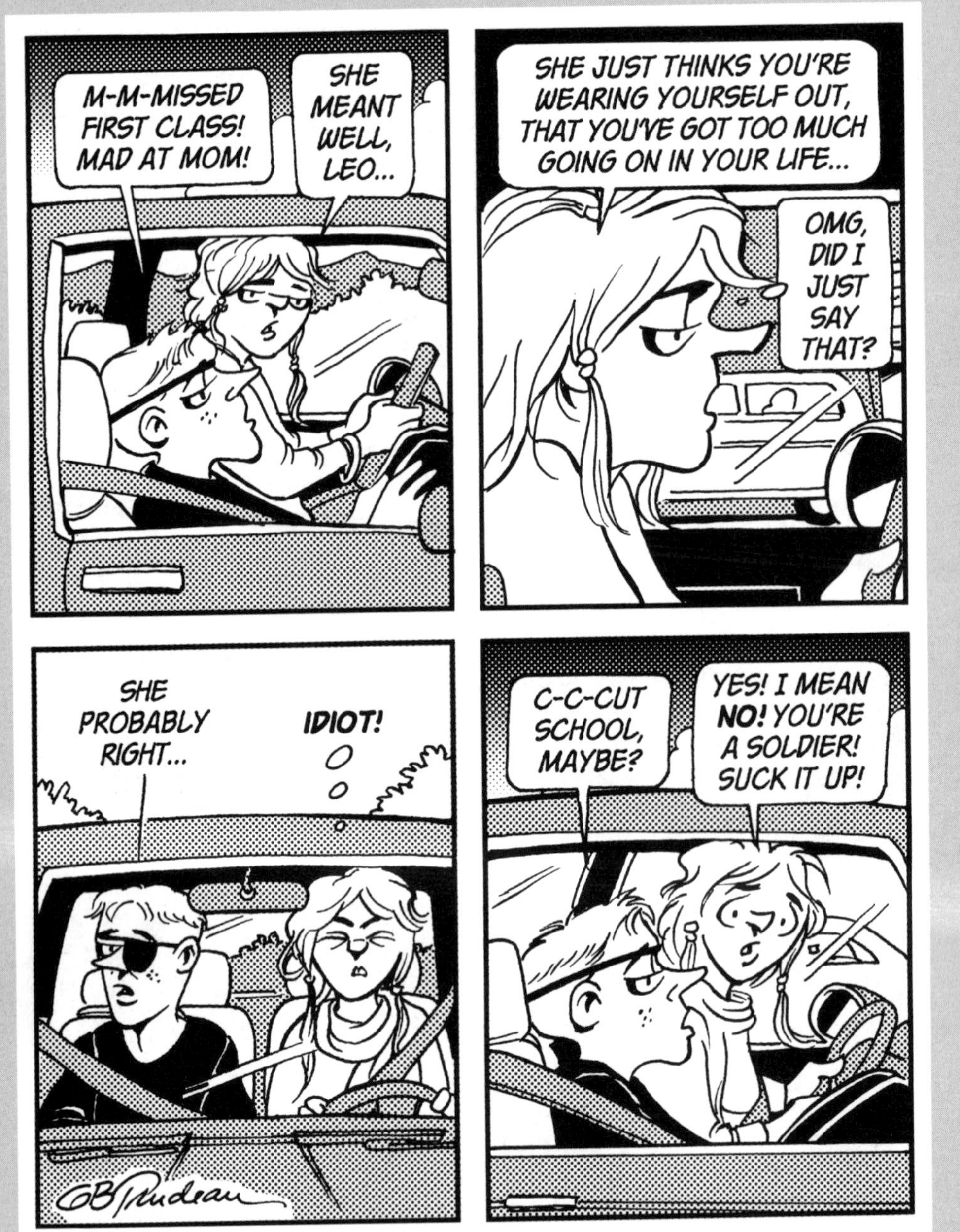
M-M-MISSED FIRST CLASS! MAD AT MOM!
SHE MEANT WELL, LEO...
SHE JUST THINKS YOU'RE WEARING YOURSELF OUT, THAT YOU'VE GOT TOO MUCH GOING ON IN YOUR LIFE...
OMG, DID I JUST SAY THAT?
SHE PROBABLY RIGHT...
IDIOT!
C-C-CUT SCHOOL, MAYBE?
YES! I MEAN NO! YOU'RE A SOLDIER! SUCK IT UP!
GBTrudeau

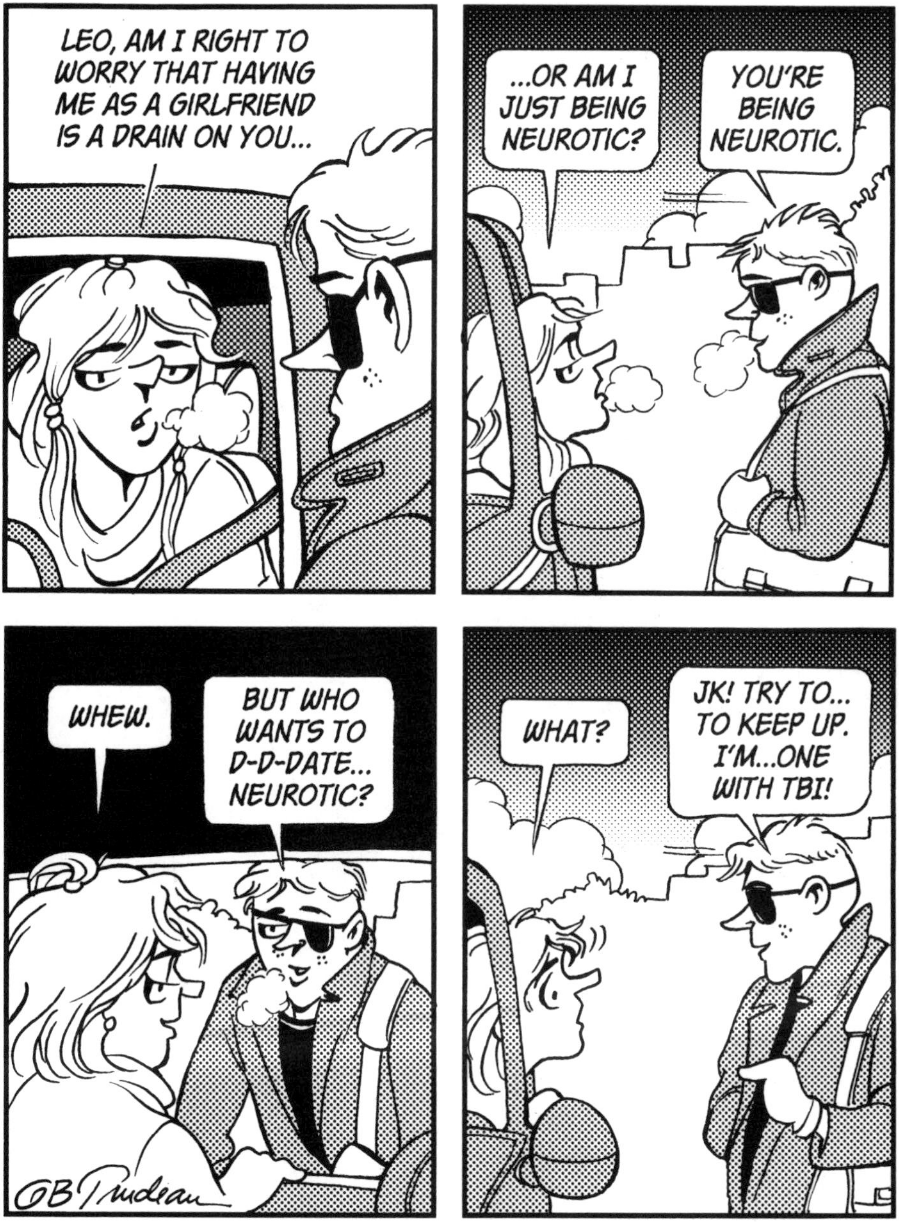

LEO, AM I RIGHT TO WORRY THAT HAVING ME AS A GIRLFRIEND IS A DRAIN ON YOU...
...OR AM I JUST BEING NEUROTIC?
YOU'RE BEING NEUROTIC.
WHEW.
BUT WHO WANTS TO D-D-DATE... NEUROTIC?
WHAT?
JK! TRY TO... TO KEEP UP. I'M...ONE WITH TBI!
©B Trudeau

FISHER HOUSE

because A Family's Love is Good Medicine

www.fisherhouse.org

A Fisher House is a "home away from home" for families of patients receiving medical care at major military and VA medical centers. As of this printing, there are forty-three Fisher Houses located on eighteen military installations and thirteen VA medical centers, with another sixteen houses under construction or in design. The program began in 1990 and has offered more than three million days of lodging to more than 120,000 families.

The Fisher House Foundation donates Fisher Houses to the U.S. Government. They have full-time salaried managers but depend on volunteers and voluntary support to enhance daily operations and program expansion.

Through the generosity of the American public, the foundation has expanded its programs to meet the needs of our service men and women who have been wounded. The foundation uses donated frequent-flier miles to provide airline travel to reunite families of the wounded and to enable our wounded heroes to go home to convalesce. They also help cover the cost of alternative lodging when the Fisher Houses are full.

For further information about these programs, to find out about volunteering, or to make a tax-deductible gift, go to their Web site at:

www.fisherhouse.org

You can also obtain information by writing them at
Fisher House Foundation, Inc.
111 Rockville Pike, Suite 420
Rockville, MD 20850

Phone: (888) 294-8560
E-mail: info@fisherhouse.org